WHERE TO WA

North West England

and the Isle of Man

ALLAN CONLIN, DR J P CULLEN, PETE MARSH,
TRISTAN REIDS, CHRIS SHARPE, JUDITH SMITH,
STEPHEN WILLIAMS

Christopher Helm
A & C Black • London

Published 2008 by Christopher Helm,
an imprint of A&C Black Publishers,
38 Soho Square,
London W1D 3HB
www.acblack.com

Copyright © 2008 text by Allan Conlin, Dr J P Cullen, Pete Marsh, Tristan
Reids, Chris Sharpe, Judith Smith and Stephen Williams
Line drawings by David Mead

ISBN: 978-0-7136-6421-8

A CIP catalogue record for this book is available
from the British Library.

Commissioning Editor: Nigel Redman
Project Editor: Sophie Page
Copyeditor: John Jackson
Typesetter: Margaret Brain
Proofreader: Mary Sheridan
Indexer: Mary Jane Steer
Maps by Brian Southern

This book is produced using paper that is made from wood grown in
managed, sustainable forests. It is natural, renewable and recyclable. The
logging and manufacturing processes conform to the environmental
regulations of the country of origin.

Printed in China by WKT Company Ltd

10 9 8 7 6 5 4 3 2 1

CONTENTS

SOUTH CUMBRIA

NORTH LANCASHIRE

SOUTH LANCASHIRE

GREATER MANCHESTER

CHESHIRE AND WIRRAL

THE ISLE OF MAN

ACKNOWLEDGEMENTS

Pete Marsh would like to thank the following for major contributions to the text: Chris Batty, Stuart Piner (Fylde), Steve White (Sefton Coast), Bill Aspin (East Lancs.) and the following for general help: Jean Roberts, Steve Martin, John Wilson, Jon Carter, Dan Haywood.

Judith Smith would like to thank S. Atkins, P. Baron, P. Berry, P. Hines, S. Hitchen and R. Travis for their help.

Allan Conlin and Stephen Williams would like to thank Colin E. Wells (RSPB Site Manager for the Dee Estuary), Peter Williams (Chairman of Hilbre Bird Observatory), Frank Duff, Phil Woolen, Dr Paul Brewster, Paul Hill and Dave Riley for reviewing early drafts of relevent sections of the text and providing comment.

Dr J. P. Cullen and Chris Sharpe would like to thank T. Abraham, R. Cope, K. Johnson, A. C. Kaye, A. Moore and S. Pimm for their help.

INTRODUCTION

The counties of Cumbria, Lancashire and Cheshire, together with Merseyside and Greater Manchester which are, for convenience, subsumed within the title of this book, make up Northwest England, running from the Welsh border and the Ellesmere moraine (limit of the last glaciation) in the south, to the Scottish border in the north. The region encompasses the mountainous Lake District, where the higher hills exceed 750 m (2500 ft) above sea level, and the western flank of the Pennine hills to the east, as well as the more fertile lowlands of the Fylde and the Lancashire–Cheshire Plain. And for the first time this guide also includes the Isle of Man. The uplands are devoted largely to sheep-rearing, with some heather management for grouse. In the south of the region, the Cheshire moors have dwindled, large areas having been converted to grazing land, while further north there has been increasing emphasis on forestry.

Hill reservoirs in the southern Pennines, constructed within the last 200 years, have suffered from the acidifying pollution that accompanied the Industrial Revolution. Many of them are steep-sided, with sparse vegetation and a limited aquatic fauna. All of them attract birds from time to time, and might reward regular coverage as a local patch, but only a selection of the more productive are included in this book.

The waters of the Lake District vary from small, clear upland tarns to large, reed-fringed meres, the best of which are ornithological sites of high quality, with excellent scenery too. Many of the Cheshire meres, also glacial in origin, are difficult of access. The cluster around Marbury, near the Shropshire border, attracts many birds but, with the exception of Marbury itself, is best left to the attentions of local watchers who can arrange ready access with landowners. Cheshire and south Lancashire contain many subsidence 'flashes', stretches of water in hollows resulting from salt or coal extraction respectively. These, like the pools caused by extraction of sand, clay and gravel, are industrial sites of benefit to birds.

The Cheshire and Lancashire lowlands contain only small fragments of ancient woodland, with further relic oak woods dotted along the southern Pennines. A thriving coppicing industry survived into the twentieth century in the Lake District, where far more broadleaved woods survive. The lowland mosses of the region, which formerly housed large heath butterflies, have now all but vanished, and some of the few remnants are still exploited for gardeners' peat, but public attitudes are changing and protection for peatlands is improving.

The coastline is for the most part low-lying, with extensive sand dunes and beaches, and estuarine mudflats.

Lying 30 miles (48 km) to the west of St Bees Head, the Isle of Man covers an area of 221 square miles (572 sq km). Hills, covered with heather and acid grassland, occupy much of the north-central area and rise to just over 2,000 feet (621 m). There are cultivated lowlands in the north and south-east. Much of the lower elevation moorland has been lost to conifer plantations during the last 50 years. Broad-leafed woodland is relatively scarce. This is an island of fast-flowing rivers and picturesque wooded glens. The coast is characterised by slate cliffs interrupted with a number of sandy bays. To the north of Peel there is a section of red sandstone giving way to sand cliffs, which are themselves replaced by dunes that border the northern lowlands. The extreme northern point consists of a bleak curving storm beach. In the south, separated from the main island by a narrow strait, is a 617 acre (250 ha) rocky islet: the Calf of Man.

The region's climate is heavily influenced by its west coast position. Winter temperatures along the Cumbrian coast and the Cheshire–Lancashire plain are a couple of degrees warmer than on the east coast, with fewer frosts, increasing the importance of these areas for wintering birds. Rainfall is typically 75–100 mm (30–40 in) per year on the plain, with 150 mm (60 in) or more in the central Lake District and locally elsewhere in the hills, where snow often lies in winter.

FEATURES OF THE REGION'S BIRDLIFE

Virtually the whole coastline from the Dee to the Duddon is connected at low tide by a series of sandbanks which, with the mudflats of several large estuaries, provide winter and passage quarters for hundreds of thousands of waders. Wildfowl too are well represented, both in the estuaries and on inland waters. The Lancashire mosslands hold huge winter flocks of Pink-footed Geese, thousands of Pochards frequent waters along the Mersey valley, and over 100 Ruddy Ducks gather on certain waters.

Seabird passage is highlighted by the north-easterly passage of skua species, Arctic Tern, Red-throated Diver and Kittiwake during the spring (especially late April to mid May). This passage uses an overland route via the Solway known as the 'Tyne Gap' and smaller numbers also migrate overland via Morecambe Bay and the Kent and Keer. Autumnal seawatching is hampered by the narrow northern entrance to the Irish Sea with the relatively shallow nature being a factor in the larger shearwaters being rare vagrants. Persistent autumnal westerly gales, however, do sometimes produce large numbers of especially Leach's Petrel. The sandy coastline mostly lacks rugged headlands, so breeding seabirds are scarce, although several colonies of terns exist, and a few gulleries, notably Europe's largest at South Walney. In contrast, the Isle of Man's predominantly rocky coastline holds an enviable Chough population, as well as a number of seabird colonies.

Walney is the southernmost sizeable breeding site for Common Eider on the west coast of Britain and St Bees the most southerly breeding site for Black Guillemot. The moorlands, especially those managed for grouse, hold significant populations of raptor species including Merlin, Short-eared Owl and (in Bowland) Hen Harrier. Black Grouse is extinct in all but the Cumbrian Pennine region but the species recovery programme will hopefully see a re-extension of range. Other species are oscillating in numbers. Lesser Whitethroat, Nuthatch, Mediterranean Gull, Little Egret and more recently, Cetti's Warbler have extended their range in or are in the process of colonizing the region. Conversely Lesser Spotted Woodpecker and Willow Tit are seriously threatened, especially outside Cheshire.

This region's birdwatchers have to work harder than their east coast counterparts to find rarities. However, small numbers of Eurasian landbird rarities do find their way through to the western coastline in the days following arrivals on the east coast. The best chance of finding a rare bird lies in persistent scanning of wildfowl and wader flocks for transatlantic strays, hence what some see as disproportionate interest by the region's watchers in wetland species. As authors, we may be accused of perpetuating this emphasis in our choice of sites. This is partly because it is difficult to convey or even justify inclusion of an area of coastal trees/shrubs on the basis of one Yellow-browed Warbler every three years. However, some sites have received persistent coverage and the observers have been rewarded ... eventually. More tangible have been the rewards for observers involved in documenting visible migration, especially the more obvious coastal locations but latterly including several strategic Pennine and other inland sites.

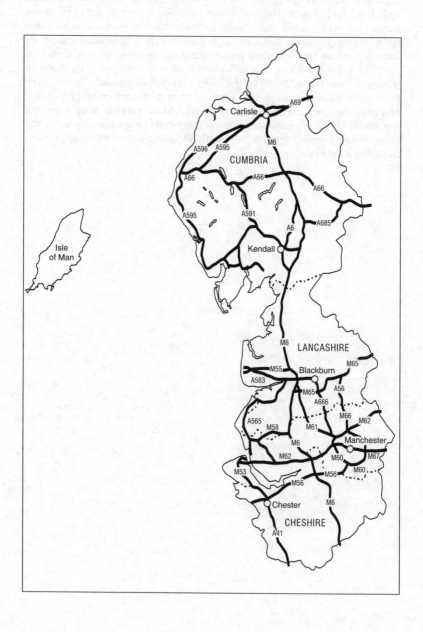

HOW TO USE THIS BOOK

The sites included in this book are grouped into regions, each with a map to give a general idea of their position. From north to south these regional maps cover Solway and the Border Country, the Vale of Eden, the Lake District, the Cumbrian Coast, South Cumbria, North Lancashire, South Lancashire (including Greater Manchester and North Merseyside) and Cheshire with Wirral, and to the west the Isle of Man.

The format standard to the rest of this series of guides has not been adopted rigidly, nevertheless for many sites the sub-headings of Habitat, Species, Access, Timing and Calendar have been employed. The Species and Calendar sections in particular were often found to overlap, and in such cases the Calendar heading has been dropped.

Habitat

A brief description of the habitat is given. The availability of habitat types is in itself a guide to which species of birds are likely to appear. For example any site with exposed mud is likely to attract waders from time to time even where these species are not specifically mentioned as occurring at that site. Any special protection or other details of ownership and status are also given. In some cases, reference is made to other aspects of natural history for which a site is noted.

Species

For each site, an account is given of the species likely to be seen through the varying seasons of the year. Speciality birds are given particular attention. There are, however, several sites in the region which, by their nature and because they are constantly watched at passage seasons, attract a number of rarities annually. Rare birds are just that. Their occurrence cannot be predicted with confidence, and a mention of past occurrences in the text does not mean that those occurrences will be repeated, even though that possibility remains.

Access

For most sites, there is a map showing access routes. In all cases access from nearby towns or main roads is described. Where we are aware of restrictions on access, these are detailed. The region contains a number of valuable orni-thological sites of industrial nature, whose accessibility depends on the consent of the owners. In many cases good relations have been built up over the years between birdwatchers and landowners or tenants. Changes in policy towards access by such landowners may occur overnight. It is vital that all visitors respect the authority and property of landowners, both to maintain good relations and good will towards the birds, and to spare us, the authors, from embarrassment.

Several of the sites in this book are accessible by permit only. Permit systems are established in order to avoid excessive disturbance at conservation sites, to provide a source of funding for conservation bodies, and in a few cases to meet the legal requirements (insurance etc.) of the landowners. Addresses are included from which permits can be obtained.

Timing

For coastal sites, visits may need to be timed to coincide with certain states of the tide. Country parks inland may be thronged with people and apparently birdless on sunny weekends. Wind direction and other weather conditions are critical at many sites. At some sites such factors matter little, but for those where they do, recommendations are made for the best times to visit.

Calendar

This section summarises in brief note form the possible highlights at each season. There is no guarantee that all the species listed will be present on any given date. At a few sites, where interest is seasonal, there may be entries for only a part of the year. This does not necessarily mean that the site is not worth visiting at other seasons. It may indicate a lack of available information.

THE MAPS

In addition to the regional maps which indicate the general position of sites, simple larger scale maps accompany most site descriptions. These are intended to help the visitor to locate the site with confidence. (Very often there will be birdwatchers present on site – northwestern birders are generally friendly and willing to share any information they may have.) Little topographical or vegetational detail is given. A key to the maps is provided below.

Key to Maps

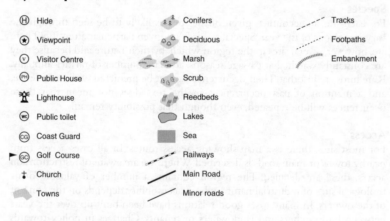

Ⓗ Hide	Conifers	Tracks
★ Viewpoint	Deciduous	Footpaths
ⓥ Visitor Centre	Marsh	Embankment
⒫⒣ Public House	Scrub	
Lighthouse	Reedbeds	
ⓦⒸ Public toilet	Lakes	
ⒸⒼ Coast Guard	Sea	
ⒼⒸ Golf Course	Railways	
✝ Church	Main Road	
Towns	Minor roads	

ABBREVIATIONS USED IN THE TEXT

CWT	Cheshire Wildlife Trust or Cumbria Wildlife Trust	NNR	National Nature Reserve
		NT	National Trust
EH	English Heritage	SPA	Special Protection Area
LNR	Local Nature Reserve	SSSI	Site of Special Scientific Interest
LWT	Lancashire Wildlife Trust		
MNH	Manx National Heritage	WWT	Wildfowl and Wetlands Trust
MWT	Manx Wildlife Trust		

THE SOLWAY PLAIN

CUMBRIA

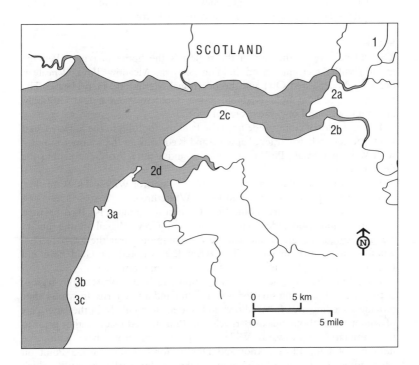

1 Longtown and Arthuret Pools
2 Inner Solway
  2A Rockcliffe Marsh
  2B Burgh Marsh
  2C Bowness-on-Solway and
     Port Carlisle
2D Grune Point and Moricambe
   Bay
3 Outer Solway
  3A Silloth Docks and Shore
  3B Mawbry Docks
  3C Dubmill Point

This area of Cumbria has not been closely studied by natural historians generally. It stretches from the slopes of the northern Pennines with their wide expanse of moorland, interspersed with large blocks of coniferous woodland, into the kinder territory of mixed cattle and sheep farms at the lower altitudes.

Moving westwards past Carlisle, into the Solway Plain, the lushness of the fields and hedgerows is punctuated by mixed woodland, remnant peat mosses, and raised bogs isolated by the advance of land reclamation. The whole area is drained by many rivers and streams. The River Esk, flowing from Scotland, is joined by the River Lyne and Liddle Water, which is for some of its length the border between England and Scotland. The River Eden having meandered through Carlisle, empties into the Solway headwater near the mouth of the Esk. Between the two is a vast expanse of saltmarsh – Rockcliffe Marsh. Further west the Rivers Wampool and Waver empty into Moricambe Bay, a very large intertidal area. From Silloth to Maryport the Outer Solway provides a coastal habitat complete with dune-slack systems and pebble-strewn shores. The farmland in this area is generally flat and uninspiring, although the occasional small tarn (lake) offers a pleasant break from this.

Species

The upland area to the east of the region is the home of typical Pennine species, with open moorland holding Skylark, Meadow Pipit, Wheatear, Lapwing, Short-eared Owl and the occasional Merlin and Hen Harrier. The forestry zones here hold Redpoll, Siskin, Goldcrest and a few Crossbills. Sparrowhawk and Long-eared Owl also occur.

The agricultural countryside from the Pennine foothills to the Solway Coast holds species such as Curlew, Lapwing and Redshank in the summer months, with Whooper Swan, Pink-footed Goose and winter thrushes roaming the fields in winter.

The mosses with alder, birch and scrub are sites for Willow Tit, Whinchat, Cuckoo, Tree Sparrow and the odd Lesser Whitethroat.

The river systems are home for Common Sandpipers, Red-breasted Merganser and Goosander, with Dipper and Grey Wagtail in the higher reaches. Kingfishers also occur but are not common. Near the lower reaches wildfowl are regular in winter. The River Esk is noted for Goldeneye and Green Sandpiper whilst in summer Little Gulls are often seen.

The saltmarshes are one of the most important bird habitats of this region, as they are the breeding sites for waders, gulls and a few terns. In winter they provide a feeding area for wildfowl and waders, particularly in the latter part of winter when thousands of Barnacle and Pink-footed Geese gather prior to their migration northwards. Wader passage is also strong here with large numbers of Grey Plover, Knot and Dunlin, for example. Grune Point on Moricambe Bay is a good migration watchpoint for smaller migrants, which in recent years have included rarer species such as Golden Oriole, Hoopoe and Barred and Yellow-browed Warblers. Offshore, Great Shearwater, Storm and Leach's Petrels and three species of Skua have occasionally been 'storm-bound' here in adverse conditions.

Along the Solway Coast large parties of Scaup are found in winter along with Red-throated Diver and Great Crested Grebe in smaller numbers. Glaucous and Mediterranean Gulls both occur here from time to time. Among the tidewrack in the dune areas small flocks of Goldfinch and Twite are regular, the odd Snow Bunting and, more unusually, Shore Lark have occasionally appeared here.

1 LONGTOWN AND ARTHURET POOLS

OS Landranger Map 85
NY37

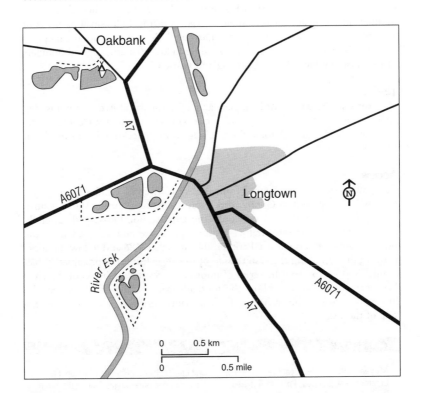

Habitat

The village of Longtown is situated 8 miles (13 km) north of Carlisle on the east bank of the River Esk. Just west of the River Esk, on the northern edge of Longtown there are three flooded gravel pits. Two are fairly exposed, while the smallest one being surrounded by an alder-fringed reedbed. Arthuret Pools is a series of pools used predominantly for fishing approximately one mile (1.6 km) to the south and lying on the west side of the river Esk.

Winter, autumn and spring are the prime times to visit. There is disturbance by anglers and dog walkers, so birds will frequently commute between the two series of pools or on to the river Esk as a last resort.

Species

During the winter period the area is an important site for waterfowl, with reasonable numbers of Whooper Swan and geese frequenting nearby fields. Smew is almost annual on the ponds and there have been records of divers and scarce grebes. Rare waterfowl have included the first Ruddy Duck for Cumbria in 1969. More recently the pools have attracted Lesser Scaup and

Blue-winged Teal. The reedbeds surrounding some of the pools have attracted wintering bittern in the past and the odd record of Reed Warbler, a fairly scarce bird this far North.

In spring the ponds attract large numbers of hirundines. Formally this area also attracted small numbers of Black Tern, but there have been very few records in recent years. The river Esk itself regularly attracts Little Gulls in small numbers in spring and an assortment of waders that includes small numbers of Whimbrel and Black-tailed Godwits. Bar-tailed Godwit and Wood Sandpiper are rare visitors. In autumn the surrounding fields often attract good numbers of European Golden Plover, Lapwing and Curlew.

Timing
Visit early in the day to avoid anglers and, in particular at Arthuret pools, dog walkers. The winter gull roost is worth checking late in the day. During south-west gales in May and October the pools are worth checking for storm-blown seabirds.

Access
Longtown Pools can be viewed from the A7 Carlisle to Edinburgh road and the A6071 Longtown to Gretna road. From Longtown on the A6071 a small muddy lay-by (NY370688) overlooks the largest pool. Please park carefully and be aware of the busy traffic. Arthuret pools are best accessed from the public footpath in Longtown. Park sensibly at NY377686 and follow the footpath south-west along the eastern side of the river Esk for approximately half a mile (800 m) to view the series of pools. To access to the banks of the river Esk north of Longtown follow the footpath from NY376689 (just over the bridge that crosses the river); the footpath runs north-east along the western side of the Esk.

CALENDAR

All year: Little Grebe, Great Crested Grebe, Common Teal, Shoveler, Pochard, Tufted Duck, Coot, Kingfisher, Grey Wagtail, Reed Bunting. and Lesser Redpoll. Rarities and scarcities have included Blue-winged Teal, Night Heron, Hobby and Mediterranean Gull.

November–March: Whooper Swan, grey geese, Pintail, Eurasian Wigeon, Common Goldeneye, Gadwall, Smew, Goosander, occasional Kittiwake, Red-necked, Slavonian and Black-necked Grebes and Long-tailed Duck. Lesser Scaup has also been recorded during this period.

March–May: Gadwall, Shelduck, Green Sandpiper, Common Sandpiper, Whimbrel, Little Gull, Grasshopper Warbler, Whinchat

June–July: Canada Goose, Mute Swan (moulting), Common Tern, Common Sandpiper and Ringed Plover. Rarities and scarcities have included Whiskered Tern, Spotted Sandpiper, Wood Sandpiper and Spotted Redshank.

August–October: Peregrine Falcon, Merlin, Chiffchaff, Linnet, Tree Sparrow, Yellow-hammer, passage waders, Gadwall. Rarities and scarcities have included Yellow-browed Warbler, Ferruginous Duck and Roseate Tern.

2 INNER SOLWAY

OS Landranger Map 85
NY15, 16, 26, 36

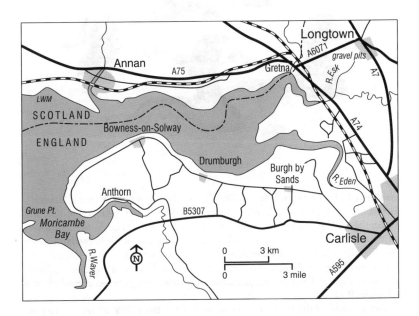

Habitat

The Solway Firth is one of Britain's major estuaries and is of international importance for both waders and waterfowl. The whole estuary is protected under European law as a Special Protection Area (SPA). The English shore has extensive salt marshes from Rockliffe to Grune Point, all scheduled as grade 1 Sites of Special Scientific Interest (SSSI). The shoreline from Port Carlisle, through to Bowness-on-Solway and then onto Cardurnock Flatts comprises expanses of sand and boulder-strewn shingle. Grune Point on the south side of Moricambe Bay is a shingle promontory with a mixed scrub cover of gorse and bramble and is a well-known Cumbrian migration point. At Silloth the Solway becomes much wider and deeper and is a site for sea ducks and seabirds.

Species

The saltmarsh on the Inner Solway is well known for wintering geese. The first Barnacle Geese arrive in October and build up to well over 10,000 birds. Pink-footed Geese used to winter in large numbers on the Inner Solway, but numbers have dropped drastically in recent years. During late winter numbers can still build up to well over 15,000 individuals before they depart in April to their breeding grounds.

Other waterbirds for which the Solway is important include Cormorant, Whooper Swan, Shelduck, Scaup and Common Goldeneye. Waders that reach numbers of international importance on the Solway include Oystercatcher, Golden Plover, Northern Lapwing, Knot, Dunlin, Bar-tailed Godwit, Curlew, Redshank and Turnstone. Up to 100,000 gulls roost in winter. Other wintering

Scaup

wildfowl and waders include Greylag Goose, Teal, Eurasian Wigeon, Shoveler, Red-breasted Merganser, Ringed Plover, Grey Plover, Black-tailed Godwit and Greenshank. The Solway can support reasonable numbers of grebes and divers in winter. As would be expected with this vast number of birds, predators such as Merlin, Hen Harrier and Peregrine Falcon are attracted here in winter. Short-eared and Barn Owls also hunt the salt marshes. Flocks of Goldfinch, Twite, Meadow Pipit and Skylark frequent the salt marsh, with very occasional records of Snow Bunting.

Gravel beds on the River Eden known as Carr Beds (NY359607) have produced some good rarities such as Greater Yellowlegs and White-winged Black Tern in the past, but access to this site is difficult.

Bowness-on-Solway is a prime site in spring, especially during a period of strong westerly winds. This is where one can experience one of Cumbria's biggest spectacles: the skua passage. Large numbers of Pomarine Skua and smaller numbers of Arctic and Great Skuas pass at close range during the right series of weather conditions. There is little to compare to the sight and experience of picking up a distant swirl of Pomarine Skuas over Criffel and watching them turn and fly in past you before gaining height and heading inland. Given suitable conditions in May you may also be rewarded with a close view of a stunning adult Long-tailed Skua; on 18 May 2007 a extraordinary flock of 21 birds was observed. On a good passage day Gannet, Fulmar, Manx Shearwater and divers can all be expected, and Common Scoter, Long-tailed Duck and Eider are often logged in small numbers

Passage waders can also be worth a check. Spring is a good time for Sanderling, Little Stint and Curlew Sandpiper. The Bowness-on-Solway area has recent spring records of Pectoral Sandpiper, Avocet and Spoonbill.

Grune point in spring can be rich with common migrants such as Northern Wheatear, Whinchat and Willow Warbler. In the past these migrants have been accompanied by scarcities such as Wryneck, Golden Oriole and Red-backed Shrike. The salt marshes of Skinburness Marsh, viewable from Grune, form a rich habitat that supports many breeding waders. Spoonbill, Little Egret and Great White Egret have appeared in recent springs. Grune Point is an important site for passage waders that hosted Cumbria's first Terek Sandpiper.

The first return migrants of autumn appear in July. As passage increases Whimbrel, Ruff, Little Stint and Curlew Sandpiper are possible. Black-tailed Godwit appears on Cardurnock Flatts and Bowness-on-Solway in numbers high enough to be of national importance during a brief few weeks in August and September, with smaller numbers wintering in recent years. Rare waders in recent years include Long-billed Dowitcher, American Golden Plover, Pacific Golden Plover and Pectoral Sandpiper. Stormy weather in October can bring storm-bound seabirds such as European and Leach's Storm-petrels, Long-tailed Skua and Sabine's Gull into the natural funnel of the estuary.

Autumn passage of passerines can be obvious, particularly at Grune Point. Large movements of winter thrushes and smaller groups of warblers and finches can be observed during the right conditions. There are records of Firecrest, Great Grey Shrike, Lapland Bunting and Yellow-browed Warbler.

Timing

A large estuary such as the Solway can be attractive to birders all year round, but the best times are spring and autumn for waders, skuas and passerines, and late winter for waterfowl. Careful study of weather conditions in April and May will help you maximise your chances of observing the skua passage. An hour either side of high tide is the best time to see most shorebirds as they are pushed onto their high-tide roosts sited on the salt marsh.

2A ROCKLIFFE MARSH   OS ref: NY334648

This is an important site for breeding waders. It is wardened throughout the summer months by Cumbria Wildlife Trust. Access is limited and *strictly by permit*. In winter the area is popular with wildfowlers. Take the A74(T) north from Carlisle 4 miles (6.4 km) to Todhills and follow the minor road to Rockciffe Village. Turn right to Castletown House and Rockliffe Cross 2 miles (3.2 km) from the village. Follow the lane half a mile (0.8 km) to the Esk Boathouse and leave your car. A track round the inner marsh runs along the top of the grass sea-protection embankment giving good views across the whole marsh.

2B BURGH MARSH   OS ref: NY328608 and NY294594

This large salt marsh, owned by the National Trust, has two access points. Follow the B5307 in Carlisle to Bellevue and take a minor road to the right to Kirkandrews and Burgh-by-Sands. At the crossroads in Burgh-by-Sands turn right for the King Edward I monument. After approximately one mile (1.6 km) there is an area to park at the top of a track on the left hand side. Park here and walk down the track to the monument for a good view over the northern part of the salt marsh. A track to the north of this point leads to the estuary of the river Eden at Olds Sandsfield.

The second access is at the west end of the village where the minor road to Drumburgh and Bowness-on-Solway follows the line of Hadrian's Wall. There are good views along the tide line and the southern half of the saltmarsh 2 miles (3.2 km) west of Burgh-by-Sands. Beware of high tides, which may cover the road. There are regular flocks of Barnacle Geese on this area during winter. Both Red-breasted Goose and Ross's Goose have been recorded.

Barnacle Geese

2C BOWNESS-ON-SOLWAY
AND PORT CARLISLE   OS ref: NY224628 and NY239623

The minor road from Burgh-by-Sands through Port Carlisle and Bowness-on-Solway follows close to the inner Solway along much of its route. As you pass through the main part of Port Carlisle, just before the road bends around to the left there is a small area to park on the right hand side of the road next to a small children's play area and just before a track. Park here and walk along the track south along the edge of the estuary for good views of the old harbour. This area is very good for viewing passage waders and terns. In recent years it has hosted White-winged Black Tern, Pacific Golden Plover, Long-billed Dowitcher, Broad-billed Sandpiper and Red-rumped Swallow. This area is best viewed an hour or so before or after high tide.

Pass through Port Carlisle towards Bowness-on-solway until just before the road bends to the left. There is a small parking area on the right (NY231629). This is another good viewpoint for the shoreline and can afford close views of waders on the rising and falling tide.

Continuing along the minor road through Bowness-on-Solway the best viewpoints are at a car park just east of the village (NY233628), the embankment of the old Solway viaduct at Herdhill Scar (NY212628) and at North Plains Farm (NY197616). At North Plains Farm you can drive down a short track to park in the RSPB car park and the walk down the track to view screens and hides overlooking pools and floods. This part of the reserve is good in winter for geese and ducks, supports breeding waders and farmland species during the summer. The reserve also attracts passage waders in spring and autumn. Rarities have included Red-backed Shrike, Purple Heron, Pectoral Sandpiper, Green-winged Teal and Ring-necked Duck.

A large stretch of the saltmarsh known as Campfield Marsh is also part of the RSPB reserve. A roadside scrape opposite Campfield Farm can be viewed from a lay-by at NY194610. This scrape can attract numbers of waders and waterfowl, and also attracts pipits and wagtails.

A short distance before North Plains Farm lies a small Cumbria Wildlife

Trust nature reserve known simply as Bowness Nature Reserve (NY205617). It contains a series of flooded gravel pits surrounded by rich mixed woodland. The reserve supports a typical array of woodland species, perhaps most notable is Willow Tit: this is perhaps the most reliable site in Cumbria for this species.

Good birds recorded on this site have included Yellow-browed Warbler, Mealy Redpoll, Ring Ouzel and Long-eared Owl. The reserve is also of interest for dragonfly enthusiasts, with not only Black Darter, Ruddy Darter and Migrant Hawker occurring in recent years but also Britain's sixth record of Scarlet Dragonfly.

2D GRUNE POINT AND MORICAMBE BAY   OS ref: NY144569

Good views of Moricambe Bay can be achieved on the eastern shore from the wireless station near the village of Anthorn. The river Wampool feeds into the bay to the east of Anthorn and can be viewed from the village. This area is a reliable site for small numbers of Yellow-legged Gull in the post-breeding flocks of moulting Lesser Black-backed and Herring Gulls in late summer.

The western shore of Moricambe bay can be covered well from Grune Point and Skinburness. To reach Grune Point take the B5302 from Carlisle to Silloth where a minor road northwards takes you to Skinburness. Park near the Skinburness Hotel and walk along the edge of Skinburness Marsh (NY128559) to Grune Point or along the shoreline from the private road behind the hotel.

CALENDAR

All year: Cormorant, Oystercatcher, Redshank, Northern Lapwing, Curlew, Common Snipe, Common Teal, Greylag Goose, Grey Heron, Grey Wagtail, Stonechat, Reed Bunting, Yellowhammer and Tree Sparrow.

November–March: Great Crested Grebe, Whooper Swan, Pink-footed Goose, Barnacle Goose, Pintail, Eurasian Wigeon, Common Goldeneye, Scaup, Red-breasted Merganser, Common Eider (rare), Sanderling, Dunlin, Knot, European Golden Plover, Grey Plover, Bar-tailed Godwit, Black-tailed Godwit, Jack Snipe, Turnstone, Kittiwake, Guillemot, Short-eared Owl, Barn Owl, Hen Harrier, Merlin, Peregrine Falcon, Rock Pipit and Twite.

March–May: Grey geese, Barnacle Goose, 10 species of duck, Green Sandpiper, Common Sandpiper, Ruff, Black-tailed Godwit, Little Gull, terns, Arctic Skua, Pomarine Skua, Great Skua, Long-tailed Skua, Northern Wheatear, Whinchat and hirundines. Scarce visitors have included Little Egret, White Stork, Common Crane, Bluethroat and Pectoral Sandpiper,

June–July: Fulmar, Manx Shearwater (during gales), Gannet, terns, skuas, Wood Sandpiper (rare), Whimbrel, Ruff, Lesser Whitethroat and Grasshopper Warbler. Recent rarities have included Pacific Golden Plover and White-winged Black Tern.

August–November: Returning geese, ducks, swans and waders, Little Ringed Plover, Little Stint, Curlew Sandpiper, Grey Plover, Black-tailed Godwit, Spoonbill (rare), Yellow-legged and other gulls, terns and skuas. Excellent passage of passerines can be expected at Grune Point. Rare and scarce visitors have included European and Leach's Storm-petrels, Long-billed Dowitcher, American Golden Plover, Pacific Golden Plover, Pectoral Sandpiper, Buff-breasted Sandpiper, Broad-billed Sandpiper, Black-winged Pratincole, Wryneck, Golden Oriole, Red-backed Shrike, Red-rumped Swallow, Yellow-browed Warbler, Barred Warbler and Lapland Bunting.

3 OUTER SOLWAY

OS Landranger Map 85
NY04, 05, 14 and 15

Habitat

This region of the Solway has a low mixed coastline of sand dunes and shingle. It offers panoramic views of the north shore across the border to Scotland. The mountain of Criffel is the most noticeable land feature. The sand dunes at south Silloth and Mawbry Banks form the two largest areas of dune slack on the English shore of the Solway and provide habitat for Natterjack Toad. The dune habitat supports a rich flora as well as bird interest. Low tide at Silloth and Allonby reveals several large scars: these banks of deposited large stones and shingle with small pools are attractive for smaller shorebirds.

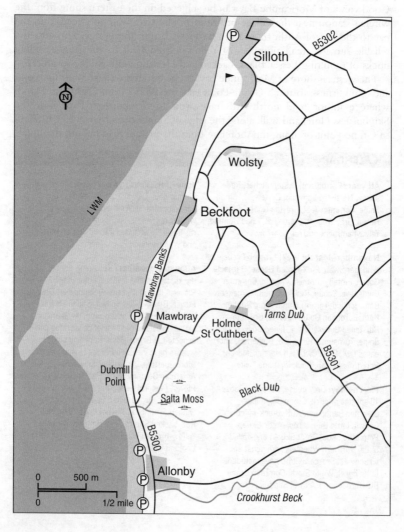

Species

The shore here holds several groups of waders and waterfowl not usually seen in the inner Solway. In autumn and winter Mallard, Eurasian Wigeon, Scaup, Common Goldeneye and Red-breasted Merganser are widespread. Ringed Plover, Bar-tailed Godwit, Sanderling and Turnstone occur in reasonable numbers and are the most numerous waders. There have been very high counts of Great Crested Grebe in recent years and Red-necked and Slavonian Grebes have been noted on rare occasions. The coastline attracts auks, and skuas occur in suitable weather conditions.

Gulls are a major feature of this section of the estuary; Mediterranean Gull and Little Gull recorded regularly. Glaucous and Iceland Gulls were regular in this area, but both have become very scarce in recent years. Rock Pipit and mixed flocks of Goldfinch, Twite and Linnet often feed on the tide line. This is an important area for breeding shorebirds such as Oystercatcher and Ringed Plover, so take care when walking on the shingle. Stonechat, Whitethroat and Lesser Whitethroat all breed. The area was formerly a breeding site for Corn Bunting, but sadly this species no longer occurs in Cumbria with any regularity. The area has attracted scarce birds such as Hoopoe, but is perhaps better known historically for hosting Britain's first Isabelline Wheatear.

Timing

The best conditions for watching the wildfowl and waders of this area occur one or two hours either side of high tide, when the waders are closer to the shore. During very big tides waders are often pushed off their traditional roosts and on to neighbouring fields. South-westerly gales may bring in divers, auks, skuas and other seabirds into the outer Solway area. Spring and autumn passage of land birds can also be notable here, as can hard-weather movements of birds.

Access

Access to the shore is good: the B5300 Maryport to Silloth road runs along the coast and has car parks at regular intervals.

3A SILLOTH DOCKS AND SHORE   OS Ref: NY105535

Habitat and species

The high and low water mark in Silloth are very close together. The promenade leading along the shoreline north east of the town to the lighthouse and beyond East Cote overlooks the whole of the Solway Firth. The town's public park has small groups of pine and ornamental shrubberies and is a good area to search for migrating land birds. In winter a good selection of wildfowl, waders and gulls can be seen in the bay. Expect good numbers of Great Crested Grebe, Scaup, Common Goldeneye and Red-breasted Merganser. Waders frequent the exposed sand banks and scars at low tide. Good numbers of Oystercatcher, Knot, Dunlin, Sanderling, Bar-tailed Godwit and Curlew occur. Mediterranean Gulls can be regular here in winter. Large numbers of gulls regularly frequent the docks, and there is often a mixed flock of finches here including Linnet, Goldfinch, Twite and sometimes Brambling. Scaup, Common Scoter, Common Goldeneye, Red-breasted Merganser, Shag, Red-throated Diver and Great Northern Diver have all visited the docks.

Access

The docks and promenade car park are well signposted from the centre of Silloth.

3B MAWBRY BANKS   OS Ref: NY083475

Habitat and species

This site is one mile (1.6 km) of fixed sand dunes with some gorse and scrub cover. The shore consists of pebbles and mussel beds. Waders on the shore include Oystercatcher, Ringed Plover, Redshank, Turnstone, Sanderling, Curlew and occasionally small numbers of Purple Sandpiper. Mallard and Eurasian Wigeon are the most common waterfowl. Grebes, Scaup, Shelduck, Common Goldeneye, Long-tailed Duck and Red-breasted Merganser occur occasionally.

Passage waders include Greenshank, Common Sandpiper, Knot and Dunlin. During summer the commoner gulls share the site with terns. The dunes provide habitat for Skylark and Meadow Pipit. Short-eared Owls may hunt the area during migration periods and in winter. Large groups of Starling roam the dune slacks in autumn and are often joined by Redwing and Fieldfare during bad weather. Spring migration produces Northern Wheatear, Whinchat amongst the resident Stonechats. Barn Owl is frequent here. Pink-footed Geese will often frequent nearby fields, especially during cold conditions. Small finch flocks mixed with Reed Bunting and Yellowhammer frequent this site during winter. Stock Dove is the commonest pigeon. Mawbry banks hosted a wintering Hoopoe during 1988–1989.

Access

The B5300 traverses the site. Access the shore from Mawbry down a track at the road junction for The Tarns (NY083469).

Pink-footed geese

3C DUBMILL POINT   OS Ref: NY076458

Habitat and species

The shoreline at Dubmill Point is dominated by Dubmill Scar, a large mussel bed and shingle bank where large groups of waders assemble at high tide. As well as the commoner waders expect to see Curlew, Bar-tailed Godwit, Knot and Sanderling at high tide. Bar-tailed Godwit can gather in hundreds. Greenshank, Grey plover, Whimbrel and Spotted Redshank may visit during migration. Red-throated Diver, Great Crested Grebe, Whooper Swan and Common Scoter are regular wildfowl visitors. Glaucous Gull has been recorded here on several occasions. The shoreline often attracts Twite during winter. Northern Wheatears use the short areas of turf during migration periods; large numbers can be encountered here.

On the landward side of Dubmill Point lies Salta Moss; this wetland area attracts Short-eared and Barn Owls, and on occasion Hen Harrier or Peregrine Falcon. Whinchat, Grey Wagtail, Reed Bunting, Lesser Redpoll and Siskin can all be found here. Roosting gulls favour the point where Crookhurst Beck runs into the sea at Allonby. Flocks of Ringed Plover, Turnstone, Redshank, Knot and Sanderling gather here at high tide to wash and feed in fresh water.

Access

Access to Allonby is fairly straight forward as there are several coastal car parks in and near the town. Dubmill Point itself is a bit more difficult and is best approached from the road or shore from Allonby.

VALE OF EDEN

CUMBRIA

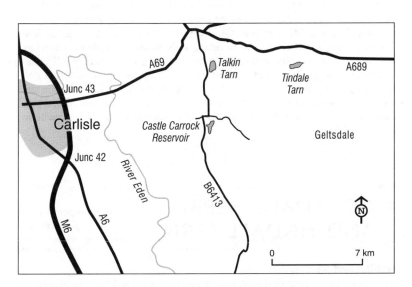

4 Geltsdale and Tindale Tarn
5 Talkin Tarn
6 Castle Carrock Reservoir
7 Eden Valley
   7A Lazonby

7B Langwathby
7C Culgaith Area
7D Kirkby Thore
7E Whinfell Forest, Cliburn

Habitat

This sheltered and agriculturally rich valley lies on the western side of the northern Pennines, which protects the area from cold east winds in winter. The valley stretches for 40 miles (64 km) from Carlisle to near the source of the River Eden beyond Kirkby Stephen. The river is the area's dominant feature as it meanders its way north. It is particularly interesting as it deepens from Appleby northwards. This area of rich pastureland and mixed arable farming it has, by and large, kept its character over the years. Many hedgerows and trees have been retained and only as the valley nears Carlisle does the trend for larger fields appear. East of Carlisle lies Talkin Tarn, a country park run by Cumbria County Council. Higher up on the lower slopes of the Pennines is the more isolated Tindale Tarn. Castle Carrock Reservoir lies at the foot of the moorland and forestry of Geltsdale.

The area where the River Eamont joins the Eden is the most interesting area for birds, particularly wildfowl. Large numbers of geese and ducks gather near Culgaith and Langwathby in winter. On the west side of the vale, at Cliburn, south of Penrith, is Whinfell Forest. This is the largest expanse of coniferous woodland in this part of Cumbria.

Species

The Eden Valley is best known for its visiting waterfowl and other waterbirds in the winter months. There are large flocks of grey geese and Whooper Swan. Cormorant, Eurasian Wigeon, Common Goldeneye and Goosander also gather in good numbers. Waders can also be prominent, especially during migration periods: Oystercatcher, European Golden Plover, Northern Lapwing, Curlew, Common Snipe and Redshank form the bulk of this movement. The river system also supports typical upland species such as Dipper and Grey Wagtail. Kingfisher and several Sand Martin colonies are also present. Common Buzzard, Sparrowhawk, Peregrine Falcon, Short-eared Owl and Raven are regular. The woodlands host typical upland species such as Common Redstart, Pied Flycatcher, Wood Warbler and Siskin. Common Crossbill is present in suitable habitats.

4 GELTSDALE (RSPB) AND TINDALE TARN

OS Landranger Map 86
NY55/65

Habitat and Species

This moorland reserve in the Northern Pennines has a wild spectacular landscape that can be truly awe-inspiring, giving one a feeling of great isolation. The fells of the King's Forest of Geltsdale are covered with moorland grasses and smaller areas of heather cover. Many parts are boggy with small streams; some of the higher areas are bare and stone-covered. This makes good breeding habitat for Merlin, Hen Harrier, Short-eared Owl, Black Grouse, Red Grouse, Ring Ouzel, European Golden Plover, Curlew and Raven.

Passage migrants at these levels include Hen Harrier, Short-eared Owl, Peregrine Falcon, Merlin, Dunlin, Twite and Snow Bunting. On the lower pastures Northern Lapwing, Skylark, Northern Wheatear and Meadow Pipit breed. Sparrowhawk, Kestrel, Common Snipe, Jack Snipe, Redshank, Whinchat, Linnet and Yellowhammer are also found here.

Along the path that passes through woodland of oak and beech, by the steep-sided rivers Gelt and Irthing are breeding Dipper, Grey Wagtail and Common Sandpiper, with Common Redstart, Pied Flycatcher, Wood Warbler and Tree Pipit in the woodlands. Tindale Tarn, a typical moorland lake, is worth a visit during winter as Whooper Swan, Pochard, Tufted Duck, Common Goldeneye, Goosander and Smew are all regular visitors. Red-veined Darter and Black-tailed Skimmer dragonflies have been recorded at this site in recent years.

Timing

This site is of interest all year round, but the moorland and woodland areas will be of most interest during spring and summer when the summer migrants have returned to breed. Tindale Tarn is at its best in winter.

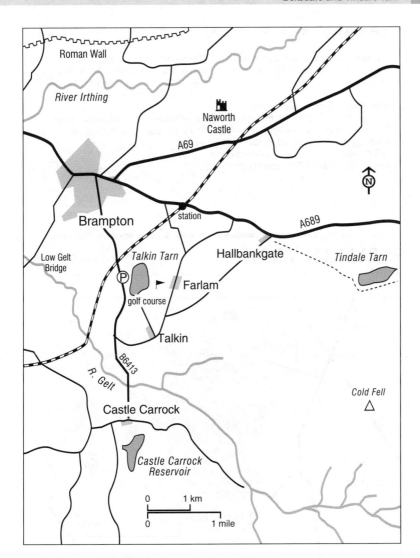

Access

There is access to three walks at all times. For Geltsdale, park at Jockey Shield on the B6413 east of Castle Carrock and walk across the River Gelt (NY542562) for the bridleways. Alternatively, from the small car park at Lower Gelt Bridge, just east of the A69 (NY520592), follow the marked path through Lower Gelt Wood or start this walk at the railway viaduct, turning west off the B6413 3 miles (4.8 km) south of Brampton. At this end it is suitable for wheelchairs and pushchairs. For Tindale Tarn park in the small car park off the A689 south of Halbankgate (NY588584) and follow footpath to tarn.

CALENDAR

All year: Red Grouse, Black Grouse, Raven, Short-eared Owl, Peregrine Falcon, Merlin, Dipper, Twite.

November–March: Whooper Swan, Eurasian Wigeon, Tufted Duck, Pochard, Common Goldeneye, Smew, Goosander and Brambling. Scarcities and rarities have included Whiskered Tern, Golden Eagle, Red-crested Pochard and Rough-legged Buzzard.

March–July: European Golden Plover, Curlew, Northern Lapwing, Redshank, Dunlin, Hen Harrier, Ring Ouzel, Common Redstart, Pied Flycatcher, Tree Pipit and Wood Warbler.

July–October: Return of wildfowl, large flocks of migrant thrushes, Brambling, Snow Bunting.

5 TALKIN TARN
OS Ref: NY545588

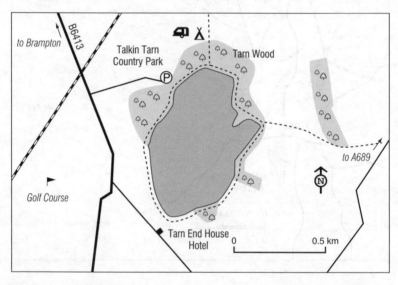

Habitat and Species

This is a small lake used for recreational purposes as part of a country park managed by Cumbria County Council. It is a well known site for waterfowl, passage waders and terns. Winter wildfowl include Greylag Goose, Eurasian Wigeon, Pochard, Tufted Duck, Common Goldeneye, Goosander and Red-breasted Merganser. Whooper Swan, Smew, Black-necked Grebe and Long-tailed Duck have all turned up in recent years. Breeding birds include Canada Goose, Tufted Duck, Grey Wagtail and Common Sandpiper.

The surrounding woodland supports breeding Wood Warbler, Common Redstart, Pied Flycatcher, Tree Pipit and Nuthatch. Passage waders and terns in spring and autumn have included Avocet, Wood Sandpiper, Green Sandpiper,

Greenshank, Black-tailed Godwit, Dunlin, Turnstone, Black Tern and Little Gull. Wintering Brambling has become a regular feature in recent years with over 3,000 recorded. Recent rarities include Lesser Scaup and Black Kite.

Access
The main car park is signposted to the left from the B6413 3 miles (4.8 km) south of Brampton, immediately after you have crossed the level crossing (NY540592). Footpaths from the car park give good access to all the lake and most of the woodland areas. Timing is important: the country park is popular at the weekends for canoeists and windsurfers.

6 CASTLE CARROCK RESERVOIR (NORTH WEST WATER)   OS Ref: N544545

Habitat and Species
The reservoir is situated south of Castle Carrock on the lower slopes of the Northern Pennines. It is planted on three sides with a mixture of conifers and

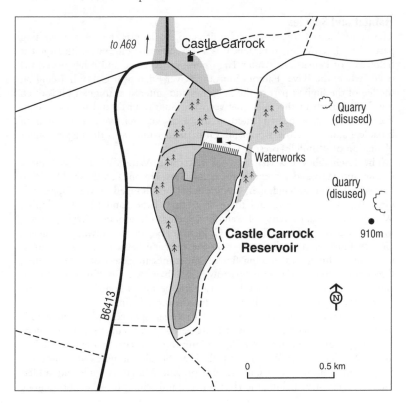

oak. The western edge has several areas of tall grasses and reeds giving food and shelter to some birds.

During winter it holds a wide selection of waterfowl including Greylag Goose, Whooper Swan, Eurasian Wigeon, Teal, Pochard, Tufted Duck, Common Goldeneye, Red-breasted Merganser and Goosander. Scarcer waterfowl such as Smew, Long-tailed Duck, Black-necked Grebe and Common Scoter have also been recorded. Passage waders and terns in spring and autumn have included Ringed Plover, Greenshank, Dunlin, European Golden Plover, Jack Snipe, Ruff, Sanderling, Black Tern and Common Tern. The conifer woodland holds Goldfinch, Lesser Redpoll, Siskin and Goldcrest. Common Buzzard, Sparrowhawk, Merlin, Peregrine Falcon, Kestrel and Tawny Owl also occur.

Access

From Castle Carrock take the B6413 south towards Croglin, turn first left on a minor road to Tottergill. Excellent views can be had of most of the reservoir (NY543540) on a footpath to Tottergill.

7 EDEN VALLEY   OS Lanranger Map 91

Habitat and Species

The central area between Armathwaite and Appleby is the most interesting part of the Eden Valley to birders. It is a mixed farming locality with large flat fields east of Penrith. In winter, large numbers of geese and other waterfowl occur where the River Eamont joins the River Eden near Calgaith. Being on the lee of the highest part of the Pennines adds interest as migrant birds often travel the length of the valley between the Solway Firth and the east coast. Forestry areas have been planted in this area with relatively new stands of broadleaf and coniferous woodland. Of particular interest is the major conifer plantation of Whinfell Forest at Cliburn.

The Eden Valley is a rich area for waterbirds. Waterfowl such as Canada Goose and Goosander breed here, as do Grey Heron, Redshank, Northern Lapwing, Common Sandpiper, Oystercatcher, and Ringed Plover. Dipper and Grey Wagtail also breed, and there are several large Sand Martin colonies. Winter sees the appearance of waterfowl such as Cormorant, Greylag Goose, Whooper Swan, Wigeon, Teal and Goldeneye. Northern Lapwing, European Golden Plover and Curlew gather on the riverside fields. Arable fields attract large mixed finch and bunting flocks, sometimes in excess of 1,000 Linnet, Greenfinch, Brambling, Tree Sparrow, Yellowhammer, Goldfinch and Reed Bunting. Small flocks of Stock Dove can also be found here. The finch flocks often attract raptors such as Peregrine Falcon and Merlin.

The deciduous woodlands are home to Great Spotted and Green Woodpeckers and Little and Tawny Owls. Long-eared Owl occurs in small numbers. Breeding migrants include Tree Pipit, Common Redstart, Spotted Flycatcher, Wood Warbler, Garden Warbler and Blackcap. Smaller numbers of Willow Tit, Siskin and Common Crossbill are also present. Migratory gulls and waders often fly west or east along the river – geese and winter thrushes also migrate

Whooper Swans

along this route, as do hirundines and other small passerines during early and late summer.

Rare and scarce birds recorded in the valley have included Black-throated Diver, Little Auk, Bean Goose, Smew, Red Kite, Grey Phalarope, Firecrest and Yellow-browed Warbler during winter and Night Heron, Black Stork, White Stork, Avocet, Wood Sandpiper, Red-backed Shrike, Wryneck and Hoopoe during the spring and summer months.

7A LAZONBY   OS Ref: NY562404

The village of Lazonby is 8 miles (13 km) north of Penrith. Take the A6 to Carlisle. At Plumpton take the B6413 to Lazonby. Pass through the village to the majestic sandstone Eden Bridge where there is a car park by the river (NY562404). The parkland to the east of the river and fields to the west often hold large flocks of Greylag and Canada Goose in winter. Whooper Swan, Common Goldeneye and Goosander are also present. Common Sandpiper, Dipper, Sand Martin, Kingfisher and Grey Wagtail are some of the summer residents.

7B LANGWATHBY   OS REf: NY565338

Take the A686 to Alston from Penrith for 5 miles (8 km) to Langwathby. The fields west of the metal girder bridge over the River Eden (NY565338) attract a herd of Whooper Swan and sometimes Bewick's Swan in winter. The fields sometimes flood and attract good numbers of Mallard, Teal and Eurasian Wigeon. Summer months bring Green Sandpiper, Goldfinch and Lesser Redpoll.

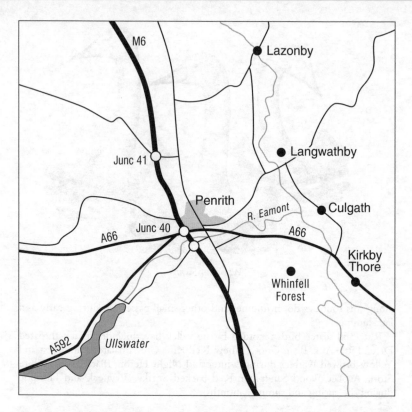

7C CULGAITH AREA   OS Ref: NY587310

The area of arable farming with large flat fields where the River Eamont joins the river Eden (NY587310) is one of the most attractive areas for birds in the whole of the Eden Valley. The hillside by the B6412 Langwathby to Culgaith road (NY588312) provides good views of this area. The river attracts good numbers of waterfowl and there is a Cormorant roost. Merlin and Peregrine Falcon often hunt here. The fields attract finches and pigeons, including Stock Dove. Less common birds that sometimes visit include Black-throated Diver, Bean, White-fronted and Barnacle Geese, Red Kite and Mealy Redpoll. If the goose flocks are not present they may be at Aigill Sike, north of the village of Culgaith (NY615317).

7D KIRKBY THORE   OS Ref: NY642240

This is another area of large fields at the river junction where Trout Beck joins the River Eden to the west of the village. The area can be viewed from two sides: from a lay-by on the A66 on the site of the old railway station (NY642240); and north along the A66 taking the first lane left. View from the railway bridge to the bend in the river. Whooper Swan, geese, Eurasian Wigeon, Short-eared Owl and Peregrine Falcon occur here.

7E WHINFELL FOREST, CLIBURN   OS Ref: NY587268

Whinfell Forest is north of the village of Cliburn. A large part of this site is a major forestry plantation with mature and semi-mature Sitka Spruce and Scots Pine. Surrounding the main forest area are several woods of oak, birch and sycamore. The track bed of the old Penrith to Darlington railway divides the forest from Cliburn moss, which is mature Scots Pine woodland with raised bog heath land flora and all the wildlife associated with such a site. The forest holds a relatively rich birdlife. In addition to the commoner species, Woodcock, Long-eared Owl, Tree Pipit, Whinchat, Common Crossbill and Willow Tit are present in varying numbers.

Access to the area is limited as large parts of the forest are private. However, a minor road to Cliburn leaves the A66 two miles (3.2 km) northwest of Temple Sowerby (NY595286) and passes through the eastern side of the forest. From this minor road a footpath through the forest starts at NY587268, leading to Sawmill Cottages and eventually to the A66.

THE LAKE DISTRICT

CUMBRIA

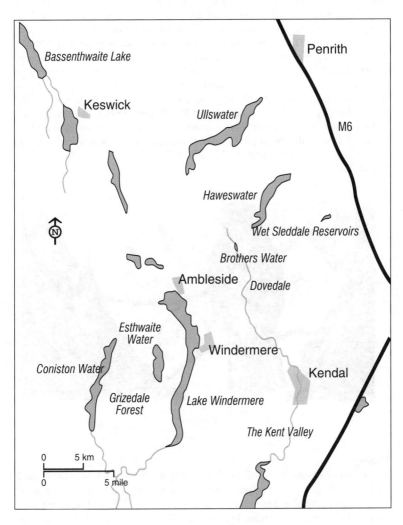

8 Bassenthwaite Lake
9 Haweswater
10 Other Lake District Lakes
   10A Brothers Water
   10B Ullswater

10C Coniston
10D Lake Windermere
10E Esthwaite Water
11 Grizedale Forest

8 BASSENTHWAITE LAKE   OS Landranger Map 90
NY23/24

Habitat and Species

Bassenthwaite Lake is most well known as an Osprey breeding site where viewing facilities have been publicised in a joint venture involving the National Park RSPB and Forestry Commission. Bassenthwaite is a SSSI and the fourth largest of the Cumbrian lakes. The southern end of the lake comprises a mixture of mire, reedbed, alder and birch scrub known as Braithwaite Bog. This is an important breeding area for waterfowl and Sedge Warbler. Grasshopper Warbler has been irregular in recent years. The bog also attracts birds of prey, sometimes including Marsh Harrier. The southern end of the lake is also important for wintering wildfowl. A good mix of the commoner species of both dabbling and diving ducks is sometimes joined by less regular species such as Green-winged Teal, Smew, Scaup, Long-tailed Duck and Common Scoter. Water Rail is scarce in Cumbria and this is one of its favoured sites. It also occasionally attracts the rarer heron species, with Great White Egret a recent occurrence. Powterhow Wood is a good site for breeding Wood Warbler.

Buzzards

Timing

The Osprey viewing point is open from early April with sightings likely until about mid-August. The Osprey centre is manned from 10 a.m. to 5 p.m. all week between April and the end of August. During sunny conditions, the light is much better in the morning. The breeding birds may chase off spring passage Ospreys. Braithwaite Bog and the nearby shallow water is worth checking in migration periods (ask the Osprey centre staff for current sightings). The other productive period is winter, especially for wildfowl at the southern end of the lake adjacent to Braithwaite Bog.

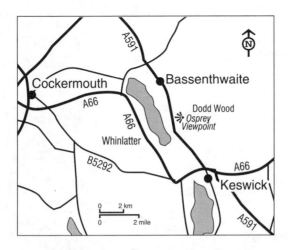

Access

The Osprey centre is 3 miles (4.8 km) north of Keswick. Turn of the A66 on to the A591, following signposts to the Mirehouse. Car and minibus parking is available at the Sawmill Tearoom opposite the entrance to the Mirehouse. There are car park charges of currently £4 per day. Coaches have to disembark passengers and arrange a returning time. From the tearoom, there is a 15 to 20 minute uphill walk to the Dodd viewpoint where a telescope is trained on the Osprey nest. Take your own telescope to view flying Ospreys and other possibilities from this superb vantage point.

There is a single hide overlooking the southern end of the lake accessed from parking in the nearby lay-by on the west side of A66. The A66 clearway is strictly enforced (including cars parked on the verge). A quick scan can be made from the south-west shoreline without visiting the hide. Lay-bys farther north along the A66 overlook less productive areas.

9 HAWESWATER   OS Landranger Map 90

Habitat and Species

The area of the Lake District around Haweswater Reservoir in the valley of Mardale is well known as the only regular site for Golden Eagle in England. Unfortunately, in recent years only a solitary male has occurred, and he is 8 to 10 years old. This geographically isolated male still showed reasonably regularly in 2007.

The area also contains most of the interesting bird species associated with Lake District habitats such as riparian, montane (including rocky gorges and crags), valley-side oak woods, conifer plantations and lakes and reservoirs. The main woodland area is Naddle Woods and this is particularly notable for Pied Flycatcher.

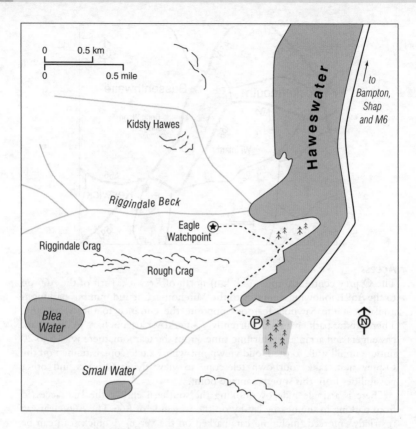

The Golden Eagle can usually be observed from a vantage point looking up the Riggindale Valley. Other montane species include Peregrine Falcon, Raven and Ring Ouzel (19 pairs in 2005). The woodlands hold Woodcock, Pied Flycatcher, Tree Pipit, Common Redstart and a few of the declining Wood Warbler. The reservoir supports a small colony of Herring and Lesser Black-back Gulls. Cormorant sometimes breeds successfully. The usual riparian and reservoir edge species include Dipper, Grey Wagtail, Common Sandpiper and Goosander. Siskin is regular in the conifer plantations and Common Crossbill regular in irruptive years. The juniper woodland on Mardale Common can be productive for migrant thrushes, including Ring Ouzel, especially during October in good berry years.

Access

Leave the M6 at Junction 39, follow the A6 north to Shap village, take the road to Haweswater and Bampton, bear left in Bampton past the church and over the bridge for Burnbanks and Mardale. The route passes the dam and then a narrow road follows the south-east flank of Haweswater (allowing views of the lake and adjoining fells). There is a small car park at the road terminus at the south end of the reservoir.

Golden Eagles

Timing

Access to the Haweswater Reserve is possible at all times. The eagle observation post is open 11 a.m. to 4 p.m. April to August. Visit the area as early as possible as the late afternoon light can be poor. Information: RSPB warden Dave Shackleton (Tel: 01931 713376).

10 OTHER LAKE DISTRICT LAKES

One of the problems with birdwatching in the Lake District is that there are many sites that do not consistently produce birds of interest. Previous publications have cited many other Lake District waters accompanied by a mouth-watering list of scarce and rare birds accumulated as a series of one-offs over the years.

The following are perhaps the best places to visit for a chance of seeing something of interest, but a regularly returning wintering Ring-necked Duck, for example, could quite easily choose one of the unmentioned lakes. It is worth checking any water body you visit, especially one with a concentration of diving or dabbling ducks. Many of the Lake District waters are bordered on at least one side by deciduous woodland dominated by oak on steep slopes that in spring and early summer may hold Pied Flycatcher, Spotted Flycatcher, Common Redstart, Wood Warbler (sporadic) and, in more open areas, Tree Pipit. Once the birds stop singing they are hard to locate in fully leaved woodland.

10A   BROTHERS WATER   OS Ref: NY402134

Attracts a reasonable variety of wildfowl and has a shoreline bordered by deciduous woodland Access from the A592 to the car park at NY402134.

10B   ULLSWATER

Wildfowl and oakwood species. There are plenty of car parks along the western side off the A592.

10C   CONISTON   OS Ref: SD290910 and SD315978

Coniston as a good track record for wildfowl. Access the western shore from car parks at Brown Howe (SD290910) and Waterhead (SD315978); there are plenty of car parks along the eastern shore, notably at SD297910.

10D   LAKE WINDERMERE   OS Ref: SD380870 and SD397965

The best areas for connecting with wildfowl species are in the secluded bays with reedbeds along the western shore, sometimes in the lee of the many islands. The best viewing points are Fell Foot (SD380870) and Cockshot Point (SD397965). Another favoured area for wildfowl can be viewed from Waterhead (NY375032), which offers good views of the head of the lake.

10E   ESTHWAITE WATER   OS Ref: SD364953

This site has sizeable reedbeds and is very good for wildfowl. The best viewing point is the car park at SD364953.

Crossbill

11 GRIZEDALE FOREST (FORESTRY COMMISSION)

OS
Landranger
Map 96

Habitat and Species

Irrruptive species such as Common Crossbill can be erratic, but Grizedale Forest (between Coniston Water in the west and Esthwaite Water in the east) is one of the few sites where this species seems to be omnipresent in greater or lesser numbers depending on the cone crop. The forest is also an excellent site for Red Squirrel and reasonably good for Hawfinch. Lesser Spotted Woodpecker and Nightjar seem to have disappeared. The forest is a huge area with many waymarked routes; a compass is advisable.

Access

Access the forest from the Grizedale Visitor Centre (SD335944). The easiest route from the M6 is along the A590 to Haverthwaite, turning right at SD340843.

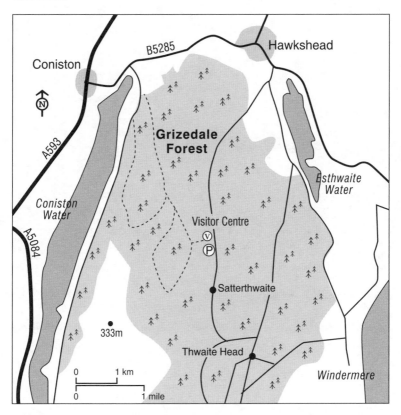

14. GRITEDALE FOREST (FORESTRY COMMISSION)

Habitat and Species

Access

THE CUMBRIAN COAST

CUMBRIA

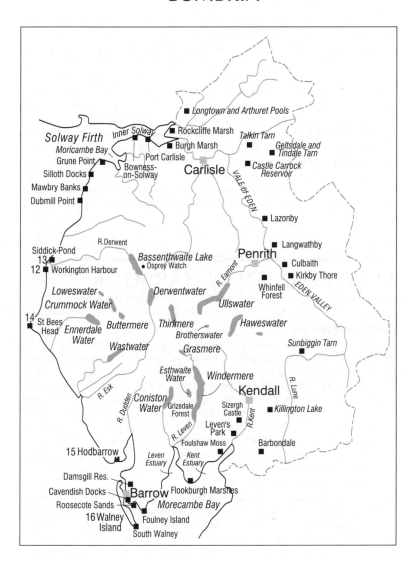

The coastline of Cumbria from Workington to Barrow-in-Furness is not generally associated with natural beauty. More often it is regarded as a polluted part of Britain's coast affected by the nuclear, chemical and coal industries. However, it has a great range of habitat ranging from the red sandstone cliffs of St Bees Head in the north, which is the point where the vast estuary of the Solway merges with the Irish Sea, to the low-lying estuarine area around Walney Island in the south.

South of St Bees, the coastline becomes less inspiring as the fields and hedgerows end on low muddy cliffs and a shingle shoreline. The skyline is marred by the dominant building of Sellafield nuclear power site, beyond which the shoreline changes to the large sand dune systems of Drigg and Eskmeals at Ravenglass. Here the estuaries of the rivers Irt, Mite and Esk meet to form a large estuary surrounded by dune slacks. From Eskmeals the narrow coastline runs close to the southern tip of the Lake District mountains, with the high bracken-covered fells of Black Combe coming close to the sea at Silecroft. Beyond Kirksanton another sand dune system starts surrounding the large estuary of the River Duddon. On the northern side of the estuary the dune slacks protect Haverigg and the man-made Hodbarrow Lagoon. The inner estuary with its large saltmarshes is very important ornithologically. On the southern shore the slacks of Sandscale Haws and North Walney are divided by the Walney Channel, which isolates Walney Island from the mainland.

12 WORKINGTON HARBOUR OS Map 89
NX 89

Habitat and Species

The harbour at Workington lies at the mouth of the River Derwent. The docks are active with coasters, fishing boats and a small marina. The surrounding area has lost all the large foundries and slag banks that were associated with the steel industry and has been landscaped. Access to the old pier on the southern side of the harbour gives good views over the whole area, as well as along the local coastline and out to sea. From the shelter of the old light station at the end of the pier one can watch Rock Pipit and Purple Sandpiper feed around the concrete block breakwater. Farther out, regular divers, sea ducks, auks, gulls and terns can be observed. European Storm-petrel has become regular in June, feeding in varying numbers offshore. Shearwaters, skuas and scarcer gull species are recorded from here on occasion.

Ringed Plover, Dunlin, Knot and Sanderling feed along the shoreline. Passage Northern Wheatear, Stonechat, Whinchat and Meadow Pipit are attracted to the landscaped grassy slopes. The northern shoreline at low tide exposes shingle and sandbanks where Curlew, Bar-tailed Godwit, Dunlin and Turnstone feed. This is also a good area for roosting gulls, with Mediterranean Gull regular. Raven occurs regularly.

From late summer through to winter Workington provides an excellent vantage point for seawatching, given suitable weather conditions. Recent years have produced large numbers of Leach's and European Storm-petrels, smaller

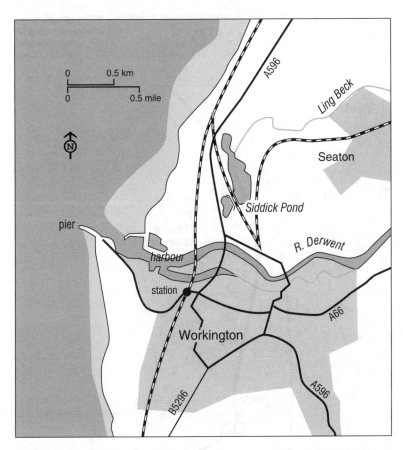

numbers of Manx Shearwater, Great, Arctic and Pomarine Skuas, and reasonable counts of Little Gull. Long-tailed Skua, Sabine's Gull and Sooty Shearwater feature more rarely. The harbour hosted a Ross's Gull in June 1994.

Timing

Workington is of interest all year round. June is the peak time for European Storm-petrel. West and south-west winds can produce excellent seawatching conditions any time from late summer through to late spring.

Access

From Workington railway station take the minor road over the railway to the harbour. This road meanders around the railway yards to the marina, where it follows the estuary of the river Derwent to the pier and coastguard lookout (NY985298).

13 SIDDICK POND

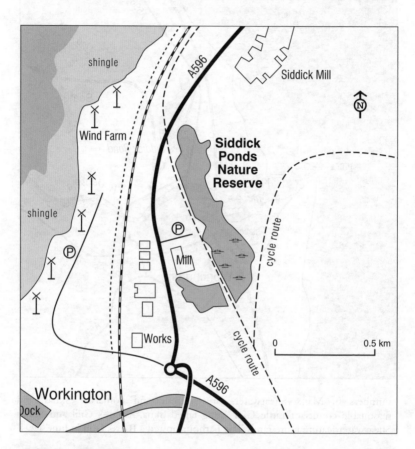

Habitat and Species

Siddick Pond lies between the northern bank of the River Derwent and the village of Siddick. It is an area of open water with a reedbed on the northern shore by an old colliery waste tip. A railway embankment bounds the western and southern fringes. To the east a large timber yard and the main Carlisle to Workington road form the boundary. The pond lies in the ancient channel of the River Derwent and is less than 10 feet (approximately 3 m) deep at the deepest point. Water passes through a culvert under the old railway to another smaller pond. A small stream known as Ling Beck feeds the whole area.

The pond fringe is predominantly reedbed with patches of rush, sedge and areas of water lily. During summer the water levels drop, exposing areas of mud that attract passage waders. The embankments behind the reedbeds are covered with bramble, gorse and hawthorn, while at the southern end a small thicket of willow acts as good shelter for passerines and raptors. The reedbeds and surrounding habitat support an array of breeding passerines such as Reed

Warbler (very scarce this far north), Common and Lesser Whitethroat, Willow Warbler, Chiffchaff, Blackcap, Grasshopper Warbler and Reed Bunting.

During the winter months a good selection of waterfowl is usually present including Pochard, Tufted Duck, Common Goldeneye, Goosander, Common Teal, Shoveler and Whooper Swan. Great Crested Grebe, Shelduck, Long-tailed Duck and Red-breasted Merganser occur on occasion. During periods of winter gales and prolonged frost scarcer species such as Red-throated Diver, Black-necked Grebe, Bewick's Swan, Scaup, Common Scoter and Smew have been recorded. Wintering Bittern has become regular at the site in recent years.

The ponds are used regularly by bathing gulls. Mediterranean Gull is recorded frequently. Barn Owl can be seen hunting along the margins of the site almost all year round and there is an irregular Long-eared Owl roost in winter. Peregrine Falcon, Merlin, Sparrowhawk and Raven are all regularly seen over the site. Water Rail is present in reasonable numbers in the reedbeds, but is heard more often than seen. Careful scanning of the reed fringes can sometimes be rewarded with a sighting of this elusive species.

Passage waders may be attracted to the site when water levels are low. Little Stint, Curlew Sandpiper, Dunlin, Ruff and Greenshank are just a few of the species that have been recorded. A large hirundine roost forms in late summer. Unfortunately, the once impressive starling roost present at this site has depleted significantly.

Scarcities and rarities recorded at this site have included Spoonbill, Little Egret, Caspian Tern, Marsh Harrier, Bearded Tit, Savi's Warbler, Firecrest, Little Bunting and Yellow-browed Warbler. This has become a regular site for Otter in recent years.

Access

There is a hide with access and a key obtainable from the security gate of the Paper Mill (the hide is on their property), the entrance gate is accessed off the A596. There is a cycleway and footpath along the old railway track, which can be accessed off the A596 by entering the Dunmail Park car park and walking behind the car sales garage to join the footpath.

CALENDAR

All year: Little Grebe, Cormorant, Grey Heron, Common Teal, Shoveler, Tufted Duck, Water Rail, Barn Owl, Kingfisher and Reed Bunting.

November–March: Whooper Swan, Eurasian Wigeon, Pochard, Common Goldeneye, Red-breasted Merganser, Goosander, Sparrowhawk, Merlin, Peregrine Falcon, Raven, Mediterranean Gull, scarcer gulls (on occasion), Bittern, Grey Wagtail, Stonechat, Linnet, Blackcap and Chiffchaff.

April–July: Garganey, lingering winter waterfowl, Reed Warbler, Sedge Warbler, Grasshopper Warbler, Lesser Whitethroat, Blackcap. There is a chance of passage Marsh Harrier, Osprey, Little Tern and Black Tern.

August–October: Returning wildfowl, migrant raptors, passage waders, hirundine roost, Bittern (latter months) and passage passerines such as Pied Flycatcher. This is the most likely time for scarce and rare visitors.

14 ST BEES HEAD (RSPB)

OS Landranger Map 89
NX91

Habitat

The immense and magnificent red sandstone cliffs at St Bees Head dominate the Cumbrian coastline. The North Head with its lighthouse is the highest point. There is a coastal path that follows the cliff tops from St Bees to Workington. Inland from the cliffs are large fields and dry stone walls with very little cover for birds. The only feature along the cliff path is Fleswick Bay, which is halfway between North Head and South Head. Fleswick is a small sheltered bay behind which a steep-sided gulley extends inland with good gorse and bramble cover. The farm at Tranflat Hall is behind North Head and forms part of the RSPB recording area.

Species

The cliffs of St Bees support over 5,000 breeding seabirds, forming the largest colony on the west coast of England. Razorbill, Common Guillemot and Kittiwake predominate in this colony with a few pairs each of Puffin and Black Guillemot. This is the only breeding site for Black Guillemot in England. Several thousand pairs of Herring Gull and Lesser Black-backed Gull breed, as do smaller numbers of Great Black-backed Gull. Shag is an irregular breeder.

During spring and autumn migration both seabird and passerine passage is notable. Divers, grebes, sea ducks, grey geese, skuas and terns are all noted here. Midsummer produces regular movements of Manx Shearwater, Fulmar and Gannet. Late summer through to autumn can be good for both European and Leach's Storm-petrels.

Passerine movement along the cliffs can be heavy during early spring, with good numbers of pipits, Skylark, chats and warblers. Hirundine and swift movements can be significant at times. Raptors such as Sparrowhawk, Merlin and Peregrine Falcon often hunt in the area at times of heavy passerine passage. Hooded Crow and Chough have been recorded among the corvid movements during late autumn. Raven breeds at this site.

Black guillemots

During winter the sea is worth checking for species such as Red-throated Diver, Great Crested Grebe, the occasional Eider, Common Scoter and over wintering auks. Peregrine Falcon is often present throughout the winter. The cliff top fields often hold flocks of winter thrushes, pipits, Linnet and Skylark. Stonechat is present throughout the year and the occasional Black Redstart may be present in the vicinity of the lighthouse. Small Blue butterfly and Speckled Bush Cricket have been recorded. Bottle-nosed Dolphin and seals add to the wildlife interest of this site.

Timing

Breeding seabirds are present from March to mid July. Although most activity occurs early in the day, many of the auks sit on the sea near the cliffs. Black Guillemots and Puffins tend to feed away from the bulk of the seabirds and are often viewable closer to the cliffs. Early morning visits are best especially when looking for spring and autumn migrants. The gulley of Fleswick Bay and the fields and low hedges behind North Head around Tarnflat Hall are particularly attractive to migrants.

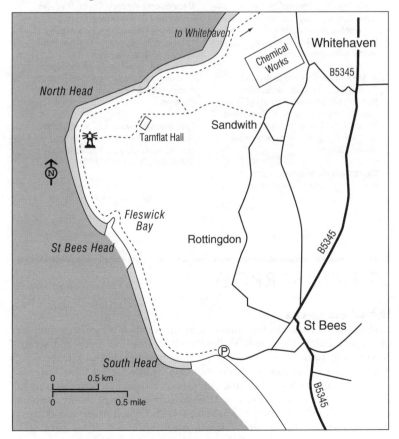

Access

From the north follow the A595 from Whitehaven for approximately 2 miles (3.2 km) to the outer edge of the built up area of Mirehouse. Take the minor road to the right across the valley to Sandwith village. In Sandwith leave your vehicle near the Post Office and walk along the private road to St Bees Head, starting at NX965147. It is around 2 miles (3.2 km) to the lighthouse and cliff path south to St Bees. The best views of the breeding cliffs are between the lighthouse and Fleswick Bay. From the south you will find the start of the cliff path in the car park in St Bees at NX961118. Stout footwear is recommended.

CALENDAR

All year: Black Guillemot, Fulmar, Cormorant, Kittiwake and other gulls, Grey Partridge, Stock Dove, Rock Pipit, Stonechat, Raven.

March–May: Divers, Manx Shearwater, Gannet, Common Scoter, Common Eider (occasional), Red-breasted Merganser, Pink-footed Goose, passage waders, skuas, terns and breeding seabirds (from mid-March). Migrants include Merlin and passerines such as chats, thrushes and warblers.

June–August: Breeding seabirds including Fulmar, Kittiwake, Common Guillemot, Razorbill and small numbers of Puffin and Black Guillemot, larger gulls, Rock Pipit and Raven. Manx Shearwater, Gannet, skuas, terns and European Storm-petrel are all possible offshore.

September–November: Seabird movements, particularly during westerly gales when scarcer species such as European and Leach's Storm-petrel can be expected. Passerine passage on the cliff tops may include Pied Flycatcher, Black Redstart and Firecrest.

December–February: Divers, sea ducks (Long-tailed Duck and Velvet Scoter are occasional), Fulmar, auks, Kittiwake and a range of other gulls, raptors such as Merlin, Peregrine Falcon and Hen Harrier (occasional), Purple Sandpiper and Turnstone. Land birds include Barn Owl, Stonechat and flocks of Meadow Pipit, Skylark and winter thrushes.

Rare and scarce species on record include Woodchat Shrike, Nightingale, Chough, Hooded Crow, Firecrest, Mediterranean Shearwater, Quail and Red Kite.

15 HODBARROW   OS Landranger Map 96

Habitat and Species

Hodbarrow is a brownfield site managed by the RSPB. It comprises a complex of lagoons and smaller pools, shallow wetland areas and open and scrub-covered slag banks. It is currently the only breeding site in Cumbria for Sandwich Tern (300 pairs in 2005), the main county site for Little Tern (46 pairs in 2005), and has a declining population of Common Tern (20 pairs in 2005). Arctic Tern used to breed at Hodbarrow, but the only county site now is Foulney Island. Breeding Black-headed Gull, Oystercatcher and Ringed Plover associate with the tern colonies. Mediterranean Gull has been seen occasionally in recent years. Other breeding species include Red-breasted Merganser, Great-crested and Little Grebes and Lesser Whitethroat.

The site is ideally located for receiving passage birds including Black Tern, Ruff, Garganey, Little Gull and skuas offshore. Black Redstart is fairly regular. The small number of wintering wildfowl can contain scarcer species such as Long-tailed Duck, Scaup and storm-blown divers.

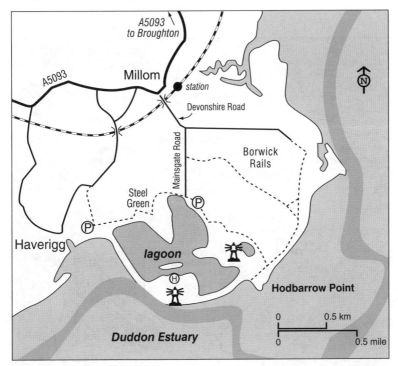

Access
Take the left fork off the A595 onto the A5093, signposted Millom (SD178854). Turn right at the T-junction in Millom by the railway station. Take the next major left turn signposted Haverigg. In Haverigg the main road takes a sharp right hand turn (SD161787), turn left here and continue towards Port Haverigg Holiday Village. Just before this complex turn right on to an unmade road that separates the lagoons from the tidal area. Access from the northern end involves a very bumpy, potholed road and is not recommended. There is a hide overlooking the ternery (see map).

Timing
Visit during late April to early July for terns and late spring passage migrants. Autumn and winter visits are best during high spring tides for roosting waders and possibly additional wildfowl. Contact: RSPB Solway 01697 351330.

16 SOUTH WALNEY AND WALNEY ISLAND

OS Landranger Map 96
SD16, 17, 26

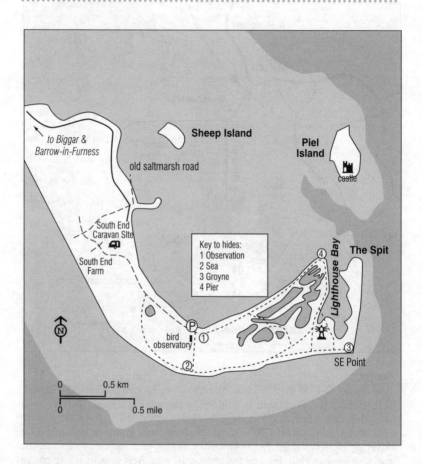

Habitat and Species

South Walney has long had a two-tier organisation. The Cumbria Wildlife Trust manages the reserve, mainly for scarce sand dune plant species, providing a sanctuary for wildfowl and wader species and conserving the huge, but unfortunately declining, large gull colony. The site is also ideally situated for receiving large numbers of visible migrants and significant falls of night migrants. A bird observatory has been in operation since 1964. The habitat comprises sand dunes in various stages of succession (including bracken, bramble and elder), fresh and brackish water lagoons, saltmarsh and mudflats. Heligoland traps were realised as the most effective way of catching small birds for the purpose of ringing at a very early stage in the history of the observatory and the vast majority of the scrub can be found within these traps.

Walney is very good for diurnal movement at both passage seasons, with Hilpsford Point perhaps the most all-inclusive location, especially in autumn. In spring, northbound birds at Rossall Point take the shortest route across the Bay to South Walney and spring movements are therefore a feature of clearer weather conditions. Marsh Harrier and Osprey have become annual spring migrants in recent years. In autumn visible migrants filter down and either continue across Morecambe Bay or, if the offshore visibility is poor, large numbers of Meadow Pipits and other migrants can be grounded on South Walney, waiting for clearer conditions.

Calm, overcast or hazy weather, especially with easterly sector winds, is most likely to produce a fall of night migrants. Because of the scant vegetation, there is a reasonably good chance of locating any scarce or rare migrants, although there is an extensive area to cover. Black Redstart and Firecrest are almost annual at both seasons. Autumn usually provides at least one scarce warbler species, especially Barred or Yellow-browed. Walney has an excellent list of much rarer vagrants such as Squacco Heron, Desert Wheatear, Paddyfield Warbler, Subalpine Warbler, Dartford Warbler, Pallas's Warbler, Greenish Warbler and White-throated Sparrow. Richard's Pipit, Wryneck and Lapland Bunting are tolerably regular in autumn and Melodious Warbler used to be, but there have been few records in recent years.

South Walney is not located as favourably for the spring passage of skuas and Arctic Tern as Rossall, Heysham and Bowness-on-Solway. Nevertheless, there is often a good range of species on offer at this time of year in a variety of weather conditions. During westerly winds and unsettled conditions from midsummer through to autumn, a good variety of seabirds can be seen: European Storm-petrel (midsummer), Leach's Storm-petrel (September to mid-October), skuas (mainly August/early October), Manx Shearwater (midsummer to early autumn) and Razorbill (late September to November). Winter seawatching can produce Common Scoter, Red-throated Diver and sometimes substantial Kittiwake movements with a handful of Little Gull. Scarcer seabirds during winter include regular Black Guillemot and Shag, and more intermittent sightings of Great Northern Diver, Slavonian Grebe, Long-tailed Duck and Velvet Scoter. Watching the later stages of the incoming tide from the Pier Hide can reveal a good assembly of wader species (number 4 on the map).

Breeding birds include Common Eider (300 nests in 2005), Lesser Black-backed Gull (11,710 pairs in 2005), Herring Gull (3, 970 pairs in 2005), Great

Eider

Black-backed Gull (70 pairs; by far the largest colony in north-west England). A census of the whole island revealed 105 to 115 pairs Common Whitethroat (2005), which gives an indication of the open nature of the terrain on Walney Island.

In winter there are spectacular congregations of waders, including regular wintering Greenshank. It is Cumbria's most reliable winter site for Little Egret, with up to six in recent years.

Access

Cross the roadbridge from Barrow-in-Furness to Walney Island, turn left at the traffic lights, and after 400 yards fork right by the King Alfred Hotel into Ocean Road. Turn left after c.½ mile into Carr Lane (signed for the caravan site) and continue for c.¼ miles to Biggar village. Just before the South End caravan site fork right, signed to the nature reserve, onto a rough track which cuts across the island past South End Farm to the reserve (stopping not permitted). South Walney Nature Reserve is open all year, 10am to 5pm (or 4pm September–April). There is a permanent warden. Entrance is by permit, and is restricted to the hides and two nature trails. A hide overlooks the gull colony and three others face the Irish Sea and Morecambe Bay, excellent for seawatching in wet and windy weather. A cottage accommodating up to eight people is available all year on a self-catering basis. Bookings are taken by the week, although October–Easter daily rates may be available, and it may be possible to accept individuals at a reduced rate. A six-berth caravan is also available.

The bird observatory includes records from the whole of Walney Island and visits to the north end during the migration seasons could be productive, especially the walk north from Earnse Point (SD171699).

TIMING AND CALENDAR

November–February: It is best to visit during calm weather as there is very little shelter. Time your visit so that the Pier Hide can be visited on the incoming tide. Check the sea for Common Scoter and Red-throated Diver.

March–June: This is the gull colony season and the gulls will flag up any raptors flying over. Calm days with easterly winds produce falls of migrants; Northern Wheatear is the most noticeable species and an indicator that other interesting migrants might be lurking in the scant cover.

August–to early November: Choose a calm day with easterly winds for a chance of land bird migrants or (mainly early morning) visible migration. Choose a wind between south west and west north west for the seabird movements over the high tide period.

Contact: Mike Douglas 01229 471066 or South Walney Nature Reserve, 1 Coast Guard Cottages, Walney Island, Barrow-in-Furness. The observatory maintains a daily blogspot (http://walneyobs.blogspot.com).

SOUTH CUMBRIA

CUMBRIA

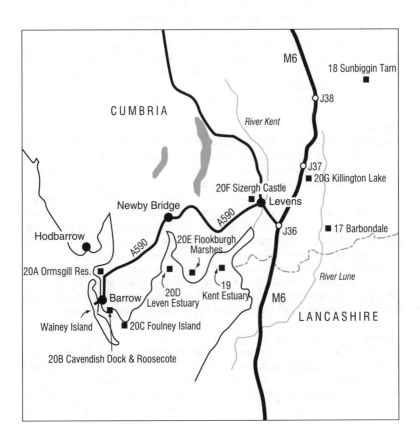

17 BARBONDALE
OS Landranger Map 97

Habitat
Barbondale is visited by many north Lancashire and south Cumbria bird-watchers to see all local fellside and upper valley oakwood species in one place without strenuous walking and private land restrictions.

The most productive area of Barbondale is a picturesque, narrow and steep-sided valley with ancient oak woodland either side of the fast-flowing Barbon Beck. The northern fell side, though sheep-grazed, has many small, scattered hawthorn trees; the southern fell side is more open. Bracken covers the lower slopes of the valley, especially on the south side. A conifer plantation dominates the narrowest section of the valley at the western end.

Species
Barbondale holds a good concentration of summer breeding visitors. The oak woodland attracts Pied Flycatcher, Common Redstart, Spotted Flycatcher and Willow Warbler. Whinchat and Stonechat find cover in the bracken-clad slopes. Northern Wheatear nests among the fallen stones and boulders. Tree Pipit abounds in the scattered hawthorns and the river attracts Common Sandpiper.

The plantation is a favoured spot for Wood Warbler, but this species is now very scarce in north Lancashire and south Cumbria and can no longer be guaranteed. Pied Flycatcher can also be difficult, especially if you do not know the song. Other summer visitors include Cuckoo and Ring Ouzel.

The variety of habitats hold a good range of species throughout the year: Raven and Common Buzzard over the fell tops; Green Woodpecker on the fell sides; Grey Wagtail and Dipper in Barbon Beck; Marsh Tit and Nuthatch in the deciduous woodland; and Goldcrest and Treecreeper in the plantation.

Timing
The best time to visit is May and early June when the summer visitors first arrive and are vocal in setting up territory. Also, at that time there are fewer leaves on the trees making the birds easier to see. Early morning can be more productive than later in the day as this area is popular with tourists as well as birdwatchers. It is advisable to avoid cloudy, calm, muggy days in June when midges abound.

Access
From Junction 34 of the M6, head north on the A683. At the junction with the A65 near Kirkby Lonsdale, turn left and then right and continue on the A683 (signposted Casterton). Continue straight on through Casterton to Barbon, turning right just before crossing Barbon Beck. This minor road takes you through the village, past the church and along Barbondale. Park near SD655826 and cross the footbridge at SD656828. Turn left and head in a westerly direction along the footpath.

The most productive section is on the north side of Barbon Beck from the footbridge to the conifer plantation. The best way to bird the area is to walk slowly, stopping at intervals for up to 15 minutes or more, scanning the trees on your left and the fellside to your right.

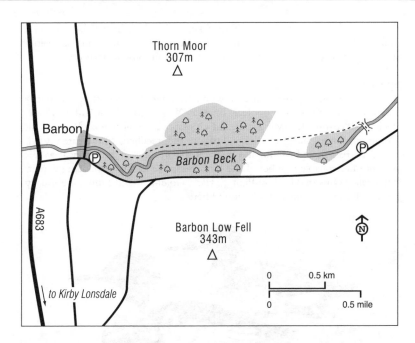

Starting at the footbridge, scan the beck for Common Sandpiper, Grey Wagtail, Pied Wagtail and Dipper. Occasionally a Goosander may fly downstream. Follow the path and just after going through the wooden gate stand for a while and study the oak trees on your right where there should be Common Redstart and Spotted Flycatcher. Look also on the fellside to your right for Tree Pipit, Cuckoo and Green Woodpecker. Common Buzzard and Raven can be seen over the fell tops. A little further westwards along the path you may see Ring Ouzel, Whinchat and Stonechat to your right. Just before the conifer plantation is the best place to see Pied Flycatcher and Nuthatch. Wood Warbler occurs at the entrance to the plantation. If you miss some species on the north side of the beck it is worth walking the road on the south side of Barbon Beck.

18 SUNBIGGIN TARN

OS Landranger Map 91
OS ref: NY61, NY676077

Habitat

Sunbiggin Tarn lies 1,000 feet (300 m) above sea level in a basin of undulating moorland surrounded by large areas of Westmorland limestone pavement and outcrops. The southern and western sides of the basin are low lying with large *Phragmites* reedbeds from which the tarn drains into the Rais Beck, a tributary of the River Lune. The Tarn covers approximately 10 acres (4 hectares) and is connected to a smaller and shallower piece of water known as Cow Dub. Between the two is a large area of floating bog and reedbed, which is the breeding site for one of the Cumbria's major Black-headed Gull colonies. To the west of Sunbiggin Tarn is Tarn Sike, which is managed by Cumbria Wildlife Trust. This is a site of botanical interest with Westmorland specialties such as birds-eye primrose, march cinquefoil and moonwort fern present.

Species

The winter months provide interest with a large range of waterfowl. Whooper Swan, Cormorant, Common Teal, Eurasian Wigeon, Gadwall, Tufted Duck, Pochard, Red-breasted Merganser and Goosander are all regular. Water Rail, Common Snipe and Jack Snipe lurk in the reedbed. Short-eared Owl, Peregrine Falcon and Merlin also frequent the area in search of prey. Raven is present in reasonable numbers. Land birds are sparse in this area during winter, but small groups of Meadow Pipit, Skylark, Goldfinch and Linnet are usually present. Twite can sometimes be found here.

Red-breasted Merganser

Spring and autumn passage brings migrant waders and waterfowl. Terns have occurred on occasion. In spring the site of the gathering Black-headed Gulls at their breeding site can be an impressive and noisy experience. Shelduck, Scaup, Pintail, Shoveler, Common Scoter, Long-tailed Duck and Black-necked Grebe have all occurred at this time, as have passage Hen Harrier and Osprey. European Golden Plover and Curlew gather on the surrounding fell sides. There is a diminishing population of Red Grouse. Passage Ringed Plover, Oystercatcher, Dunlin, Ruff, Greenshank and Common Sandpiper are all regular. Smaller numbers of Curlew, Snipe and Redshank often stay to breed.

More unusual passage waders recorded in recent history include Dotterel, Grey Plover, Sanderling, Pectoral Sandpiper, Little Stint, Turnstone and Red-necked Phalarope. Passage terns have included Common, Little, Arctic and Black. Kittiwake and Fulmar have been recorded in stormy conditions and Little Gull may appear during mid to late summer.

The reedbeds attract large numbers of roosting hirundines in late summer. Sedge Warbler breeds in fluctuating numbers. Passage land birds have included Kingfisher, Dipper, Common Redstart and Grasshopper Warbler. Scarcities recorded at this site have included Bittern, Ring-necked Duck, Rough-legged Buzzard, Red Kite and Osprey. Gadwall, Common Teal and Tufted Duck breed regularly and Shoveler and Eurasian Wigeon do so occasionally.

Timing

The tarn is the centre of a local shooting and fishing syndicate so visits to this site are best made in the close season. During passage migration early mornings or late afternoons are the best times to visit as feeding or bathing activity will be at its highest. Suitable weather conditions during spring or autumn can produce a rarity.

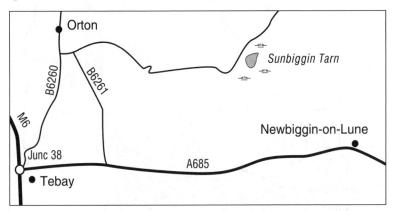

Access

Suitable views can be achieved from the minor road overlooking the tarn. Take the Orton road at the junction of the M6 and the A685 north of Kendal. Leave Orton on the B6261 and after 0.5 miles (0.8 km) take the minor road to Raisbeck and Sunbiggin. The tarn is 4 miles (6.4 km) onto the moor along the road to Little Asby from Raisbeck. Tarn Sike can be viewed from the track that leaves the road at the cattle grid (NY666074). A high viewpoint on the moorland (NY674077) looks over the reedbed and the Cow Dub.

CALENDAR

All year: Common Teal, Gadwall, Eurasian Wigeon, Tufted Duck, Sparrowhawk, Common Buzzard, Peregrine Falcon, Red Grouse, Coot, Common Snipe, gulls and Raven.

November–March: Cormorant, Whooper Swan, Shoveler, Pochard, Common Goldeneye, Red-breasted Merganser and Goosander. Pintail, Scaup, Long-tailed Duck, Merlin and Short-eared Owl are all possible. Winter thrushes and Stonechat.

June–August: Little Grebe, Shoveler, Ruff, Black-tailed Godwit, Kingfisher, hirundines, Sedge Warbler and Twite; Common Scoter, Common Tern, Little Gull and Wood Sandpiper are recorded on occasion.

April–May and July–October: Grey Heron, Ringed Plover, European Golden Plover, Common Sandpiper, Greenshank, Shelduck. Black-necked Grebe, Dotterel, Sanderling, Little Stint, Whimbrel, Spotted Redshank, Green Sandpiper, Turnstone and Black Tern are occasional visitors.

19 KENT ESTUARY

OS Landranger Map 97
SD47 and 48

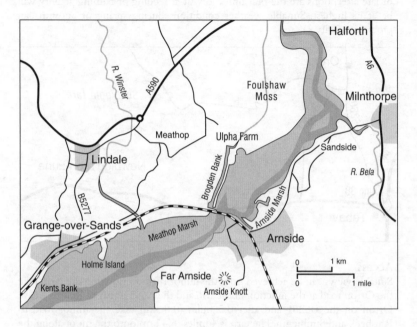

Habitat and Species

There are several strands of interest in this area. The restoration of Foulshaw Moss is still in its infancy; it may prove to be an excellent birding site in years to come. The topography of the estuary acts as a funnel in inner Morecambe Bay, leading to a wide variety of transient species on normal spring migration (skuas and Arctic Tern) or storm-blown during lengthy periods of autumn or winter south-westerly gales (Leach's Storm-petrel). In addition, the funnel effect has also led to a good track record with respect to scarce passage wader species. Other than Curlew and Northern Lapwing, the ratio of scarce wader species to their more common cousins is probably higher than at any other site in Morecambe Bay, so it is worth double-checking the identity of any small or medium sized waders.

The agricultural fields on the east side of the estuary remain one of the few regular Yellow Wagtail breeding sites in the north west, including derivatives from a former nesting Blue-headed Wagtail. These hybrids are colloquially known as "Channel" Wagtails. There is also a substantial gull roost on the Kent Estuary. When intensive checks are made in late summer and early autumn, these have contained a significant number of Mediterranean Gulls. The regular Greylag Geese are mainly of feral origin, but the recently restored Foulshaw Moss was the original site for the Morecambe Bay wild population that now frequents the Leighton Moss area. There is always the possibility that this flock may transfer back to the restored suitable habitat along the Kent.

Vagrants on the Kent Estuary have included Baird's and Pectoral Sandpipers, and Laughing and Ring-billed Gulls.

Access

Foulshaw Moss can be accessed off the A590 at SD459838, where there is a car park. The Cumbria Wildlife Trust website contains further details of this developing site.

The recommended routes to the Kent Estuary itself are:

Access on the east side can be made at Halforth (SD477838), where a log-book is kept. Take the minor road off the A6 by the Bluebell Inn at Heversham and follow to Halforth Farm. After visiting Halforth, return along the road and take the right turn about a mile (1.5 km) from the A6. Carefully check all fields either side of this road and park near the old railway line at SD489815. Walk north east along the old railway line and view the sewage works for wagtails. A male Subalpine Warbler was located in nearby bushes on one occasion. On the other side of the road the Bela estuary can be viewed. The B5282 runs alongside the estuary at Sandside and again at Arnside. There are several viewing points along this road (park carefully as it is very busy).

Nearer the estuary mouth, the area around New Barns and Blackstone Point can be accessed on minor roads from Arnside (SD442778). Blackstone Point is quite productive on good skua days as they are funnelled up the Kent on spring migration (peaking in late April to early May). This movement can also include Arctic Terns. On the west side of the estuary there are various vantage points between Grange and Kents Bank with reasonable numbers of wildfowl off-shore, notably a regular gathering of more than 1,000 Pintail.

Most of the interest in the Kent Estuary and Foulshaw Moss area is during the summer months. The limestone outcrops and associated woodland are the best sites in northern England for butterflies, including five species of true fritillary, Duke of Burgundy Fritillary and (at Arnside Knott) Scotch Argus.

Timing

There is interest at all times of the year, although, as with many other Morecambe Bay estuarine sites, it is perhaps best to avoid the very high tides.

20 OTHER SOUTH CUMBRIAN SITES

20A ORMSGILL RESERVOIR   OS Ref: SD192704

This is located in the north-west suburbs of Barrow (SD192704) and can be easily accessed off the A590. Records over the years have included Red-rumped Swallow and Black Tern.

20B CAVENDISH DOCKS–ROOSECOTE SANDS AREA   SD203687

This area is accessed by taking a minor road off the A5087 (SD203687) and following the road between Ramsden Dock and Cavendish Dock. Park by the

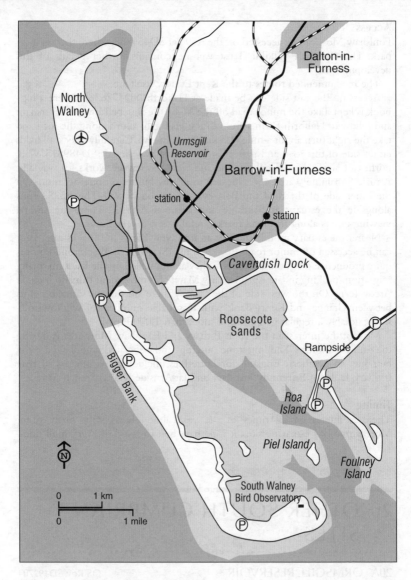

south-west corner of Cavendish Dock. A visit on an incoming tide should connect with a good variety of waders and wildfowl on Roosecote Sands, including Black-tailed Godwit. Cavendish Dock regularly supports one or more scarcer species such as Slavonian Grebe. At the eastern end of Cavendish Dock, reedbed and wetland habitats support Reed Warbler. The area between here and Westfield Point (accessed via the Cumbrian Way and Cistercian Way) has attracted some rare passerines, notably Woodlark and Dusky Warbler. There are several development proposals for the Cavendish–Ramsden area so access may change, but none of these threaten the existing bird life of Cavendish Dock and Roosecote Sands.

20C FOULNEY ISLAND   OS Ref: SD233656

Foulney Island is managed by Cumbria Wildlife Trust on a seasonal basis because of the tern colony. Unfortunately, there are only around 40 pairs of just one species: Arctic Tern. However, the site is very good for winter birdwatching and has a good track record for wader, Light- and Dark-bellied Brent Goose (off nearby Rampside) and occasional Slavonian Grebe, Black Guillemot and commoner waterfowl.

Brent Geese

Access
Take the A5087 coast road from Ulverston to the roundabout at SD243664. Take the minor road through Rampside towards Roa Island. Park at SD233656 where an informative sign indicates the potential dangers of visiting Foulney Island. Visitors will be cut off for a lengthy period of time on tides of 31 feet (9.5 m) or above. Access is not possible over the higher high tide periods. Visiting the island involves an approximately 2.5 mile (4 km) round trip with no shelter.

20D LEVEN ESTUARY

All the vantage points marked on the map can be productive at the appropriate stage of the incoming or receding tides for all the usual wildfowl and wader species associated with the Morecambe Bay estuaries. This used to be the most regular site for Scaup in Morecambe Bay, but these have become more erratic in recent years.

20E FLOOKBURGH MARSHES

This whole area is very important for roosting waders, but viewing and counting them accurately for WeBS counts can be very difficult as the birds are

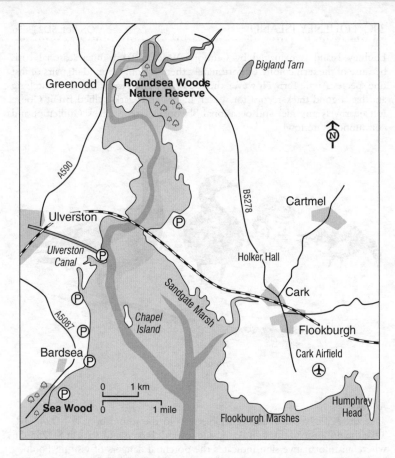

often only in range on the highest tides. The three main sites are West Plain, East Plain and Sand Gate Marsh.

20F SIZERGH CASTLE (National Trust)   OS Ref: SD498879

The limestone woodlands contain a high density of Marsh Tit. There are several sites for regular Hawfinch, perhaps the best of which in Cumbria is the walled garden at Sizergh Castle (SD498879) during winter early mornings. Access for Sizergh Castle is well signposted off the A590 by the junction with the A591.

20G KILLINGTON LAKE   OS Ref: SD587915

This lake used to have an excellent track record for rare species accompanying a reasonable-sized diving duck flock. However, in recent years the lack of semi-resident birds of interest has led to fewer birders visiting and connecting with passage birds, which undoubtedly must still pass through. Rarities have included Caspian Tern, Common Crane and Ring-necked Duck. Disturbance from recreational activities has been cited for the poor recent track record. There is still a significant Black-headed Gull colony. This site is easily checked by anyone in transit on the nearby M6. Leave at J37 and head east. Take the first turn on the right and immediately right again and view the lake after about 550 yards (500 m). Alternatively, you can scan some of the lake for Black Tern from the nearby motorway services.

20H LEVEN'S PARK   OS Ref: SD573858

This is an excellent site in winter with Dipper and Grey Wagtail on the River Kent and Brambling in good beech mast years. This was formerly a reliable site for Lesser Spotted Woodpecker, but they seem to have disappeared. Parking is available nearby.

NORTH LANCASHIRE

0524 701601

LANCASHIRE

P.C. LA5 0SW

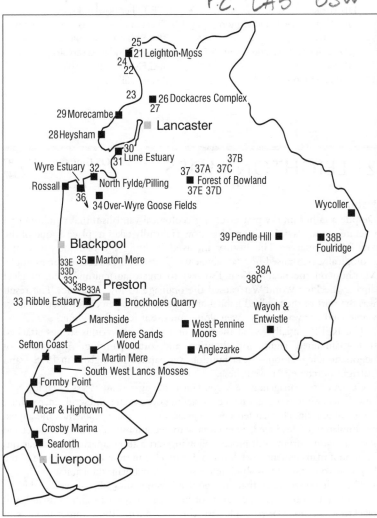

21 Leighton Moss
22 Carnforth Marsh
23 Hest Bank
24 Jenny Brown's Point

25 Woodwell
26 Dockacres former Gravel Pit
    Complex
27 Hare Tarn

21 LEIGHTON MOSS

OS Landranger Map 97
SD47

Habitat

Despite a rather murky past involving ecological vandalism that would not be tolerated these days, Leighton Moss now rightfully takes its place as one of the top RSPB reserves. The history involved draining the extremely rare and ecologically rich raised bog (a habitat which can still be seen at, for example, Meathop on the nearby Kent Estuary) to create agricultural land. Neglect during the First World War caused the drainage to lose efficiency. The result was the start of the reedbed habitat and a subsequent perception that the most viable land use was to leave well alone and use it for wildfowling.

The RSPB initially leased the land in 1964, with various strings attached that maintained rights for shooting and otter hunting. A mixture of negotiation, legislation – otter hunting was banned in England in 1978 – and outright purchase removed these.

Current site management is a constant battle against a process of rapid vegetation succession to prevent reed encroaching open water and scrub encroaching the reeds and florally rich fen-edge vegetation. The main problem is the annual accumulation of dead reed, which is slow to decompose, raises the litter level and starts a gradual drying out process, allowing scrub to encroach. Please bear this in mind if management work leads to disturbance in front of one or more of the hides on your visit: this is absolutely essential to maintain the habitat.

The valley sides are clothed in woodland comprising ash, oak, yew and birch interspersed with more open areas of limestone pavement and grassland, and blackthorn scrub. Many people visit this area during the summer months to see insect and botanical specialities that include Duke of Burgundy, High Brown and Pearl-bordered Fritillaries and dark-red helliborine.

Species

Leighton Moss is most famous for its breeding Bitterns, Marsh Harriers and Bearded Tits. There are many other species of interest such as omnipresent

Marsh Tits on the feeders by the centre, Water Rails and a good selection of wildfowl. Mammal interest includes regular Red Deer and the recent return of up to two Otters after a lengthy absence of records. The status of Bittern is a cause for concern with just one male and two females thought to comprise the local breeding population. Many of the extra Bittern sightings during the winter months are of visitors from eastern Europe.

Regular passage migrants at Leighton Moss include Spoonbill, Osprey, Black Tern and Little Gull. Numerous rarities have included Red-footed Falcon, several Purple Herons, three or four records of Caspian Tern and rare passerines such as Penduline Tit and Great Reed and Savi's Warblers. A ringing programme has revealed many scarce migrants lurking in the scrub alongside the paths. Captures have included Barred and Yellow-browed Warblers and Wryneck. Check the many tit flocks for any scarce warbler species that may join them, especially from September to early November.

Marsh Harriers

Timing

Leighton Moss is at its best for general bird watching during spring and early summer, when there is a chance of hearing Bittern booming, seeing Marsh Harriers at their most active and the greatest likelihood of passage visitors such as Osprey and Black Tern. More specialised visits are advised as follows:

For Bearded Tits, follow the public causeway for 165 yards (150 m) to view the specially installed grit trays. Almost 100 colour-ringed individuals were recorded during 2006. The best time is September and October. Ask at reception for more details.

Bittern sightings are most likely in winter when continental migrants join the local birds. The best locations vary so ask at reception for advice on which hides give the best chance of a view at the time of your visit.

Water Rails and Water Pipits are most conspicuous during freezing conditions when they may visit the area in front of the Lilian's Hide on a regular basis.

Autumn 2007 saw over 20 Little Egret and a Great White Egret roosting overnight on the island visible from the Lower Hide. Time will tell whether this will be a regular feature.

Woodcock can be seen roding in spring and early summer and heading from roosting to feeding areas in the winter months, when up to seven may cross the road at dusk (SD489759). On an evening visit you may also connect with a Starling roost and attendant raptors. The Starlings sometimes roost at alternative sites such as Pine Lake, so again it is best to ask at reception for the current situation.

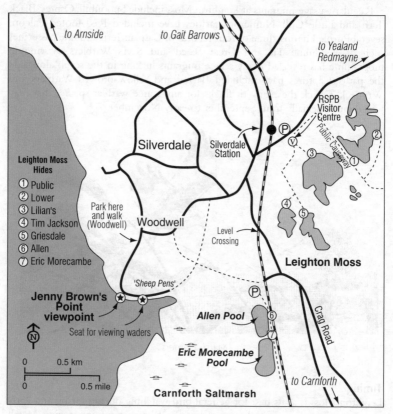

Access

Exit the M6 for the M601 at junction 35. This route also allows the option of visiting Pine Lake and other pits in the Dockacres complex. There are two recommended alternative routes from here, both reached by heading north on the A6, turning left at Borwick crossroads and left again at the T junction in Warton village.

From there, take the 'Crag road' by turning right at the Black Bull inn or continue and turn right at the Silverdale road junction (SD494720). Follow signposts to the reserve.

Alternatively, head north on the A6 – perhaps including a stop by at the seasonal water at Holmere (SD512744) – then turn left at the crossroads (SD513758) and right at the T junction in Yealand Redmayne. Stay on this road and you will reach Leighton Moss, perhaps via a roadside scan of the northern reedbed area from SD485757.

CALENDAR

All year: Bittern, Bearded Tit, Marsh Tit, Gadwall, Water Rail.

Late November–early March: Best time for Bittern; Water Pipit, Siskin, Lesser Redpoll, Hen Harrier (occasional), Little Egret; large numbers of common wildfowl (unless the shallow meres are frozen).

Late March–May: Marsh Harrier, Reed Warbler, Sedge Warbler, Black-headed Gull (breeds). Mediterranean Gulls sometimes accompany the breeding Black-headed Gulls.

Regular passage species include Osprey, Black Tern, Garganey (sometimes breeds) and Little Gull.

June–July: Marsh Harrier (with young), Garganey (some years). Starling and Swallow roosts in late July attract common raptors and sometimes Hobby.

August–early November: Large numbers of common wildfowl; regular evening roosts of Starlings (throughout) and Swallows (to late September).

22 CARNFORTH MARSH

OS Landranger
Map 97

Habitat and Species

These are brackish pools on the inner edge of Carnforth saltmarsh. The salt inhibits colonisation by invasive water plants, so the site retains areas of open shallow water and mud with relatively little management. Gravel islands have been constructed and these hold nesting Black-headed Gulls and Avocets. This is arguably the best of the north Lancashire sites for passage wader species, providing there are no storm-surged high tides or periods of prolonged mid-summer drought. Passage waders seek out the most suitable available habitat and sometimes this is on the flood at the eastern end, which unfortunately cannot be viewed easily from the hides.

Almost any species of wader is possible, although the track record for Nearctic species other than Pectoral Sandpiper is poor. Icelandic Black-tailed Godwit occurs in very large numbers and most of the *Tringa* species are well represented, including regular Wood Sandpiper in autumn. Ruff, Little Stint and Curlew Sandpiper are annual visitors. Rarities have included Wilson's Phalarope, White-rumped Sandpiper and Black-winged Pratincole. Little Egrets are regular outside the breeding season. Spoonbills appear on an annual basis in spring and early summer and Great White Egret has occurred.

Significant numbers of wildfowl can be found, notably Eurasian Wigeon and Common Teal. This is perhaps the best site in the area for Gadwall and Shoveler. Many wildfowl visit the flooded fields alongside the access road and may be joined there by Black-tailed Godwits and other waders during low water levels.

The bushes between the car park and hide are always worth checking for migrant passerines. On one memorable occasion they attracted a Woodchat Shrike.

Timing

The winter months are best for high counts of wildfowl, but checking the dwindling numbers in spring can be profitable as these may include passage birds including Garganey and perhaps a Green-winged Teal.

April to May and July to early October are best for passage waders, but the late autumn can be poor if there has been flooding by high tides. High tide visits are recommended for waders but are by no means absolutely necessary, especially if attractive feeding areas exist on the pools. As usual with passage waders, a visit in wet unsettled conditions in April and May or July and August is recommended. Unsettled weather may encourage terns to drop in. Next best is during cloudy weather. Hot sunny conditions often lead to bad light and a significant heat haze at the Eric/Allen hides.

The Black-headed Gull colony sometimes has attendant Mediterranean Gulls in April and May. Nesting Avocets are on show from mid or late March to mid August, but this species does not winter in the region.

Access

Take the left turn at SD477738 and then consider the height of your vehicle. Saloon cars can progress under the railway bridge to the car park. If you have a camper van, minibus or similar vehicle, park carefully along the stretch of track before the rail bridge. The hides are approximately 0.3 miles (0.5 km) from the car park and 0.6 miles (1 km) from the road junction. Viewing the flooded fields alongside the road from Warton to Crag Foot is exceedingly dangerous and not recommended. Instead, view from the track to the Allen and Eric Morecambe hides.

CALENDAR

All year: Regular Icelandic Black-tailed Godwit, Raven and Peregrine Falcon.

Late November–early March: Little Egret, Merlin, Gadwall, Pintail, Eurasian Wigeon, Common Teal, Red-breasted Merganser, Common Snipe and Kingfisher. Greenshank and Spotted Redshank winter occasionally. The flock of Greylag Geese is considered the most southerly wintering population of wild Icelandic birds; they are invariably more wary than and usually keep separate from the large feral population.

Late March–May: Breeding Avocet. Wildfowl sometimes include Garganey and Green-winged Teal. Passage waders include Ruff, Greenshank, Spotted Redshank, Green Sandpiper and occasionally Little Stint and Pectoral and Curlew Sandpipers. Mediterranean and Little Gulls may frequent the Black-headed Gull colony. Spoonbill is fairly regular and may linger.

June–July: Depending on the water levels, early return-passage waders may include Pectoral and Wood Sandpiper. Adult and juvenile Avocets remain. Marsh Harriers predate Black-headed Gull chicks

August–early November: Passage waders may include Ruff, Wood Sandpiper, Green Sandpiper up until mid-October. Little Stint and Curlew Sandpiper rarely appear before late August. Wildfowl increase in numbers and species from early September.

23 HEST BANK

OS Landranger Map 97
SD46

Habitat and Species

This area of saltmarsh and intertidal mudflats has lost some of its roosting smaller waders to the Morecambe sea defence groynes, but high tides provide spectacular views of Knot, Oystercatcher, Curlew and sometimes Bar-tailed Godwit. Rock Pipit, Skylark and sometimes Twite are forced off the saltmarsh by the high tides. This is the site the RSPB use for high spring tide wader watch events, which can include the walk south along the shoreline to Teal Bay (see Morecambe).

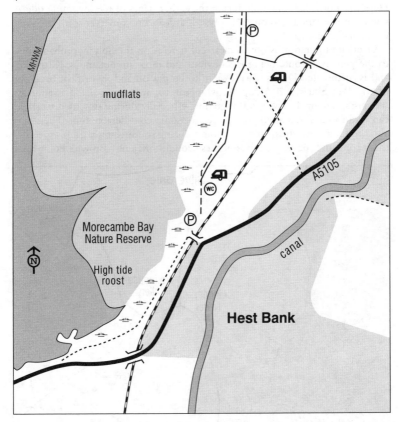

Access

Via Hest Bank level crossing at SD468665 (off the A5105).

Timing

Good during high spring tides during late July to early May. Winter months are best for large flocks of waders.

24 JENNY BROWN'S POINT

OS Landranger
Map 97 SD47

Habitat and Species

Jenny Brown's Point is a vantage point 10 minutes drive from Leighton Moss. The point overlooks Morecambe Bay, notably the inner section of the main arterial water, the Kent channel. It is building up a deserved reputation as an excellent spring seawatching station, especially for close views of skuas as they attempt to migrate overland via the Keer flightline, over Leighton Moss or up the nearby Kent Estuary. This site is best visited from about two and a half hours before high tide to one hour after the tide, perhaps following a visit to Heysham north harbour wall during the earlier stages of the incoming tide. A telescope is essential, although it is best if at least one observer scans the skies for high-flying birds.

Overland migration is not so clear-cut here as on the Solway, probably due to the perceived route being less obvious and more mountainous. Kittiwakes and Red-throated Divers usually seem to be put off and fly or float back out of the Bay. Skuas and Arctic Terns appear to migrate overland eventually. Indecision about the overland migration, especially during unsettled weather, can lead to skuas remaining on the sea for some considerable time. The site is also productive for storm-blown seabirds during southwesterly gales, especially the second and subsequent days of these conditions. Jenny Brown's Point has a

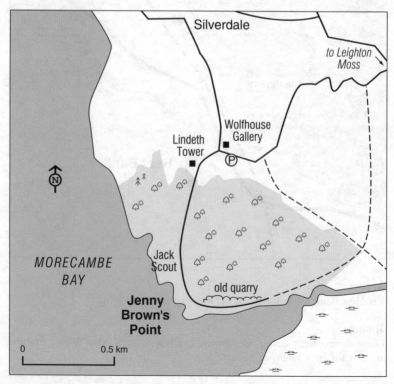

similar track record to Heysham, but if the wind is west of south-west birds may not be blown this far into the Bay. There is no shelter.

The mudflats and especially the inlet just north east of the seawatching point can be productive for waders, especially in late summer and autumn when Avocet, Whimbrel and Curlew Sandpiper can be found. These can be viewed from a seat next to the vehicle turning point.

The bushes and trees, especially those surrounding the sheep pens, have a reasonable track record for migrant passerines including Firecrest, Yellow-browed Warbler and once a long-staying Pallas's Warbler.

Access
Parking is limited and many pedestrians use the final section of the road so access is difficult. Try to share a car from Leighton Moss and follow minor roads to SD462734. You may have to progress another 220 yards (200 m) to park. Many observers watch from the road using the wall as shelter; others watch from the nearby grassy bank.

Timing
Visit from about two and a half hours before high tide to about one hour after the tide. Spring seabird movements peak at different times: late March for Kittiwake; early to mid April for Red-throated Diver; and mid April to mid May for skuas.

CALENDAR

All year: A variety of wildfowl and wader species linked to the populations at Leighton Moss and the Allen and Eric Morecambe pools.

November–February: Occasional wintering Red-throated Diver; regular Scaup and Common Eider. Purple Sandpiper is irregular on the groyne at high tide.

March–early April: Peak passage of Red-throated Diver and Kittiwake, with early Common Scoter and occasional Great or Arctic Skuas.

Mid April–early June: The peak time for passage skuas, Common Scoter and Arctic Tern; also still Red-throated Diver and Kittiwake.

June–July: European Storm-petrel and Manx Shearwater influxes during south-west gales; winds of lesser strength are good if visibility is poor.

August–early November: Unproductive unless there are strong onshore winds, when Leach's Storm-petrel (September–early October) and a variety of common seabirds including Arctic and Great Skuas occur. Migrant passerines visit nearby bushes and trees, especially during east winds and in sheltered sycamores still retaining leaves late in the season.

25 WOODWELL

OS Landranger Map 97
SD47

This is a good, if rather over-visited and well-known site for Hawfinch and Marsh Tit. People have not always respected the privacy of residents here. Observers are asked to stay on the road and not stand in gateways. Hawfinch can be found anywhere along the length of the road. Park at the entrance (SD463744) and walk. Hawfinch, Marsh Tit and other woodland species are present all year, but the former is much easier to find in the leafless winter months, especially if observers familiarise themselves with its 'tick' call before visiting.

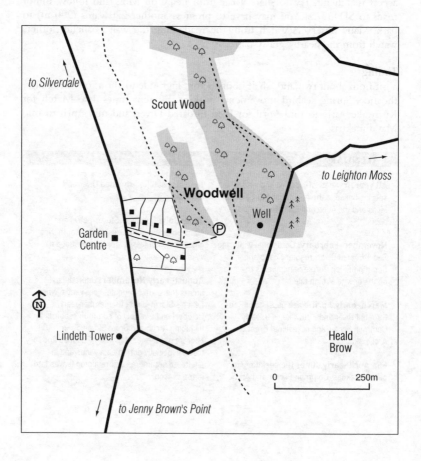

26 DOCKACRES FORMER GRAVEL PIT COMPLEX

OS Landranger
Map 97
SD57

Habitat and Species

The former gravel workings at Dockacres lie in the centre of the Keer valley flight line and attract many interesting birds. Pine Lake is by far the most important for wintering wildfowl. The other water bodies have become less attractive to birds because leisure interests have altered the character.

The main feature here is a large assembly of Pochard, especially in late autumn. The birds are highly mobile and there is sometimes a mass exodus to Leighton Moss during periods of intensive water sport activity. There is also a significant population of Tufted Duck. These tend to move between Pine Lake and the Fountain Pool to the north. Careful checking through Tufted Ducks and Pochards over the years has produced rarer wildfowl. A Lesser Scaup accompanied the Tufted Ducks during autumn 2006 (the second record for the site). Other notable records include two Ring-necked Ducks, two Ferruginous Ducks, several Long-tailed Ducks and Scaup. Rare grebes and inland divers

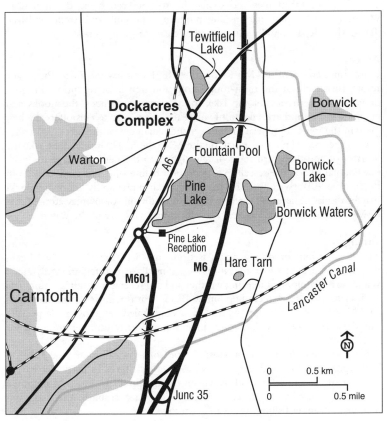

have never been particularly regular here, but have included Pied-billed Grebe. Smew was annual during the 1980s and 1990s, but there have been few records since 2000. Huge numbers of Coot accompany the diving ducks and can make the search for scarce visitors a lengthy process.

Pine Lake is a very productive site during hard weather. It tends to be the last of the local fresh waters to freeze over and there can be mass displacement of dabbling ducks from Leighton Moss and other sources. Because the area lies under a natural flight line, short-staying passage birds are a regular feature. There is little habitat for waders, but the area has a good track record for Osprey, Black Tern and Little and Mediterranean Gulls. White-winged Black and Whiskered Terns have occurred.

Passerines do not feature strongly here, but Borwick Waters and Pine Lake attract White Wagtails in mid–late April, occasionally accompanied by Yellow Wagtails (now very scarce).

In wet, drizzling conditions during the spring and early summer huge numbers of hirundines and swifts can be found feeding over Pine Lake and Borwick Waters. Check these for the possibility of a Red-rumped Swallow or an even longer shot such as a rare swift species. Soaking wet drizzle with poor visibility in spring and early summer is very productive weather for many inland gravel pits, reservoirs and other waters. Besides creating good feeding conditions for hirundines and swifts, the weather can bring down passage waders to any muddy margins and produce Little Gull and Arctic or Black Terns. Most depart rapidly if the weather clears to sunny conditions.

Access

From Junction 35 of the M6 follow the M601 motorway spur to Pine Lake resort. Turn right at the mini-roundabout and sign in at reception. Progress down the eastern side of the lake, making sure you check the nooks and crannies at the southern end, until you reach an open area. This offers the best view in the most appropriate light over the remainder of the lake.

For other waters progress north on the A6 to the A6070 roundabout, take the fourth exit and then turn immediately right into the Leisure Village to check the Fountain Pool. Please call in at reception beforehand and view only from the south side. Borwick Waters is less attractive than previously but diving ducks may be displaced here and the tiny Black-headed Gull colony may attract Little or Mediterranean Gulls. Passage Black Terns may visit any of the waters.

Timing

The best period for diving ducks is from mid-September to early March, especially mid-September to November. Pine Lake is often the only open water during prolonged freezing weather and can receive a significant numbers of displaced wildfowl, including Smew. Black Tern is regular during late April and May when south east winds are accompanied by showers (especially thunderstorms). Drizzly conditions in spring and early summer are good for hirundines and swifts.

If you are visiting Leighton Moss in April or May, call in at Pine Lake on both your incoming and outgoing journeys. Black Terns in particular have a habit of turning up after midday. Given the proximity to inner Morecambe Bay, strong onshore winds can sometimes displace seabirds: this has even included a Gannet fishing successfully on Pine Lake.

CALENDAR

September–March: Waterbirds, especially diving ducks and Coot. Large numbers of Tufted Duck and Pochard may include less common species, including Scaup and Ruddy Duck.

Mid March–early June: Most productive during wet drizzling weather or intermittent showers and thunderstorms when large numbers of hirundines and swifts and regular Black Tern (mid-April to May) and Little Gull (April to early June). Possibility of passage Black-necked Grebe.

July–August: Lots of watersports activity and few birds but worth checking during unsettled weather with strong winds; wildfowl numbers may start to build up during the last week of August.

27 HARE TARN   SD517717

This seasonal water can be incorporated into any spring visit to the Dockacres complex. It can be very productive for passage waders and hirundines during the drying out process, which leaves extensive muddy edges. A good site for Little Ringed Plover and Icelandic Black-tailed Godwit.

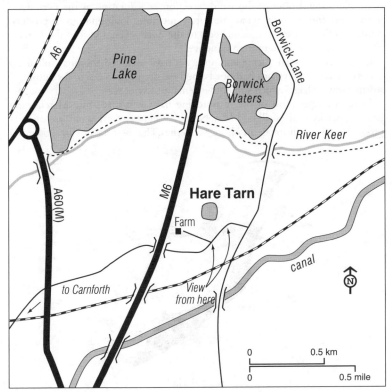

Access
Access from the minor road north from Carnforth or south from Borwick Lake.

28 HEYSHAM AREA, INCLUDING THE BIRD OBSERVATORY AND NATURE RESERVE

OS Landranger Maps 97 and 102
SD35, 36, 45 and 46

Habitat and Species
This area has been flagged up in several publications as one of the top sites for Leach's Storm-petrel in north-west England during south-west and westerly gales in September to October. However, due to its location inside Morecambe Bay – which faces the wrong direction in autumn – at least two days of strong onshore winds are required to produce any numbers of this species. The views can be excellent as the birds pass close by the north harbour wall. Observers must take careful note of the wind direction and duration as the periods of south-west and westerly winds are often not quite long enough to produce numbers of seabirds. If the wind veers to the north-west a visit to the Mersey or Wirral coasts will be more productive.

Other seabirds seen during autumn gales have included Sabine's Gull and a variety of skuas. Heysham harbour is the best site in the county for autumnal storm-blown Shags, which sometimes remain to winter.

In recent years most of the seawatching has taken place mid March–early June, especially mid April–mid May. Note that light easterly winds are often as productive as traditional on shore westerlies. The best tactic for observing

Sabine's Gull

seabird passage is to watch from Heysham north harbour wall during the first 3 to 4 hours of the incoming tide, then travel round to Jenny Brown's Point for the high tide period. This has proved an excellent recipe for connecting with flocks of Kittiwakes, Arctic Terns, Red-throated Divers and Pomarine, Arctic and Great Skuas as they attempt to deal with the obstacle provided by the British Isles to their north-easterly orientated migration. Skuas and Arctic Terns usually spiral up and head overland when they reach the inner bay; Red-throated Divers and Kittiwakes usually turn round and fly over or around Walney Island before heading up the Cumbrian coast and perhaps overland by the less mountainous Tyne Gap (see Solway entry).

Occasional periods of unsettled weather with onshore winds in June and July may bring European Storm-petrels close to Heysham harbour mouth and power station outfalls at all stages of the tide. The birds are attracted to invertebrates cooked as the cooling water passes the reactors and along the outfalls. Keep in touch with information services as, unlike many seawatching phenomena, an influx often lasts long enough for people within reasonable range to arrive in time to view the birds.

Winter gales usually produce large numbers of Kittiwake and Little Gull; Little Auk, Grey Phalarope and Great and Pomarine Skuas are possible. Like many west coast sites, Heysham received an "every 50 years" event in the form of an unseasonal Leach's Storm-petrel influx in December 2006. Waiting to see what is following incoming boats, notably the midday Isle of Man passenger ferry, can be productive at this time of year.

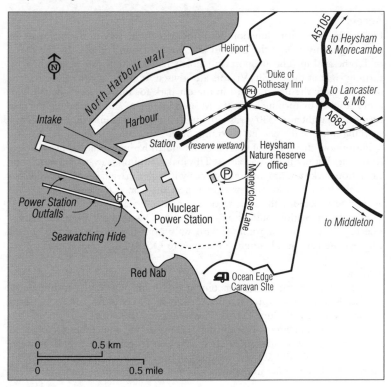

The power station outfalls should be checked on the incoming tide, but not on a high spring tide when the birds disperse, including anything roosting on the nearby Red Nab. The main features are: Common and Arctic Terns during spring and early summer; Mediterranean Gulls (including good numbers of juveniles) during late summer; and Little Gulls and Kittiwakes during autumn and winter

The heliport hosts a spectacular high tide roost of Knot during the winter. months, especially after the turn of the year when counts have reached over 25,000. Spring passage of Turnstones, resplendent in summer plumage, can be observed by looking down on to the skears alongside the north harbour wall during April and May. This site also provides one of the best opportunities in the county to see the declining Purple Sandpiper. The former wintering population is long gone.

The bushes, trees and open ground around the power stations, including the wildlife trust reserve, can receive considerable numbers of grounded migrants, especially during easterly winds and poor visibility preceding a weather front approaching from the south. Rarities in the last few years have included Wryneck, Tawny Pipit, Thrush Nightingale and Icterine, Melodious, Dusky and several Yellow-browed Warblers. Visible migration includes common diurnal migrants such as Meadow Pipit and just occasionally a scarce migrant, most notably Serin, Woodlark, Common Crane and European Bee-eater. A winter Twite flock is a fairly reliable feature of the area, especially around the feeding station on the north harbour wall. A colour ringing programme has shown the birds to be mostly of inner Hebridean origin.

Access

Follow the A683 from Junction 34 of the M6 all the way to the major set of traffic lights just before the harbour and power station complex by the Duke of Rothesay Inn. The heliport and north harbour wall can be reached by turning right at these lights. Visitors are advised to call in at the nature reserve office or view the notice board in the car park for further access details. The office reached by turning left at the Moneyclose lights and then taking the first turn on the right after 330 yards (300 m). It is usually manned during weekday working hours and weekend mornings during migration time.

Please note that the final section of the north harbour wall has been closed to vehicles but not pedestrian access. This makes autumn seawatching from your car a more awkward proposition, especially if anglers have taken all the available space along the narrow section of road near the gate. Car-based observers are advised to park along the wide section of road and watch from there.

The Power Station outfalls are a 1.2 mile (2 km) walk from the nature reserve car park, or a 0.6 mile (1 km) walk from the car park at the end of Moneyclose Lane just before the entrance to Ocean Edge caravan park.

Timing

Spring seabird passage on the incoming tide from mid March to mid April (mainly Kittiwakes and divers), mid April to mid May (skuas and Arctic Tern) and late May to early June (Manx Shearwater and late skuas).

Autumn seawatching is best during September and sometimes October on the second and any subsequent days of strong to gale-force winds between south-west and WWNW. Even low tide can be productive, especially for Leach's Storm-petrels remaining in the main channel off the north harbour wall.

Avoid visiting the outfalls on high spring tides. The best time to visit is the early to middle stages of an incoming tide.

Migratory passerines are best searched for during early to mid-morning between mid March and early June and from mid August to mid November.

CALENDAR

November–February: Kittiwake and Little Gull in the harbour or around the outfalls. Shag in or around the harbour (up to 27 in 2006–2007). Mediterranean Gull on the outfalls or along the north harbour wall. Twite along the north harbour wall

March–early June: See under Jenny Brown's Point for seabird timing (the two sites often share the same individuals), but Arctic Tern is more common (including feeding on the outfalls) and Manx Shearwater and auks are more regular at Heysham. Visible migration notably includes Lesser Redpoll in late April and early May.

Late June–August: Large numbers of Black-headed Gulls on the Power Station outfalls accompanied by good numbers of Mediterranean Gulls and one or two Little Gulls. A few lingering Common and Arctic Terns, especially in unsettled weather. European Storm-petrel during strong onshore winds in June and July

September–October: Visible migration of passerine species and Pink-footed Goose. Mainly Meadow Pipit, often with good numbers of Grey Wagtail, in September followed by finches, thrushes and Starlings in October.

Information: Visit http://heyshamobservatory.blogspot.com
Nature reserve office tel. 01524 855030.

29 MORECAMBE PROMENADE

OS Landranger Map 97
SD46

Habitat and Species

The main interest is in wintering wader and wildfowl, including Common Eider, Black-tailed Godwit and fairly regular Scaup. There have been some radical changes in the last few years with the addition of many sea-defence groynes, the extension of the Stone Jetty and the complete closure of the old-fashioned sewage outfalls. This has reduced the number of some species, notably Common Goldeneye.

The new groynes have increased the number of roost sites and made it more difficult to locate wintering birds such as Spotted Redshank and Purple Sandpiper, but without increasing the number of Turnstone and other rocky shore species. Perhaps the main advantage of the groynes for birding is to create areas of slack water on the leeward side during strong winds. The groyne next to the Stone Jetty car park is perhaps the best site in such conditions.

Morecambe Promenade was formerly noted for wintering Common Golden-eye, regular Long-tailed Duck, Great-crested Grebe and occasional Red-throated Diver. The most ubiquitous species is now Common Eider. Small numbers of Red-breasted Merganser and greatly reduced numbers of Great-crested Grebe can be found. Common Goldeneye rarely numbers more than 20. Scaup is a regular but highly erratic winter visitor.

Gulls often loaf on the sea and foreshore next to the promenade. There are one or two regular wintering Mediterranean Gulls. Larger gulls frequent the fisherman's slipway next to the Lifeboat Station and have included Iceland Gull.

The best groynes for roosting waders are by the Battery, Stone Jetty, Broadway and at the northern end of the promenade (often referred to as Teal Bay).

The rocky shore regularly holds Northern Wheatear at migration time. Rock Pipit is elusive but present each winter. Black Redstart and Snow Bunting are occasional on migration, especially late autumn. The bushes next to the Stone Jetty regularly hold wintering Blackcap. The seaward end of the Stone Jetty is a good visible migration vantage point during late March to May and August to November. Substantial flocks of Pink-footed Goose can be sometimes be seen from late January.

Access

The car park at the Battery (SD422637) is a good vantage point. The car park at the Stone Jetty (SD432645) can be used as a base from which to check the high tide roost on the nearby groyne and, after a 550 yard (500 m) walk, to scan the sea and mudflats from the end of the jetty. The areas to the north of the Stone Jetty are favoured by wader species, which are easily visible from the promenade even at low tide. One option is to leave your car and walk the 1.9 miles (3 km) along the promenade to Teal Bay, checking the inshore mudflats and tidal channels along the way. This walk, or a series of vehicular stops along the promenade, is also an option at high tide when the birds will gather on the groynes at SD441651, SD445650, SD455657 and SD463661. Parking on the

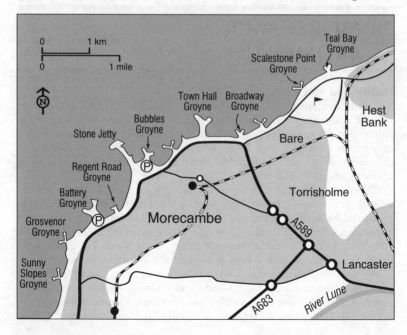

promenade is not usually a problem in the winter months. Please do not park in the Leisure Centre when visiting the Teal Bay area.

Timing

Morecambe Promenade is most productive between September and April, although returning Mediterranean Gulls usually arrive back in mid July and there is a possibility of irregular late spring and early autumn migrant wader species roosting on the groynes.

As is the case with several Morecambe Bay sites, observation of waterfowl in the low tide channels and waders on the mudflats can be equally or more productive than high tide visits. This is especially the case with ducks and grebes which may retreat to the centre of the bay at high tide. Stone Jetty is best about four hours before high tide to watch the early stages of the tidal flow. Wildfowl that feed in the low-tide channel just to the south will float past and allow very good views. The other productive time to watch is at high tide when the waders gather on the groynes. Scaup may remain close inshore, usually in the region of Scalestones Point (SD455657).

Strong winds from the south or east can cause problems when viewing the roosting waders on the groynes as they shelter out of sight on the seaward side. Conversely, north or north-west winds and associated rougher seas will push the birds within view from the promenade.

The Stone Jetty is a recommended seawatching base (see Heysham for details of timing). Stone Jetty is especially good for very close views of Leach's Storm-petrels after two to three days of south-westerly gales. It is also a good vantage point for observing the spring skuas and Arctic Terns.

CALENDAR

November–March: Ducks and waders, including occasional Spotted Redshank and Purple Sandpiper; Kittiwake and Little Gull during strong onshore winds and wintering Mediterranean Gull.

March–early June: Seabirds (see Jenny Brown's Point); Common Eider numbers increase; migrant passerines in the bushes (especially by Stone Jetty) and any undisturbed open ground.

August–October: Possibility of Leach's Storm-petrel and other seabirds during onshore gales. Migrant passerines (same sites as spring) have included Black Redstart and Snow Bunting.

---

30 THE LUNE ESTUARY
OS Landranger Maps 97 and 102
SD45 and 46

This chapter includes the tidal section of the Lune as far north as Skerton Weir. The outer estuary boundaries for this section are Middleton Sands and Glasson. Recent years have seen several major changes in this area. Jet ski disturbance and closure of the rubbish tip are detrimental for birding; the borrow pits comprising Conder Pool and the as yet unnamed pools at the northern end of Aldcliffe Marsh enhance the area. Wildfowlers have created pools that are good for passage waders. These can be observed from the Aldcliffe Marsh embankment. Freemans Wood and the cover alongside the cycle track is good for breeding Lesser Whitethroat and boasts single records of Subalpine and Yellow-browed Warblers.

The Lune Estuary is bordered by extensive saltmarshes that attract large flocks of Northern Lapwing, Redshank, Curlew, European Golden Plover and Eurasian Wigeon, along with smaller numbers of Common Teal. Up to 15 Little Egret can be found scattered along the estuary in the winter months, but not as yet during the breeding season. The cattle-grazed saltmarshes of the western side hold good numbers of breeding waders, notably Redshank and Northern Lapwing. A small Common and Arctic Tern colony maintains a precarious foothold on Colloway Marsh, with no evidence of successful breeding in recent years. The wide section of the estuary between Glasson and Conder is very good for European Golden Plover, Bar-tailed Godwit (including a small summering flock) and gulls, including a returning late summer Yellow-legged Gull first noted in 1995. Conder Pool and Estuary are good sites for passage waders and have held Spotted Redshank in recent winters. Glasson Marina supports small numbers of diving duck, including regular Scaup.

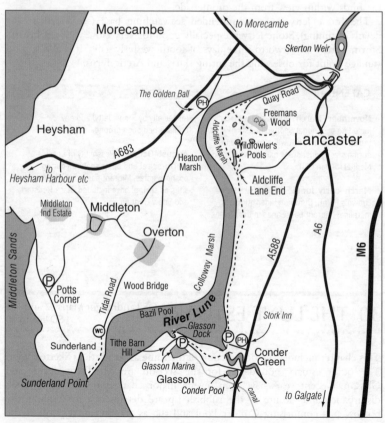

The Middleton Sands wader roost is huge, but difficult to observe and the light conditions are often unfavourable. The upper tide line from Potts Corner to Sunderland Point can be productive for open-ground passerines, especially Northern Wheatear during spring and autumn migration. The tidal road to Sunderland can offer very close views of waders, including Whimbrel, and is one of the most reliable sites for Curlew Sandpiper in autumn.

The upper estuary lost its main attraction when the rubbish tip was closed in December 2006. It is worth checking the Skerton Weir area (SD483634).

Access

The western side of the estuary has very little access. The private Colloway Marsh can only be observed at long range from the eastern bank of the estuary. The tidal road from Overton to Sunderland is best observed from a vehicle to avoid disturbance. Close views of waders can be obtained from Wood Bridge (SD429569) and anywhere along the final 440 yards (400 m) before the car park by the toilet block (SD427563). There is no vehicle access beyond here, so leave your car and walk (with telescope) through Sunderland village where the road affords good views of both sides of the estuary. Make careful note of the timing before visiting the Sunderland peninsula (see next section). For Middleton Sands park at Potts Corner (SD413572) and walk along the tide edge.

Apart from extremely muddy access via Yenham Lane (SD438580), the west side of the Lune can only be viewed from the tidal road running north east and signposted to the Golden Ball public house (SD444608). The start of this road gives an excellent high vantage point.

The eastern side of the estuary has much easier access. For a full day view Conder Green and Conder Pool (SD458557) and perhaps scan from Tithe Barn Hill (SD443559) then park at Glasson Dock by the Marina (SD446562) and walk the bridle track as far as Aldcliffe Lane End (SD459602). Here you have a choice of continuing along the embankment or the bridleway. The embankment affords good views of the saltmarsh and the wildfowlers pools on the inland side. You can return via the bridle track, where a large maize field in crop or stubble can contain Tree Sparrow and other passerines.

The best vantage points for vehicle-based observers are (south to north): from the embankment across the road from the Glasson Marina car park, Conder Green car park (SD457562), Aldcliffe Lane End (SD459602) and anywhere along Lancaster Quay. The best overall views of Skerton Weir are from the west side (SD480632).

Timing

Relatively narrow estuaries such as the Lune are often more productive on the lower stages of the tidal cycle, when the birds are on the mudflats. However, the birds can be distant and camouflaged on distant skears or hidden in channels. Many observers favour the early stages of the incoming tide, especially when viewing the wider section from Glasson embankment. Another favoured time to watch the estuary is on a very high spring tide as this pushes some of the more elusive saltmarsh species out into the open and inshore, notably Little Egret and (Scandinavian) Rock Pipit. Avoid the Sunderland tidal road at this stage of the tide.

The Lune estuary can provide good general birdwatching at all tidal stages. It is not essential to correlate visits with high tides. Winter produces a nice selection of waders and wildfowl throughout, usually including Whooper Swan, Spotted Redshank and small numbers of Pink-footed Goose.

Late January to March sees much larger numbers of Pink-footed Goose passing through. The best viewing points are from Aldcliffe Lane Ends or the southern end of the Golden Ball tidal road. Concentrate on the outer estuary sites, notably the Sunderland village area and between Crook Farm and Cockersands Point in April and May or late July to early September. Passage flocks of Dunlin and Ringed Plover can act as carriers for more unusual species.

CALENDAR

November–March: Estuary and fields hold wildfowl and waders; Kingfisher, Spotted Redshank and perhaps Greenshank around the Conder Green and Pool area; Bewick's and Whooper Swans on Aldcliffe Marsh or Glasson Basin; large European Golden Plover flock around Glasson basin; Little Egret. High spring tides offer views of (Scandinavian) Rock Pipit. Late winter sees Pink-footed Goose flocks on the saltmarshes and other geese are annual, with Barnacle Goose and European White-fronted Goose the most regular.

April–July: Small numbers of Common and Arctic Terns attempt to breed, usually on Colloway Marsh near to the pylon crossing. Common Eider is starting to colonise the estuary as a breeding species. Passage waders can be found at Conder Green, Conder Pool and the Aldcliffe wildfowler's pools. Lesser Whitethroat and other summer visitors are at the footpath along the eastern side.

July–October: Passage waders at Conder Creek – favoured by juvenile Curlew Sandpiper from late August onwards – and the nearby Conder Pool. Careful checks with a telescope of the Lune mudflats between Glasson and the Conder Estuary are recommended, especially scrutiny of any Dunlin flocks. Gulls have included a returning autumn Yellow-legged Gull since 1995. The Aldcliffe wildfowlers pools can also be productive.

31 COCKERSANDS

OS Landranger Map 102
SD45

Habitat and Species

The Cockersands area comprises a mixture of arable fields and three main wader and wildfowl vantage points are joined by coastal pedestrian access. The most northerly fields in the area are retained as winter cereal stubble and have attracted significant numbers of Skylark and the occasional Lapland and Snow Buntings. Snow Bunting has also been found on passage on a small spit at Cockersands Point. A wide-ranging flock of Twite can often be found along the seawall. There is usually at least one singing male Corn Bunting in the area during early summer. Tree Sparrow is regular at all times of the year. A variety of waders and gulls visit the fields in wet conditions, including Icelandic Black-tailed Godwit. Merlin regularly hunts this area in autumn and winter.

The mudflats between Cockersands Point and Crook Farm and along the Cocker Estuary often hold significant numbers of Ringed Plover and Dunlin on spring and autumn passage. Wader flocks sometimes include Sanderling (spring), Curlew Sandpiper and Little Stint (mainly autumn). A Broad-billed Sandpiper was found here in spring 2006.

Large numbers of Eurasian Wigeon and Common Teal and significant numbers of Pintail can be found along the whole stretch. Rarer ducks have included single Green-winged Teal and American Wigeon. The fields along Jeremy Lane often support a winter Mute Swan herd and this is one of the most reliable sites in Lancashire for Bewick's Swan. The swans regularly commute to the Lune estuary at Glasson port, presumably to feed on grain spillage.

Access
There are two main routes. For both turn left off the A588 at Upper Thurnham (SD560545) or follow Jeremy Lane from Glasson (SD450558). At the fork in the road (SD433541), you can turn left for route one and park at Bank Houses (SD434529). Here you can telescope the Cocker Estuary in situ or walk east to Bank End or west along the seawall round to the Crook Farm. Alternatively turn right at the fork in the road (SD433541) and use the car park next to Lighthouse Cottage (SD429543). Walk along the road to Crook Cottage and Farm. You can also walk from the car park to Bank Houses.

On very high tides the best site is Bank End saltmarsh. Walk from Bank Houses and scan from SD442528 or walk farther along the embankment. Vehicle access to Bank End Farm is not recommended: parking here is not only intrusive but also you run the risk being cut off during incoming spring tides. On very high spring tides, scan from the vehicle at SD449528.

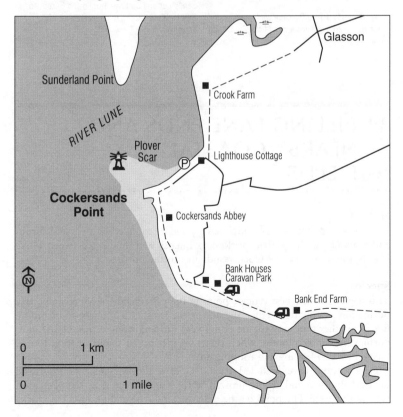

Timing

By far the largest variety of birds is found at low tide, but they can be distant. Try to time your visit about 3 or 4 hours before a spring tide or 2 or 3 hours before a neap tide. Either choose one of Bank Houses and Lighthouse Cottage or split your time between the two. If doing both locations, check the main Dunlin flocks from the Lighthouse Cottage car park before driving to Bank Houses and watching the tide cover the remaining mudflats before walking round to observe the high tide fare from Bank End Farm. Lighthouse Cottage car park is worth another look from about an hour and a half after high tide to observe the waders arriving on the newly exposed mudflats, perhaps then returning to Bank Houses for a similar process.

CALENDAR

October–March: Eurasian Wigeon, Common Teal, large flocks of waders, especially European Golden Plover, Northern Lapwing. Check gull flocks for Mediterranean, especially during the February and March muck spreading. Swans gather at Jeremy Lane. Twite occurs in winter and Snow Bunting in late autumn and early spring.

April–early June: Passage waders may include scarce species among flocks of Dunlin and Ringed Plover. The wader flocks have potential to attract scarce species but are not often checked.

July–September: Passage waders including Little Stint, Curlew Sandpiper, Ruff, Greenshank, Spotted Redshank. There is a chance of scarce species such as Pectoral Sandpiper and Dotterel. Dunlin and European Golden Plover flocks might reward careful scrutiny.

32 PILLING LANE ENDS AND NEARBY COASTAL FIELDS

OS Landranger Map 102
SD44

Habitat

The Lane Ends amenity area includes a pond surrounded by trees and shrubs and a popular car park that overlooks saltmarsh and mudflats between Fluke Hall to the south and the Cockersands area to the north.

Species

This is probably the best vantage point in the eastern side of Morecambe Bay during high spring tides, especially during the last 2 to 3 hours of an incoming tide. The other times to visit are either very early morning or just before dusk during the winter months, when there are spectacular flights of Pink-footed Geese between feeding and roosting areas.

Rare visitors have included Pacific Golden Plover, Richard's Pipit and Lapland Bunting, and Yellow-browed Warbler and Firecrest in the plantation around the pond. The pond has held Slavonian Grebe and Long-tailed Duck.

In recent years, the fields between Pilling Lane Ends and Fluke Hall have been very attractive for waders and wildfowl. Favoured fields vary, but the ones alongside Fluke Hall Lane have consistently held a good variety of birds, especially Whooper Swan during the winter months. The fields are also regularly utilised by Pink-footed Geese, and the easy viewing enables other species to be located amongst the hordes, including both forms of Bean Goose, White-fronted Goose, light- and dark-bellied Brent Goose, Snow Goose and regular Barnacle Goose. There was a lengthy stay by a Glossy Ibis in late autumn 2006 and a good variety of waders, including Buff-breasted Sandpiper, have been observed over the years.

Access

Saloon cars, but not camper vans or minibuses, can access the amenity area car parks (SD415494). Large vehicles park just before the entrance. Many observers prefer walking west to watch the incoming tide in the region of the sluice (SD406495), but this is an exposed position in poor weather. Turn right in Pilling village (SD404487) for Fluke Hall Lane.

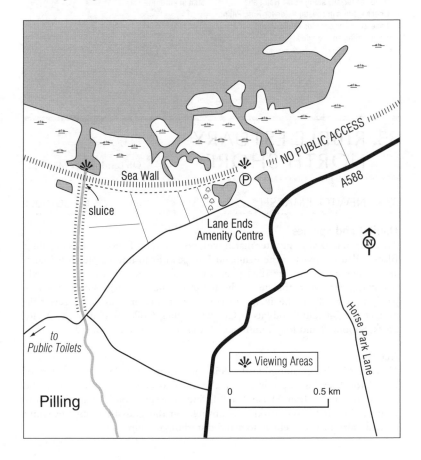

Timing

Visit during the latter stages of incoming spring tides. The dropping tide feeding areas are not generally within viewing range and the wet saltmarsh can produce a severe heat haze. Visit Lane Ends during the high tide period in between checking the Cockersands sites on the incoming and dropping tides. The coastal fields at Fluke Hall Lane and elsewhere can hold birds at all stages of the tide. Large numbers of waders can be displaced to Fluke Hall Lane on high spring tides, especially when storm surges cover the saltmarsh at Fluke Hall. Apart from perhaps mid to late June, there is usually something of interest to see here on all high spring tides. Viewing may be obstructed by heat haze in sunny conditions during the summer months.

CALENDAR

October–March: Flights of Pink-footed Goose over Lane Ends in late evening and early morning; swans and geese in coastal fields, especially along Fluke Hall Lane. Check waders in coastal fields for Ruff. Pilling Lane Ends car park for wildfowl and waders on incoming spring tides.

April–May and July–October: High spring tides may produce a variety of passage waders such as Curlew Sandpiper, and Little Stint in autumn.

33 RIBBLE ESTUARY
NORTH SHORE   OS Landranger Map 102

33A NEWTON MARSH   OS Ref: SD456293

Habitat and Species

This area of grazed freshwater marsh with pools is most famous for its breeding Black-tailed Godwits of the mainland European form limosa. Newton Marsh also retains significant breeding populations of Northern Lapwing and Redshank. In recent years this site has hosted several notable rarities during May – partly as a result of the increased coverage at this time as volunteers help protect the breeding godwits – Citrine Wagtail, Collared Pratincole, White Stork, Spoonbill and four Temminck's Stints have all been recorded.

Access

Newton Marsh lies alongside the A584 just over a 1 mile (1.6 km) east of Freckleton. Viewing is possible from the A584 westbound laybys or from the minor road to Clifton Marsh Landfill Site accessible south from the traffic lights at Marsh Garage. Parking is possible on the grass between the white bollards. Stay in your vehicle to avoid disturbing the birds.

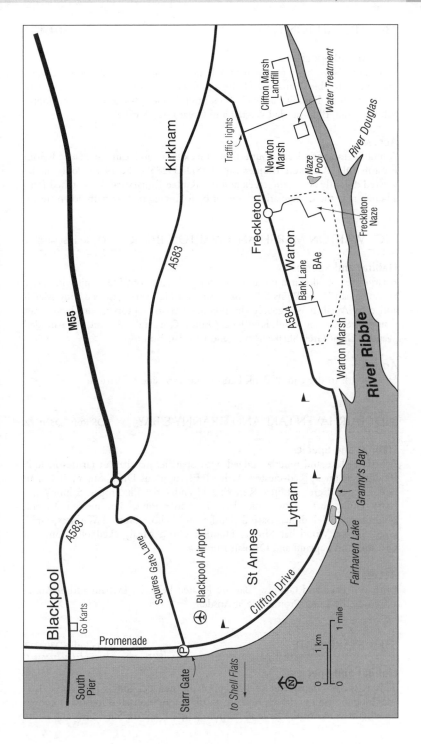

33B   FRECKLETON NAZE   OS Ref: SD434272

Habitat and Species
Freckleton Naze has a freshwater pool and a convenient access point to view the upper Ribble Estuary and the confluence of the River Douglas. Past rarities include Ruddy Shelduck, Spoonbill, Honey Buzzard, Osprey, Hobby, Sabine's Gull, Blue-headed Wagtail and Great Grey Shrike.

Access
A public footpath leads south from Freckleton and can be reached from Preston Old Road on Bunker Street (SD434283). The Naze Pool can be viewed distantly across the creek and the Ribble Estuary can be watched from a bench near the triangulation point or by following the footpath downstream.

33C   WARTON MARSH AND WARTON BANK   OS Ref: SD404274

Habitat and Species
A large area of saltmarsh most famous for gatherings of Water Pipit with a few Scandinavian Rock Pipits for comparison, on high spring tides during March and early April. It is arguably the premier site for raptors in the Fylde. Past rarities include Spoonbill, Red Kite, Osprey, Corncrake, Avocet, Blue-headed Wagtail, Great Grey Shrike, Raven and Ortolan Bunting.

Access
Head south to the end of Bank Lane at the west side of Warton.

33D   FAIRHAVEN LAKE AND GRANNY'S BAY   OS Ref: SD340272

Habitat and Species
A boating lake and mudflats edged with Spartina marsh. Past rarities include Ruddy Shelduck, Red-crested Pochard, Ferruginous Duck, Smew, Slavonian Grebe, Little Egret, Osprey, Red-necked and Grey Phalaropes, Sabine's and Ivory Gulls, Turtle Dove, Shorelark, Richard's Pipit, Blue-headed Wagtail, Nightingale, Melodious, Barred, Dusky and Yellow-browed Warblers, Great Grey Shrike, Woodchat Shrike, Hooded Crow, Mealy Redpoll, Common Crossbill and Lapland and Ortolan Buntings.

Access
Fairhaven Lake and Granny's Bay are located between Lytham and St Annes alongside the Inner Promenade at Ansdell.

33E   STARR GATE   OS Ref: SD303317

Habitat and Species
This is the southern end of Blackpool promenade, and is a favoured sea-watching location in the appropriate weather conditions. It is most well known for distant views of the large Common Scoter flock on Shell Flats and is the

most reliable site in Lancashire for Velvet Scoter and Long-tailed Duck. Nearby upper beach has hosted Snow Bunting but is heavily disturbed.

Access

From South Pier drive south until you reach the go-kart track. If coming from out of town follow Squires Gate Lane off the M55. Starr Gate car park is through the lights at the end.

CALENDAR

Late November–early March: Newton Marsh acts as a winter refuge for flocks of Eurasian Wigeon and Common Teal with smaller numbers of Black-tailed Godwits and Shoveler. Warton Marsh regularly hosts Hen Harrier and Merlin, and Short-eared Owl during spring tides. Spring tides often push Water Pipits off the marsh, where they can be viewed on the fence line at the end of Bank Lane.

Small flocks of Little Egrets gather at Freckleton Naze, often roosting on the pool. The fields behind the pool often have grazing Whooper, Bewick's and Mute Swans and flocks of European Golden Plover, Northern Lapwing and Curlew.

March–May: Newton Marsh is an important location for passage waders. European Golden Plover and Black-tailed Godwit gather in large numbers during March and April, with small parties of Whimbrel often present towards dusk in late April and early May. Little Ringed Plover breeds nearby and can often be seen on the marsh during spring and summer, when Garganey can be found occasionally. Freckleton Naze is one of the Fylde's last strongholds for Cuckoo, which is reliable in early May. Garganey and Yellow Wagtail are possible in spring.

June–July: Green Sandpiper is a regular visitor to Newton Marsh in small numbers. Wood Sandpiper has been seen on several occasions. At Freckleton Naze good views of both Common and Arctic Terns can be had as they fish the main channel.

August–early November: From Naze Point it is worth checking the large trees washed up onto the marsh opposite for Peregrine Falcon. Return wader passage in late summer can bring summer plumaged Spotted Redshank and Greenshank to Freckleton Naze. Marsh Harriers often hunt over Warton Marsh.

Early morning visible migration watches from Fairhaven Lake and the nearby dunes see large movements of migrating passerines, particularly Skylark, Swallow, House Martin, Meadow Pipit, Grey Wagtail, Pied Wagtail, Redwing, Fieldfare, Starling, Chaffinch, Greenfinch, Goldfinch, Linnet and Reed Bunting.

34 OVER WYRE GOOSE FIELDS

OS
Landranger
Map 102

Habitat and Species

This farmland supports feeding Pink-footed Goose and Whooper Swan during autumn, winter and spring. There is a healthy resident population of farmland birds such as Yellowhammer, Reed Bunting, Corn Bunting, Tree Sparrow, Skylark, Stock Dove and Little and Barn Owls.

Access

Access is along a network of narrow country lanes between the villages and towns of Garstang, Cockerham, Pilling, Preesall and Out Rawcliffe. The main

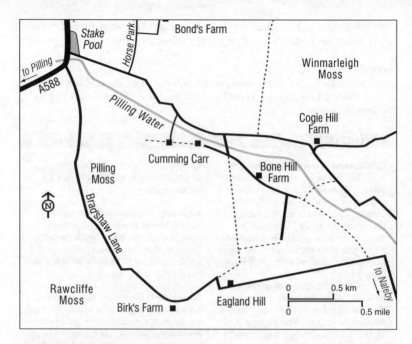

A588 is a busy and potentially dangerous road, but many of the minor roads that criss-cross the farmland are ideal for birdwatching. Take great care not to inadvertently disrupt any farming activities. The hamlet of Eagland Hill (SD430452) serves as a good starting point when searching for the characteristic species of the area.

TIMING AND CALENDAR

Late November–early March: Large numbers of Pink-footed Geese visit north Fylde at this time, particularly from late January through to a winter peak in late February. Many of these geese will have spent a proportion of the winter in Norfolk before relocating northwest en route to Scotland in the spring and Iceland in the summer.

Pink-footed Geese roost each night on Pilling Marsh before leaving en masse at dawn to feed in the fields; the exact field preference varys from year to year depending on crop rotation.

In most winters the flocks of Pink-footed Geese carry small numbers of other goose species, most often Barnacle Goose. Eurasian and Greenland White-fronted, Pale- and Dark-bellied Brent and the occasional Tundra Bean Goose are all possible. Vagrant Taiga Bean Goose, Todd's Canada Goose, Lesser Snow Goose and Ross's Goose have also accom-

panied the flocks in recent winters. Spotting rarer species can be difficult among the large flocks of Pink-footed Geese and a telescope is essential. Use your car as a mobile hide to avoid disturbance when searching the lanes Over Wyre to best enjoy a wild goose chase.

Winter passerines gather in flocks. Corn Buntings often favour the hedgerows adjoining New Lane, east of Eagland Hill (SD438453). Tree Sparrow, Yellowhammer and Reed Bunting gather at designated feeding sites – currently Bradshaw Lane Head (SD415460) and New Lane – where they not only provide excellent views but also attract Sparrowhawk and Merlin.

March–May: Pink-footed Geese remain in the fields until early April, then spend much of their time on the nutrient-rich saltmarsh. March is the optimum time for searching for rare geese.

Late April–early May: Ploughed fields attract migrant Northern Wheatears and Whimbrel. Dotterel has been seen in the past. Corn Buntings and Yellowhammers sing from many hedgerows. Tree Sparrows become harder to see as they breed in nextboxes in the many small woods.

June–July: Cereal fields attract singing Quail, which are best listened for on warm still evenings or during the night. Barn Owls hunt roadside field margins. Corn Buntings and Yellowhammers sing in hedgerows and a

few pairs Curlew have young.

August–early November: A relatively quiet period before the Pink-footed Geese return in early September, although Marsh Harriers are increasingly being seen over cereal fields in early autumn. Flooded stubble fields can be very attractive to passage waders such as Black-tailed Godwit and Ruff, with Spotted Redshank, Greenshank and Little Stint a possibility. A Lesser Yellowlegs and Pectoral Sandpiper feeding together graced a flood by New Lane, Eagland Hill, in September 2002.

35 MARTON MERE

OS Landranger Map 102
SD33

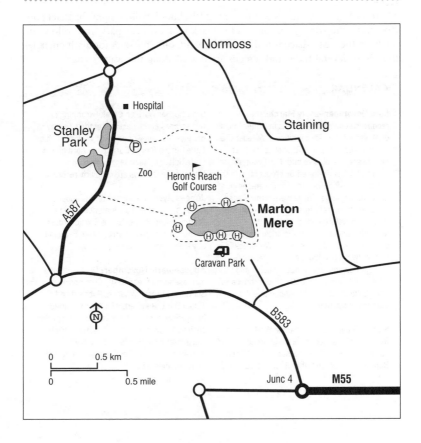

Habitat and Species

Marton Mere (SD344353) formed at the end of the last Ice Age and is one of only two kettleholes in northwest England. The southern bank is now a caravan park and the northern bank, a former rubbish tip, is covered by scrub and grassland. Around 200 species of birds have been recorded, over 130 annually. The site, which is an SSSI, is owned and run as a local nature reserve by Blackpool Borough Council.

The site is well known for its long and impressive list of rare and scarce birds, including: American Wigeon, Green-winged Teal, Red-crested Pochard, Ferruginous Duck, Smew, Red-necked, Slavonian and Black-necked Grebes, American Bittern, Little Bittern, Night Heron, Glossy Ibis, Spoonbill, Honey Buzzard, Montagu's Harrier, Goshawk, Osprey, Hobby, Spotted Crake, Corncrake, Common Crane, Collared Pratincole, Temminck's Stint, Pectoral Sandpiper, Long-billed Dowitcher, Lesser Yellowlegs, Red-necked and Grey Phalaropes, Ring-billed and Laughing Gulls, Roseate, Whiskered and White-winged Black Terns, Turtle Dove, Hoopoe, Wryneck, Red-rumped Swallow, Cetti's, Savi's, Great Reed and Barred Warblers, Firecrest, Bearded Tit, Golden Oriole, Great Grey Shrike, Hooded Crow, Common Redpoll, Hawfinch and Lapland Bunting.

Access

Marton Mere is two miles east of central Blackpool. Follow signs for Blackpool Zoo from the M55 Junction 4. Use Blackpool Zoo car park and follow the tracks to the east, adjacent to Herons' Reach Golf Course. A footpath encircles the Mere. Several hides and screens are dotted along the water's edge.

CALENDAR

Late November–early March: The reedbeds support Water Rails in winter (most often seen during icy conditions). At least one Bittern is usually present: dusk is the best time to see this elusive bird. Most winters see a communal Long-eared Owl roost form in the scrub just inside the northern perimeter of the nature reserve. These well-camouflaged birds are never easy to see but, with patience, they can usually be watched from the footpaths: under no circumstances enter the scrub in search of this species. Woodcock is frequently seen in flight over the reserve. Whooper Swans feed in nearby fields and often visit to roost and bathe. Stonechat can often be found below the embankment at the east end of the mere.

March–May: Blackcap, Sedge Warbler and Reed Warbler arrive in spring to breed in good numbers, alongside small numbers of Reed Bunting, Lesser Whitethroat and occasionally Grasshopper Warbler. Careful scanning of the two scrapes at the east end of the site may produce Garganey or passage waders such as Little Ringed Plover. During late April and May Little Gull and Black Tern can occur. Northbound Ospreys are regularly recorded.

June–July: Late summer brings about a build up in Coot and duck numbers and a Starling roost. If a nocturnal Swallow roost forms it can attract Sparrowhawk, occasionally Merlin and, in the past, Hobby.

August–early November: Duck numbers increase further, especially Common Teal, Shoveler, Eurasian Wigeon, Pochard and Tufted Duck. Hundreds of gulls come in to bathe. Scan through for less common species, such as Mediterranean Gull. Autumn fruits can attract good numbers of migrant thrushes. Flocks of Goldfinch and Long-tailed Tit roam the area.

36 WYRE ESTUARY   OS Landranger Map 102

Habitat and Species

Rossall Point (SD312478) forms the southern boundary of Morecambe Bay, and the whole area provides year round interest for the birdwatcher. A high tide wader roost forms near the disused coastguard station (subject to tide height and disturbance). Past rarities have included Black-throated and Great Northern Divers, Red-necked and Slavonian Grebes, Sooty Shearwater, European Storm-petrel, Shag, Osprey, Kentish Plover, Grey Phalarope, Long-tailed Skua, Sabine's and Ross's Gulls, Black Guillemot, Little Auk, Puffin, Hoopoe, Desert Wheatear, Hooded Crow, Common Crossbill and Lapland Bunting.

Fleetwood Golf Course (SD314475) is private but can be viewed from the promenade footpath running along the north and western margin or the pavement of Princes Way. Past rarities have included American Golden Plover, Pomarine Skua, Ross's Gull, Hoopoe, Richard's and Tawny Pipits, Blue-headed Wagtail, Desert Wheatear and Lapland Bunting.

Fleetwood Marine Lakes (SD324482) consists of two open access pools, a boating pool and a smaller model yacht pool.

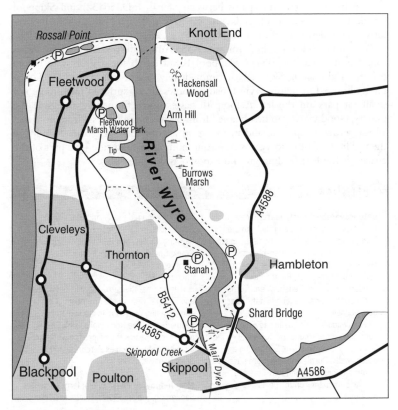

Stanah is the local name for the west side of the Wyre Estuary between Thornton and Skippool Creek. Rarities seen here include Ruddy Shelduck, Little Egret, Hobby, Avocet, Turtle Dove and Common Crossbill.

Skippool Creek (SD412358) is where the Main Dyke flows into the Wyre Estuary west of Shard Bridge. The mudflats provide good feeding for the flocks of waders that roost in the highest parts of the estuary. Past rarities include Smew, Little Egret, White-rumped Sandpiper (twice), Great Knot and Ring-billed Gull (thrice).

Knott End (SD350486) beach is best watched at high tide during neap tides or on the flowing or ebbing tide during spring tides. A gull flock often gathers near the Esplanade and regularly contains Mediterranean Gull. On neap tides the best times to visit is probably two hours before high tide or one hour after high tide to low water. Tides over 29 feet (9 m) normally displace the waders upstream and downstream. Past rarities include European Storm-petrel, Kentish Plover, Grey Phalarope, Waxwing, Chough, Hooded Crow and Common Crossbill.

Access

For Rossall Point there is a car park on Princes Way near the Beach Road roundabout. Paths lead to the promenade. Much of the Wyre Estuary can be viewed from the riverside paths between Stanah (SD356432) and Skippool Creek. The Wyreside Ecology Centre car park and picnic site at Stanah overlooks the widest part of the estuary.

Skippool Creek is reached from the A585 Amounderness Way–Mains Road roundabout. Take the B5412 Skippool Road north for a short way before turning right along Wyre Road immediately before the Thornton Lodge public house. Just before Wyre Road becomes an un-surfaced track there is a small car park on the left. A footpath passes north from here alongside the estuary. Good views can be obtained from between the jetties. Please note that all the jetties are private and many are in a poor state of repair: do not use them. The best time to visit is from one hour after high tide (this part of the estuary is the first feeding ground exposed as the tide ebbs).

CALENDAR

Late November–early March: Rossall Point has small numbers of Red-throated Diver, Great Crested Grebe, Common Eider, Common Goldeneye and Red-breasted Merganser offshore. The wader roost may include Oystercatcher, Ringed Plover, Sanderling, Dunlin, Redshank and Turnstone. Snow Buntings can be found on the beach occasionally.

Fleetwood Marine Lakes has a high tide Turnstone roost around the pools and on the island in the boating lake. Sanderling and, occasionally, Purple Sandpiper are possible. Common Goldeneye and Red-breasted Mergansers gather on the pools and give excellent views.

Dunlin, Ringed Plover and Black-tailed Godwit join the large flocks of Northern Lapwing, Curlew and Redshank at Skippool Creek. Shelduck and Mallard are the commonest wildfowl; a few Common Teal are often present.

The saltmarshes attract flocks of finches and Skylark, with smaller numbers of pipits and wagtails. Water Pipits are sometimes seen amongst the Rock Pipits. Jack Snipe often accompanies the Snipe. The whole area attracts raptors such as Peregrine, Merlin and Sparrowhawk.

March–May: At Rossall Point large parties of Sanderling, Ringed Plover, Knot and Dunlin with smaller numbers of Grey Plover and Bar-tailed Godwit on the shore. Northern Wheatear and Whinchat are regular at Fleetwood Golf Course; Ring Ouzel is a possibility and Stonechat likely.

Varying numbers of Ringed Plover, Dunlin, Black-tailed Godwit, Greenshank, Whimbrel and Common Sandpiper at Skippool Creek.

June–July: During late July and August the Sandwich and Common Terns that gather at high tide occasionally attract Arctic and Little Terns, particularly in the evenings; Black and Roseate Terns have been recorded.

The planted areas at Stanah and the riverside hedgerows attract passerine migrants. Breeding birds include Reed and Sedge Warblers, Lesser and Common Whitethroats and Willow Warbler.

August–early November: At Rossall Point seabirds including Fulmar, Gannet, Manx Shearwater, Arctic and Great Skuas and terns can be seen offshore with, from late August onwards, southwest gales driving Leach's Storm-petrels inshore or even over the beach in severe gales. The promenade is a good vantage point for daytime migrants such as Swallow, House Martin, Meadow Pipit, Grey Wagtail and finches moving south.

Skippool Creek has influxes of Curlew Sandpiper and sometimes Little Stint, Ruff and Spotted Redshank, and parties of Ringed Plover, Dunlin, Black-tailed Godwit and smaller numbers of Greenshank, Ruff, Whimbrel and Common Sandpiper.

Knott End is not a prime seawatching location, but Leach's Storm-petrels may pass the shelters during strong westerly winds in September and early October.

37 FOREST OF BOWLAND OS Landranger Map 41

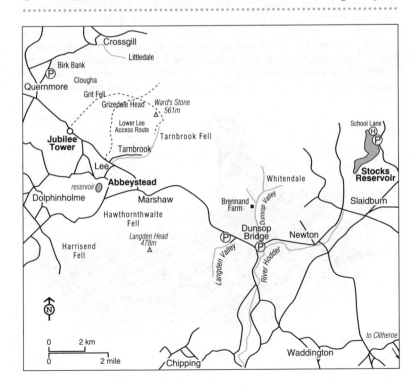

The Forest of Bowland is an area of outstanding natural beauty worthy of full exploration. The following sites highlight the most suitable areas for seeing the whole range of regular bird species and habitats in the area.

37A   WARD'S STONE AND AREA   mainly SD55

Habitat and Species

Ward's Stone is the highest point in west Bowland at 1,840 feet (561 m). It comprises managed heather moor, bilberry, wet flushes with eroded peat hags and stony areas on the summit. It was a reliable Dotterel site to rival Pendle in numbers until the foot and mouth epidemic of 2001, which led to a temporary removal of sheep grazing the summit that limited areas of suitable habitat. The spread of the gull colony nearer to the summit may also deter Dotterel. The restoration of grazing should lead to this site becoming productive once again.

Ward's Stone offers good views of the large Lesser Black-backed Gull colony on the Tarnbrook peat. European Golden Plover nests regularly on the summit. Greenland subspecies Northern Wheatears are regular on passage during the Dotterel season.

The lengthy walk to the summit during the Dotterel season could produce Hen Harrier, Merlin, Peregrine, Short-eared Owl, Stonechat, Raven, Northern Wheatear and other fauna such as Emperor and Fox Moths and Green Hair-streak butterfly. The summit provides excellent views of North Wales, Isle of Man and sometimes the Mourne mountains in Northern Ireland.

The access route from Lower Lee passes woodland for the first 0.3 miles (0.5km). Spotted Flycatcher and Redstart are regular. A visit to this area at Dotterel time should always include a check of the undulating rough pasture at SD550575 (best viewed from the side road and main road). Dotterel has occurred and there may be a flock of the northern form of European Golden Plover.

Golden Plover

Timing
The ideal time to visit is at the end of the first week in May during easterly winds, but any time from the last week of April to mid May could be productive.

Access
There are two lengthy walks here and several much longer options (for example via Tarnbrook at SD588557 or Littledale) for access to the start of the upland path (SD549611). The most popular choice is to park at Jubilee Tower (SD543573) and use the path via Grit Fell. The start of this track is off-putting with wet flushes and deep channels in the peat. More recently, the fell road running from Lower Lee (SD564556) has been designated for pedestrian access. Follow the track to Grizedale Head (SD566582) and take the left fork until the intersection between the fell road and footpath (SD564588). Take the footpath to your right for another 1.2 miles (2 km) until you reach Ward's Stone summit. The plateau is a large area and a Dotterel flock known to be present once took three well-spaced observers an hour to find; allocate at least an hour for a careful search.

37B   STOCK'S RESERVOIR AND
SURROUNDING AREA   OS Ref: SD75

Habitat and Species
Stock's Reservoir is at an altitude of 590 feet (180 m). It is around 2 miles (3 km) long and up three-quarters of a mile (1.2 km) wide. The surrounding mixture of habitats ranges from deciduous and coniferous woodland to heather moor, meadows and wet flushes.

Stock's is an isolated body of water and has acted as a magnet for many short-staying visitors over the years. The most bizarre of these was a wing-tagged White-tailed Eagle in 2003 from the release scheme in Scotland and the rarest the first Isabelline Shrike for North-west England in November 1996.

Regular species of interest include Osprey (Stock's is probably the best site in the county for lingering birds in spring and early summer). In summer the site hosts a large Black-headed Gull colony with one or two pairs of Mediterranean Gull. Twenty-one species of ducks have been recorded, including a formerly winter resident Ring-necked Duck and two more recent Green-winged Teal. Eleven of the 28 species of wader recorded breed in the area, including Little Ringed Plover.

The occurrence of scarce wader species relies on the water level and available mud. Favourable conditions, usually in spring, have produced four records of Pectoral Sandpiper, two of Temminck's Stint and a few Wood Sandpipers.

The surrounding woodlands are a mixture of commercial coniferous plantations and deciduous, mainly oak. Regular species include Spotted and Pied Flycatcher and Common Redstart. As elsewhere in Lancashire, the seemingly suitable oak wood habitat only occasionally attracts Wood Warbler nowadays. Coal Tit is abundant in the coniferous forest. Significant numbers of Common Crossbill arrive during irruption years with a good cone crop. Brambling is another irregular species that is sometimes present in good numbers during autumn and winter. Open areas support a few pairs of Grasshopper Warbler, Whinchat and Stonechat, and a few passage Ring Ouzels.

At least one Great Grey Shrike has been regular during recent winters (but not in 2006–2007). Raptors include reasonably regular Marsh Harrier, Hen Harrier, Hobby, Goshawk and Red Kite, and a single record of Rough-legged Buzzard.

Common, Arctic and Black Terns occur almost annually in spring and early summer; Kittiwake and Little Gull are less regular, usually in spring. Other seabird species have occurred on two or less occasions and have included Black-throated Diver, Arctic Skua and Manx Shearwater, along with overland-migrating Common Scoters. There is a large winter gull roost of mostly Black-headed and Common Gulls.

Timing

Spring provides the best variety of birds. Cloud and periods of rain with westerly winds can be particularly productive for grounded migrants. South-east winds in late April and May can be productive for Black Tern.

Access

Approach the northern end of the reservoir via the unclassified road that runs north to north-west from the B6478 at Stephen Moor Crossroads (SD748542) between Tossside and Slaidburn. Park after about 1.5 miles (2.4 km) at School Lane car park (SD732565). Follow the trail from the gate at the north-west corner of the car park and take the left-hand fork down to the hide (SD730567). A logbook and photographs of recent sightings adorn the walls inside. There is an 8-mile (12.8 km) circular walk around the reservoir and extensive trails through the adjacent Gisburn forest. Paths can be muddy at any point beyond the footpath to the hide.

CALENDAR

Winter months: Possibility of a passing Hen Harrier or Brambling and Common Crossbill in the woodlands. The reservoir may be unproductive.

Redstart, Grasshopper Warbler and Pied Flycatcher breed. Wood Warbler is occasional. Mediterranean Gulls in the Black-headed Gull colony.

March–early June: Passage waders, passage Osprey may linger. Regular Common Scoter and Black and Arctic Terns. Common

July-October: Possibilities of passage birds, but fewer than in spring.

37C DUNSOP VALLEY   OS Ref: SD66

Habitat

Dunsop Valley is an upland valley in the heart of Bowland with conifer planta-tions on both sides and some clearfell. The head of the valley comprises steep grassy slopes, pasture and cloughs. The River Dunsop runs through. Heather moorland surround the area on three sides, with the Hodder valley to the south.

Species

This well-known raptor site is good for several regular species and provides an outside chance of a Red Kite or passage Osprey. Summer migrants include

Common Sandpiper, Ring Ouzel, Cuckoo, Northern Wheatear, Whinchat, Common Redstart, Tree Pipit and Pied and Spotted Flycatchers. Residents include Red Grouse, Short-eared Owl, Raven, Dipper, Grey Wagtail, Stonechat, Siskin and other common woodland species. It is a good location for Common Crossbill in irruption years and there can be a sizable winter finch and thrush roost.

Timing
Mid February to April is the peak time for raptor watching and late March to May is best for summer migrants.

Access
From the car park in the village of Dunsop Bridge (SD660501) head right along the road, turning right just before the bridge over the river. A path runs adjacent to and eventually crosses over to meet the road, which runs up the valley. Alternatively, continue over the bridge and follow the road turning left at SD659500. Walk past the houses and head up the valley road. A circular route at the head of the valley allows you to rejoin the valley road back towards the village. The walking is easy and the road surface good until the track forks to Whitendale and Brennand Farms (SD653535). The route between the farms requires more stamina and appropriate outdoor footware.

A favoured spot for raptor watching in the valley is to the left of the road at SD651521, marked "witcher well" on the OS Map. There is strictly no unauthorised vehicular access along the Dunsop Valley road.

37D LANGDEN VALLEY   mainly SD66

Habitat
A steep-sided upland valley comprising a beck, ash and stunted oak woodland cloughs and mature heather moorland.

Species
Several species of raptor a day are possible in the valley proper at the right time of year, including Hen Harrier. Summer visitors include Cuckoo, Ring Ouzel, Whinchat, Northern Wheatear, Common Redstart and Tree Pipit. Meadow Pipit is super-abundant. Common Sandpiper, Oystercatcher, Dipper and Grey Wagtail frequent the beck. A supporting cast including Curlew, Raven, Red Grouse, Short-eared Owl and Stonechat also frequent the area.

The larches on the approach to the valley (SD631511) are worth checking for Common Crossbill in irruption years. Wood Warbler can sometimes be heard singing during the spring passage period. Pied and Spotted Flycatchers are a distinct possibility. This area is a reliable site for Lesser Redpoll and particularly Siskin in most seasons.

Langden Head (SD5851) sometimes attracts a trip of Dotterel. Increased coverage of this area during both passage periods may produce more records.

Timing
April is best for raptors and arriving summer migrants.

Access

Situated off the main Dunsop Bridge to Lancaster road at the heart of the Trough of Bowland. There is ample parking space on the roadside verge at SD631512. Take the footpath across the bridge and follow the track through the Larches. The valley itself opens up shortly afterwards.

The upper path at the valley mid-section (SD6050–SD6350) provides a higher viewing position for watching raptors, but is a fairly strenuous ascent. Stout walking boots and appropriate outdoor clothing are recommended. A snack van operates by the parking area at weekends.

37E   OTHER BOWLAND SITES

SCANNING THE NORTHERN SLOPES OF HAWTHORNTHWAITE

This can be undertaken from anywhere along the road running south west from Marshaw, but is best around SD570532. With patience you may connect with a patrolling Hen Harrier or Short-eared Owl as well as more regular Raven and ubiquitous Red Grouse. Turning around, you can scan the woodlands around Abbeystead for the omnipresent Common Buzzard; Red Kite has occurred.

Timing

Winter and spring are the most productive.

THE TROUGH OF BOWLAND

This road passes through well-spaced pine trees giving a passable imitation of Speyside. There are also stands of beech and oak. Notable birds include: Brambling around the beech trees in winter; Common Redstart and Spotted Flycatcher during the summer months; and Crossbill from late summer during irruptive years. The more open higher areas produce regular roadside Stonechat. The wooded area runs from SD595535 to SD614538. Check the beeches around SD584537 in winter when the surrounding fields are favoured by flocks of winter thrushes.

DM

Brambling

BIRKBANK CAR PARK/CLOUGHA

An area of pleasant scenery that is good for Stonechat and Red Grouse. The surrounding woodlands (SD525604) hold Common Redstart and the occasional Pied Flycatcher. Best in spring.

HARRIS END FELL

This viewing point has a good track record for raptors, Raven and Stonechat. Red Grouse is ubiquitous. Merlin and Peregrine Falcon are regular. Park at SD531500. An all-year site.

38 SELECTED EAST LANCASHIRE RESERVOIRS

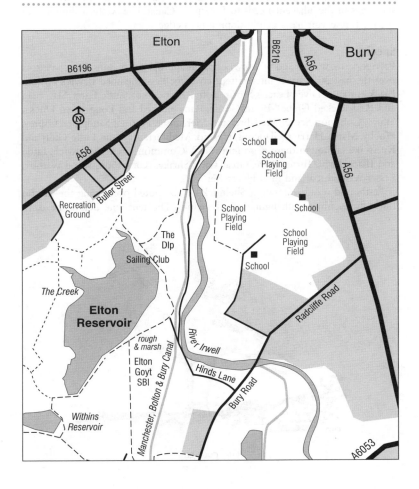

Overview

Regular coverage, reading the weather and an awareness of what is happening ornithologically elsewhere inland are essential factors in getting the most out of the reservoirs of east Lancashire. A muddy edge for waders is essential, but dependent entirely on the weather in each year.

Weather overview

Periods of moderate to strong westerly winds in conjunction with clouds and patches of rain during passage periods are the most productive conditions for grounding migrants. South-east winds in late April and May can be productive for Black Tern.

38A   RISHTON RESERVOIR   OS Ref: SD715300

Habitat

The 37-acre (15 ha) Rishton Reservoir was built in 1828 to solve water shortages in the adjacent Leeds to Liverpool Canal. The western shoreline of the main reservoir has a gently sloping field edge.

Species

Passage terns, waders and wildfowl occur at appropriate seasons. Scarce visitors over the past 30 years of intermittent coverage have included Bewick's Swan, Black-throated Diver, Leach's Storm-petrel, Arctic Skua, Little Egret, Slavonian and Red-necked Grebes, Brent Goose, Ring-necked and Long-tailed Ducks, Smew, Common Scoter, Red-breasted Merganser, Pectoral Sandpiper, Osprey, Hobby, Marsh Harrier, Glaucous, Iceland, Mediterranean and Little Gulls and Kittiwake (although there is no gull roost), Common, Arctic, Sandwich, Little and Black Terns, Turtle Dove, Great Grey Shrike, Rock Pipit, Wood Warbler, Lesser Whitethroat and Pied Flycatcher.

Eastbound moult-migrating Shelduck can be noted over-flying the site on fine July evenings with light westerly winds. The fenceline below the dam,

Glaucous gull

viewable from Cut Lane, is worth checking for passage Whinchat and Stone-chat in autumn.

Timing
The site is prone to disturbance by anglers, dog walkers and sailing, so an early morning visit is advisable.

Access
The Reservoir is 2 miles (3.2 km) east of Blackburn at SD715300. From the large roundabout adjacent to junction 6 of the M65 take the A678 towards Rishton. After about 1.7 miles (2.7 km), turn left and park on Cut Lane in the vicinity of the phone box. Take the path through Cut Wood down past the football pitch to view the reservoir from the small promenade on the eastern shoreline.

38B FOULRIDGE RESERVOIRS   OS Ref: SD888417

Habitat
Lower Foulridge Reservoir is bordered by large suburban gardens and pasture. Willows fringe the reservoir. Upper Foulridge Reservoir is surrounded by pasture.

Species
Notable visitors have included Red-throated, Black-throated and Great Northern Divers, Shag, Arctic and Pomerine Skuas, Manx Shearwater, Little Egret, Black-necked and Red-necked Grebes, wildfowl including Bewick's

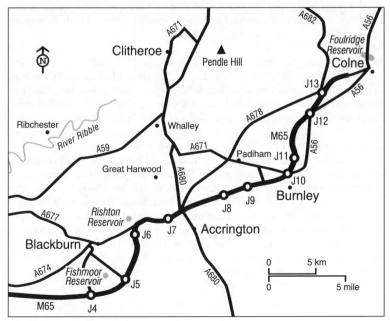

Swan, Garganey, Ring-necked Duck, Common Eider, Common Scoter and Scaup, Iceland, Glaucous, Mediterranean and Little Gulls, Black-legged Kittiwake, passage terns (of five species), Spotted Sandpiper, Red-necked Phalarope and passage waders, Osprey, Hobby and Black Redstart.

The vegetation fringing the reservoir can be productive for finches, tits and passage warblers. Black-headed and Common Gulls dominate the winter gull roost.

Timing
Early morning is best.

Access
Take the A6068 from Junction 14 of the M65. Turn left at the second set of traffic lights on to the A56 towards Skipton for about a mile (1.6 km). Upper Foulridge Reservoir (SD895412) is private. It can be viewed from the A56 at SD890413 and from the causeway at the eastern end (SD896412), which separates Upper Foulridge from the smaller Brownhill Reservoir. Lower Foulridge Reservoir (SD888417) has access all round. Park carefully on the pavement by the A56 (SD890414) and on the lane at the north-west end outside the sailing club (SD880419).

38C FISHMOOR RESERVOIR   OS Refs: SD700260 and SD704258

Habitat
The main holding reservoir for the Blackburn water supply, Fishmoor is a stone-sided water-body that has seen significant encroachment by urban development in the past decade. A thin strip of farmland at the southern end still exists at the time of writing. The adjacent smaller water is Guide Reservoir.

Species
Best known for the winter gull roost. Between 1993 and 2005, the many Herring, Black-headed, Common and up to 150 Great Black-backed Gulls here drew in scarcer species such as Kittiwake, Little, Iceland, Glaucous, Mediterranean and Yellow-legged Gulls. Rarer still were two Ring-billed Gulls, Lancashire's first fully documented Caspian Gull and a Kumlien's Gull. Since December 2005 the number of larger gulls roosting at Fishmoor has fallen dramatically, seemingly as a result of changes in tipping practice and/or bird scaring tactics at the main local landfill site at Whinney Hill Tip, Altham. If this trend continues, occurrences of the scarcer large gulls at Fishmoor will most likely reduce.

Low water levels are rare at Fishmoor, but waders have included American Golden Plover, Spotted Redshank, Little Stint, Knot, Turnstone, Whimbrel, Sanderling and Ruff. Notable waterbirds have included Bewick's and Whooper Swans, Red-necked Grebe (two), Shag, Smew, Scaup and Common Scoter.

Passerines include regular Stonechat in autumn. The surrounding walls should be checked for Northern Wheatear and Whinchat in passage periods. There is one record of Black Redstart.

Timing

The gull season begins as early as mid July when birds begin to disperse from breeding colonies. The period from mid July to October is the most reliable time to connect with Mediterranean Gull, although they are relatively frequent in winter. July to October is also the best time for Yellow-legged Gull. Mid-November to March is best for Iceland and Glaucous Gulls.

Access

From Junction 5 of the M65 follow signs for Shadsworth. Go straight through the first two roundabouts and at the third turn left at the JJB store (SD700260). Rather than continuing into the main car park in front of the store, turn right on to the area running down the side of the building and park at the end overlooking Fishmoor. Parking is possible outside the car park entrance when the car park barrier is closed outside shop opening hours. There is pedestrian access all around the reservoir.

Alternatively, park outside the car park of The Willows public house (SD704258) accessed by turning left at the second roundabout from the M65, and walk around Guide Reservoir.

Gulls at Fishmoor do not roost overnight on the water. Instead they prefer to roost on the large factory roof to the south of the site. To view the gulls on both the factory roof and the water go to the north-west corner of Guide Reservoir (SD700258).

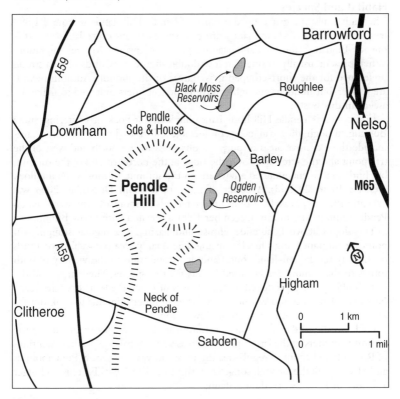

Dotterel

39 PENDLE HILL
OS Landranger Map 103
SD795410

Habitat and Species

The high, millstone grit-capped summit of Pendle Hill stands at around 1,890 feet (577 m) and is a dominant feature of the east Lancashire landscape. It is one of England's most reliable staging posts for spring Dotterel migration. When present, usually in single or low double-figure trips, birds show a strong preference for the short-cropped grassy areas of the summit. Autumn records are scarcer, but frequent enough to give hope to birders prepared to make the ascent in this season.

In most years Pendle Hill hosts Lancashire's largest flock of wintering Snow Bunting, though they can take considerable effort to locate. Favoured areas include the extensive areas of purple moor-grass to the north and west of the trig point and the scree areas over the ridge at the northern end of the summit, but birds can be encountered anywhere on the summit. In most years the flock averages 10 to 20 birds. A count of more than 80 in December 2003 was exceptional. Two of east Lancashire's three records of Shorelark have occurred on Pendle summit. The first, in December 1990, associated with Snow Buntings.

The slopes above Pendleside House and Farm are a regular stopping-off point for migrant Ring Ouzel in spring. The quarry area (viewable two-thirds of the way up the left-hand route) and dry-stone walls in the vicinity of both routes to the summit are favoured haunts for this species. These areas and the farm buildings have produced several records of Black Redstart over the years. Northern Wheatear and Whinchat are other summer migrants to look out for in this area. Stonechat breeds on the lower slopes.

Red Grouse and a few pairs of European Golden Plover breed on the summit; numbers of the latter species increase during passage periods. Sightings of Raven have become a regular feature in recent years. Meadow Pipit abounds and Skylarks fill the air with song. Sadly, since the late 1990s Twite is no longer a feature of Pendle's breeding avifauna.

CALENDAR

Late April–mid May: Dotterel.

October–March: Snow Bunting.

Last week of March–April: migrant Ring Ouzel.

Access

From the north, Pendle is best approached from the A59. Drive through the village of Downham. Approach from the south by leaving the M65 at Junction 13 on to the A682, then through the villages of Roughlee and Barley.

Park on the roadside along Barley Lane (SD815416) outside the entrance of Pendleside House and Farm, about 1 mile (1.6 km) north east of Barley village. Follow the track towards the farm, avoiding the private left-hand branch towards Pendleside Farm. After passing a barn on the right-hand side, pass through a wooden gate on the right and then an iron gate at the top of the field.

There are two routes to the summit. The left-hand route runs parallel with the left-hand wall and is longer but considerably less strenuous than the punishing stepped footpath that runs to the right. If taking the left-hand route, bear right at the top towards the trig point. Descend by either route. Stout footwear and appropriate clothing are recommended.

Timing

Weekdays have considerably less human traffic and fewer disturbances than weekends. For migrants on the slopes, an early morning visit is recommended.

SOUTH LANCASHIRE

LANCASHIRE

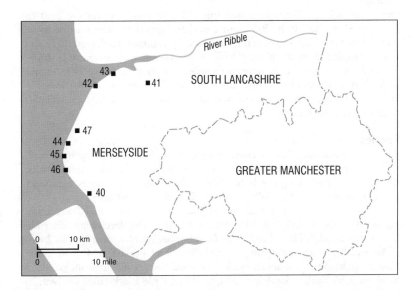

40 Brockholes Quarry
41 Seaforth Nature Reserve and Crosby Marine Park
42 Mere Sands Wood
43 Marshside
44 The South Ribble Marshes
45 The Sefton Coast
46 South-West Lancashire Mosses
    46A Rimrose Valley Country Park
    46B Martin Mere
47 West Pennine Moors

47A Rivington, Anglezarke and Yarrow Reservoirs
47B Belmont Reservoir
47C Jumbles Country Park Reservoir
47D Wayoh Reservoir
47E Turton and Entwhistle Reservoir

40 BROCKHOLES QUARRY
LWT RESERVE

OS Landranger Map 102
SD585305

Habitat

Lancashire Wildlife Trust purchased this 261 acre (106 hectare) site next to junction 31 of the M6 in 2007 when sand and gravel extraction came to an end. The series of lagoons is being colonised by common reed, reed mace and other conspicuous water plants. Public access commenced in summer 2007, but birds and dragonflies have been recorded systematically since 1998 thanks to limited access to observe the non-operational lagoons. It stands alongside 163 acres (66 hectares) of ancient woodland, which the wildlife trust will also be involved in managing.

Species

This new site already has an enviable reputation after monitoring by a small team of experienced birders. As well as the attractions of the wetland habitats, the site is situated along the Ribble Valley flight line and receives significant numbers of migrants, especially waders, wildfowl, gulls and terns.

Breeding birds include Great-crested and Little Grebes, Ringed and Little Ringed Plovers, Skylark, Reed Bunting and Linnet. The developing waterside habitats attracted five Reed and three Grasshopper Warbler territories in 2006.

An excellent roost of spring passage Whimbrel peaked at 401 in 2003. Twenty-eight other species of wader recorded since 1988 have included 63 Sanderling, 55 Curlew Sandpiper, 30 Little Stint, 1,138 Black-tailed Godwit, 20 Spotted Redshank, 30 Knot, 18 Grey Plover and 46 Turnstone. Rarer records have included an impressive 18 Wood Sandpipers, 3 Pectoral Sandpipers, a Temminck's Stint and the first county record of Semipalmated Sandpiper.

Shoveler and Gadwall counts of 61 and 44 respectively suggest that breeding will take place in the near future. It is a regular site for Garganey (16 records). Accompanying up to 500 Coot is a significant diving duck flock of up to 60 each of Tufted Duck and Pochard, joined occasionally by Scaup. There is a single record of Ferruginous Duck.

Sanderling

Other species of interest have included regular Little Egret and a reputation as probably the most reliable site in Lancashire for Hobby sightings during the summer months. Other raptors, which reflect the conscientious level of recording and the location on a major flightline, include 12 different Honey Buzzard records during September 2000 and 14 different Osprey records. Other passage raptors have included Marsh Harrier, Hen Harrier and Red Kite.

Gulls and terns are well represented and have included Lancashire's first Laughing Gull (1999) and a Ring–billed Gull (2003). The Ribble valley is a known flight line for Little Gull and Arctic Tern on spring passage. Inclement weather has produced several site records along with 26 records of Kittiwake. Mediterranean Gull is regular, especially from March to August. Black Tern has been an increasing feature of both passage periods.

Brockholes is an inland site that gives the birder the sense of anticipation that one could encounter the unexpected at any time. A prime example of this was the appearance of a White Pelican of unknown origin during autumn 2006.

Access

Exact access details to this new site are currently uncertain, but will involve exiting the M6 at Junction 31. Please check with the Lancashire Wildlife Trust on their website (www.lancswt.org.uk), by phone (01772 324129) or by post (Lancashire Wildlife Trust, The Barn, Berkeley Drive, Bamber Bridge, Preston PR5 6BY).

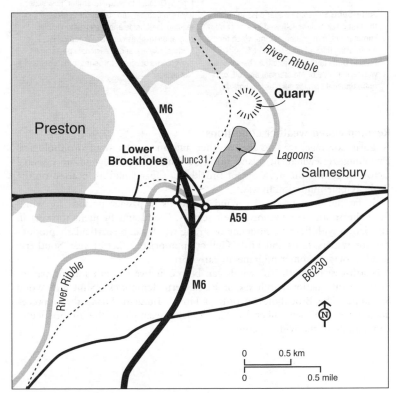

CALENDAR

January–March: Wildfowl and gulls, including a significant pre-roost of Black-headed and Common Gulls in March with a good chance of Mediterranean Gull. Double-figure numbers of Oystercatcher in January and triple-figure numbers of Curlew roost from Feb, peaking in March and continuing into April. Early migrants including Little Ringed Plover, Sand Martin, Common Chiffchaff, Blackcap and Northern Wheatear typically arrive from the third week of March. Rock Pipit is a possibility in March. Kittiwake is annual in small numbers between February and May. Common woodland species include Green Woodpecker.

April–May: Further arrivals of summer migrants. Chance of passage terns and waders. The first Whimbrels arrive from mid-April, with the roost peaking late April to early May. Chance of Osprey, especially in April. Small numbers of Little Gull are annual. Possibility of Hobby from late April.

June–Sept: Still some wader passage during the first week of June followed by a brief mid-summer lull in migration, during which time a summering flock of first-summer Black-headed Gulls perhaps offers the chance of a wandering Little or Mediterranean Gull, or more unusual species such as the one-day Ring-billed Gull in 2003. August can be the best month for Little Egret. Autumn wader passage is evident from mid-June with the first small flock of Northern Lapwing and perhaps a Green Sandpiper. Wader passage in this season is prolonged, but dependant on suitable weather conditions. Sightings of Hobby until the third week of September. Careful scrutiny of Common Teal can occasionally reveal Garganey from July. Wildfowl passage more noticeable from the last week of August.

Significant visible migration is dominated by hirundines; Meadow Pipits feature as September progresses. The first Water Rail of the autumn may put in an appearance from mid-September. Very occasional sightings of Long-eared Owl have occurred at dusk in late summer to mid autumn.

October–December: Wildfowl passage continues, with a chance of Whooper Swan and Scaup or other scarce waterbirds. Rock Pipit in October to early November. Low water levels in October can sometimes reveal feeding Jack Snipe and Water Rail. Visible migration involves corvids, Woodpigeon, finches, Skylark and occasional spectacular movements of winter thrushes in October and November.

Recommended weather conditions

Regular coverage, reading the weather and an awareness of ornithological happenings elsewhere in inland northern England and beyond are essential factors in getting the most out of Brockholes Quarry and its location on the River Ribble migration flyway.

By far the most productive wind directions in passage periods are winds from the south-west to north-west sectors. Cloud and frequent showers in association with fresh to moderate or strong winds can be particularly productive for waders, terns and Little Gull at appropriate times of year. Southerly winds provide summer migrants in early spring.

North-east to south-east winds can be productive in both seasons, particularly during national influxes of Black Tern, Temminck's Stint and Wood Sandpiper. The Brockholes records of Honey Buzzard during the unprecedented events of September 2000 are a classic example of the importance of being aware of the wider picture.

41 SEAFORTH NATURE RESERVE AND CROSBY MARINE PARK

OS
Landranger
Map 108

Habitat and Species

Seaforth Nature Reserve lies in the northern Liverpool Docks at the mouth of the River Mersey. The reserve comprises two lagoons surrounded by a mosaic of grassland, scrub, saltmarsh and reedbed. It is a regionally important roosting site for gulls and waders, holds large numbers of wintering ducks including Scaup and is nationally important for passage Little Gull in spring. The site is owned by Peel Holdings and managed under licence by the Lancashire Wildlife Trust. Seaforth forms part of the Mersey Narrows and North Wirral Shore Special Protection Area and is designated principally for Redshank, Common Tern and Cormorant.

Seaforth used to be known solely as a gull hotspot, with 15 species recorded, including an impressive total of five Bonaparte's Gulls and two or three Ring-billed Gulls annually. It is still rightly famous for its large spring passage of Little Gull during the *Chironomid* midge hatch. However, with 243 species recorded the site has much more to offer than just gulls. In recent years the headline birds have included rare waders and migrant landbirds, notably three Nearctic 'boat-hoppers' – Song and White-crowned Sparrows and Blackpoll Warbler – and more conventional vagrants such as Bluethroat, Icterine Warbler and Pied Wheatear.

Waders at Seaforth include significant high-tide roosts of Redshank and Oystercatcher and smaller numbers of Dunlin. Regular passage waders include Little Ringed Plover, Curlew Sandpiper and Little Stint. Rarer species recorded in recent times include Pacific Golden Plover, Long-billed Dowitcher and Buff-breasted, Marsh and Terek Sandpipers. Regular winter wildfowl flocks mostly comprise Common Teal, Tufted Duck, Pochard, Scaup and Common Golden-eye. Rarer species have included Long-tailed Duck and Smew.

Little Gull – first winter

The provision of rafts has resulted in a healthy population of breeding Common Tern and up to 2,000 migrant birds a day in late summer. The Common Tern flocks regularly attract smaller numbers of Sandwich, Arctic, Black, Little and Roseate Terns. White-winged Black Tern has been recorded on five occasions and Forster's Tern once.

Crosby Marine Lake is an area of variably brackish water within Crosby Marine Park. It is owned by Sefton Council and lies immediately to the north of Seaforth. When the freshwater content is favourable to hatches of *Chironomid* midges, it shares the spring Little Gull passage with Seaforth and is also favoured by passage Black Tern. Crosby has a good track record for storm-blown waifs such as Grey Phalarope, divers and the rarer grebes; these often give excellent views. Despite being a public park, the surrounding rough grassy areas and mature dunes have played host to migrant or winter passerines such as Snow Bunting, Lapland Bunting, Shore Lark and Richard's Pipit.

Visible migration sometimes involves very large numbers of Meadow Pipits, thrushes and finches in autumn. Occasional large raptors add variety, including 14 Honey Buzzards in September 2000 and fairly regular Ospreys.

During north-west winds in autumn, large numbers of seabirds may be forced into the Mersey Narrows. In these conditions, Leach's Storm-petrel can be seen in large numbers along with a good chance of Sabine's Gull and Long-tailed Skua among larger numbers of Arctic Skua. There was a Little Shearwater in 1992. Midsummer European Storm-petrel influxes are a feature of fresh to strong winds.

Access

Under government regulations relating to security of all ports, access to Seaforth Nature Reserve has been restricted since July 2004. All visitors must book in advance, giving seven day's notice. You will need to supply the names of everyone in your party together with make, model and registration number of any vehicles. Arrangements will then be made with the Port Police for your admission and day passes will be issued at the nature reserve office. Contact swhite@lancswt.org.uk or ring 0151 920 3769 during office hours to make your booking.

Having sorted out the administration, access to Seaforth is via the well-signposted entrance to the Freeport (SJ327967). Exit the M57/M58 at the northern/western terminus (Junction 7) and take the A5036 south west. At the junction with the A565, exit the dual carriageway and follow signs to the Freeport. Please call in at the office before using the hides (see map).

Crosby Marine Park is reached by heading north from the Freeport on the A565 and turning left at the next set of traffic lights after about 440 yards (400 m).

Seawatching can only be carried out from the shoreline of Crosby Marine Park, with the south-west corner near the Radar Tower favoured. There is no seawatching access from Seaforth.

If you are not able to book in advance, parts of Seaforth can be observed through a lengthy section of perimeter fence that separates the dockland property from Crosby Marine Park.

Timing

Little Gulls pass through from the last week of March to the first week of May, peaking during the third week of April. Leach's Storm-petrel and skua species

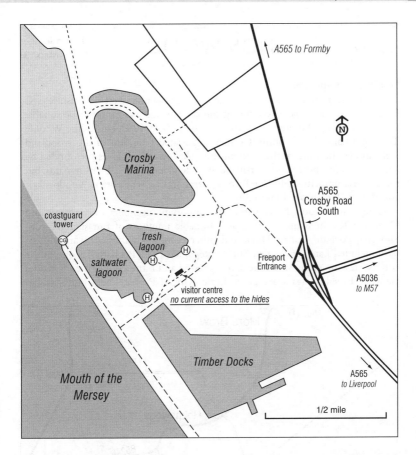

are recorded during strong west to north-west winds between the last few days of August (unusual) throughout September and early October (peak period) to late October (regular) and (rarely) November to early December. If Sabine's Gull occurs it is usually before mid-October. Strong onshore winds in June and July can produce European Storm-petrel.

Transitory landbirds such as Northern Wheatear and White Wagtail can be encountered between mid March and early June and from mid July to early November. Visible migration of passerines peaks between late September and early November. Passage waders occur mostly between April and early June and mid July to early October.

The spring passage of Common Gull peaks between mid March and May; rare smaller gulls such as Ring-billed and Bonaparte's may travel with this species. The future status of larger gulls is very difficult to predict. Reorganisation of landfill sites may signal the end of regular Iceland and Glaucous Gull sightings.

Midwinter brings good numbers of wildfowl, notably Scaup, to the lagoons at Seaforth. Little Gulls and Kittiwakes are possible in the Mersey Narrows during strong north-westerly winds, while thoughts of Seaforth's three records of Ross's Gull keep winter gull-watchers on their toes.

42 MERE SANDS WOOD

OS Landranger
Map 108

Habitat and Species

This wildlife-rich haven in the heart of agricultural west Lancashire was formed when sand deposited during the last Ice Age was found to be suitable for glass making. The site was quarried from 1974 to 1982. Lancashire Wildlife Trust and Lancashire County Council negotiated retention of the woodland areas and landscaping of the sand pits into shallow-edged lakes surrounded by a mixture of dry heath and marshland. A wide diversity of habitats remains, but the site has unfortunately lost Red Squirrel and Lesser-spotted Woodpecker, and Willow Tit is now a rare visitor.

Mere Sands Wood hosts nationally important numbers of Gadwall and Common Teal in winter, as well as reasonable numbers of Eurasian Wigeon, Shoveler, Pochard, Tufted Duck and other common wildfowl. Rare visitors have included Lancashire's first Surf Scoter since 1882. Pochard has one of the county's few breeding sites here. Great-crested and Little Grebes breed, as does Gadwall. Breeding waders include Little Ringed Plover. The whole site has

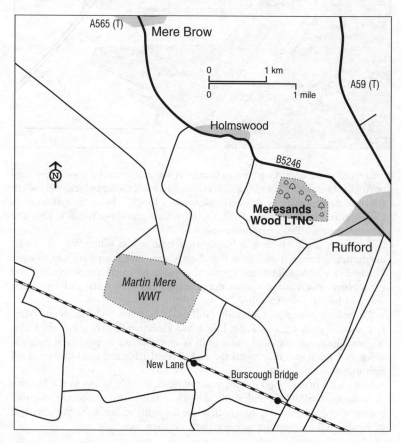

about 60 breeding species, including a good variety of the commoner warbler species. The surrounding woodlands support Lesser Redpoll and Siskin in winter. This is one of the best sites in Lancashire for dragonflies.

Access
Leave the A59 in Rufford and join Holmeswood Road (B5246). After 1 mile (1.6 km), turn left at the Nature Reserve and Meresands Kennels signs. The car park is at the end of the lane. There are three circular nature trails with up to six hides and a viewing platform for dragonflies. The white trail is suitable for motorised wheelchairs. There is a well-equipped visitor centre operated by the Lancashire Wildlife Trust and a picnic area near the car park.

Timing
The visitor centre is open from 9 a.m. to 5 p.m. The car park opens until 8 p.m. Easter until the end of August.

CALENDAR

April–August: Sunny days between mid May and the end of August are recommended for a good mix of dragonflies and birds, with several visits needed to see all the dragonfly species. Early May is best for singing birds. Look out for passage birds such as Garganey on the pools.

November–February: Winter visitors such as Siskin and Lesser Redpoll, with a possibility of Common Redpoll in some years and, on one occasion, Arctic Redpoll. Winter wildfowl.

43 MARSHSIDE   OS Landranger Map 108

Habitat and Species
Marshside RSPB reserve lies at the northern end of the Sefton Coast on the shores of the Ribble Estuary. It is a 272-acre (110 ha) area of reclaimed grazing marsh. Rimmer's Marsh is south of Marshside Road and Sutton's Marsh to the north. A further block of around 620 acres (250 ha) of neighbouring saltmarsh will hopefully extend the RSPB reserve during 2007.

Marshside and the adjacent golf course and foreshore has an impressive list of 250 recorded species. Recent additions include Black Stork, Glossy Ibis, Smew, Long-eared Owl and, if accepted, Pallid Harrier. Much of the marsh floods in the winter and attracts spectacular numbers of waterfowl, especially Eurasian Wigeon (over 21,000 in winter 2006–2007), Common Teal, European Golden Plover, Northern Lapwing and Black-tailed Godwit. Pintail, Shoveler, Snipe, Curlew and Ruff visit in smaller numbers. Large flocks of Pink-footed Goose may bring a Greenland White-fronted or Barnacle Goose with them. Storm-driven roosts of gulls can number into the thousands.

The reserve has one of the highest densities of breeding waders in lowland Britain, with around 80 pairs of Northern Lapwing and 25 pairs of Redshank.

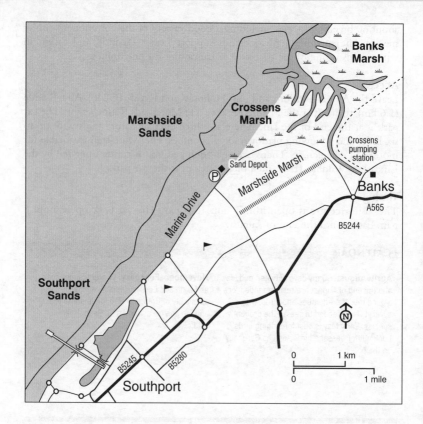

Since 2001, Avocet has established its strongest breeding population in north-west England: 24 pairs reared 38 chicks in 2006. Garganey regularly over-summers. Shoveler, Gadwall and Tufted Duck breed regularly and Common Teal does so occasionally.

Many Skylarks breed on the marsh along with smaller numbers of Sedge and Reed Warblers, Reed Bunting and Linnet in the ditches and scrub.

The saltmarsh and mudflats at Marshside are internationally important for Knot and Bar-tailed Godwit and nationally important for Dunlin, Grey Plover, Oystercatcher and Shelduck. Raptor activity can be impressive in the winter months, especially at high tides when Merlin, Peregrine Falcon, Sparrowhawk and Kestrel can be expected, along with a good chance of seeing Hen and Marsh Harriers. Short-eared and Barn Owls are regular. There were up to 12 Little Egrets in winter 2006–2007.

Rarities over the past 30 years have included Lesser White-fronted Goose, American Wigeon, Night Heron, Purple Heron, Cattle Egret, Black Stork, Common Crane, Glossy Ibis, Black-winged Stilt, American Golden Plover, Kentish Plover, Baird's, White-rumped and Broad-billed Sandpipers, Long-billed Dowitcher, Lesser Yellowlegs, Marsh Sandpiper, White-winged Black Tern, Ross's Gull and Savi's Warbler.

Recent scarce migrants have included Leach's Storm-petrel, Mediterranean, Ring-billed, Glaucous and Iceland Gulls, Grey and Red-necked Phalaropes,

Bluethroat, Richard's and Red-throated Pipits, Yellow-browed Warbler, Red-backed Shrike, Great Grey Shrike, Lapland Bunting and more or less annual Spoonbill, Green-winged Teal, Temminck's Stint and Pectoral Sandpiper.

Access
Marshside is accessed via Marine Drive, the coastal road that runs 2 miles (3.2 km) north of Southport town centre. Various access alternatives from the main A565 can be seen on the map. There are plenty of vantage points along the whole of the reserve boundary, two hides, a viewing platform, a car park and toilet facilities. The hides are open from 8.30 a.m. to 5 p.m. all year. Most of the birds can be observed from the reserve footpaths at all times. Reserve entry is free and RSPB membership is encouraged. For further information telephone the reserve office on 01704 536378 or email the warden (graham.clarkson@rspb.org.uk).

CALENDAR

March–June: Sand Martin, Northern Wheatear, White Wagtail and Common Sandpiper pass through; Northern Lapwing begins to nest. In May, Redshank begins breeding and migrants such as Little Gull, Ruff, Ringed Plover and Dunlin move through. Avocets breed and as water levels fall the marshes are full of wader chicks feeding alongside Gadwall and Shoveler ducklings.

September–February: A high tide visit can be rewarded with one of Lancashire's wildlife spectacles as huge numbers of waders and wildfowl concentrate on the reserve and adjacent estuary. Raptors are a constant feature, along with large flocks of skylarks and linnets.

44 THE SOUTH RIBBLE MARSHES
OS Landranger Map 108

Habitat and Species
The saltmarshes and sand and mud flats of the Ribble Estuary form one of the most important wetlands for wintering and passage waterfowl in Europe, and the most important in Britain after the Wash and Morecambe Bay for waders, ducks, geese and swans. Sixteen species regularly achieve internationally important totals and the smoke-like flights of waders to and from their high-tide roosts are one of our greatest natural spectacles, attracting birdwatchers from far and wide.

The south side of the estuary has one of the largest extents of saltmarsh in Britain, with around 5,000 acres (2,000 ha) representing 20 per cent of the total intertidal area. In addition to the nutrient-rich mudflats, the grazed saltmarsh provides ideal feeding for wintering Eurasian Wigeon, which have exceeded 100,000 on occasion – by far the largest assembly in the country. The ducks are often accompanied by large flocks of Pink-footed Geese and Whooper Swans. A wide variety of other birds uses the saltmarsh in winter, including Skylark, Meadow Pipit, Scandinavian Rock and Water Pipits, and

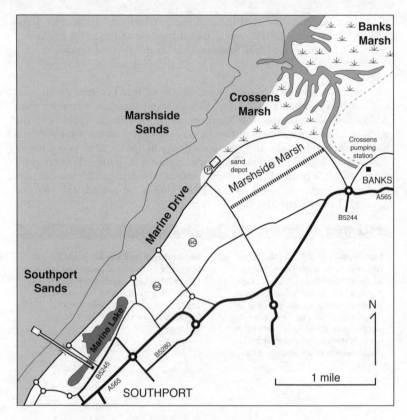

Twite (ringing suggests the Ribble Twites are mainly of Pennine origin). These and the waterfowl attract birds of prey, particularly Merlin, Peregrine Falcon, Marsh and Hen Harriers and Short-eared Owl.

The Ribble Estuary holds nationally important colonies gulls and Common Terns, mostly on the south bank of the river. Black-headed Gulls have decreased from a peak of 20,000 pairs in 1989, but the colony includes at least five pairs of Mediterranean Gull. In contrast, the large gulls have increased.

There is also an important population of nesting Redshank on the marshes, although 231 pairs in 2003 is a significant reduction on the 400 pairs estimated in 1974. Black-tailed Godwits used to breed at Longton Marsh, but are now confined to Newton Marsh. Ruff is a sporadic breeder. Avocets have colonised since 2003 and in 1999 the Ribble hosted the first successful breeding by Spoonbills in Britain since the 17th century.

Access to any part of the Ribble Estuary is difficult and significant numbers of scarcer species undoubtedly pass through unnoticed by birdwatchers. This situation is likely to be improved when the RSPB's plans to restore 370 acres (150 ha) of reclaimed arable land at Hesketh Out Marsh to estuarine habitats. Nevertheless, the list of rarities, especially waders, in the past 50 or so years is impressive. On the south bank of the river these include Great White Egret, Stilt and Broad-billed Sandpipers, Lesser Yellowlegs and Wilson's Phalarope.

45 THE SEFTON COAST   OS Landranger Map 108

Between Southport and the northern suburbs of the Liverpool conurbation at Crosby is an area of wide, sandy beaches, backed by a dune system of outstanding botanical, herpetological and entomological interest. The extensive sand flats linking those of the Ribble to those of North Wirral Shore and the Dee provide feeding and roosting grounds for large flocks of waders. The dune system is the largest in England. It provides shelter for a wide range of migrants in both spring and autumn, especially in areas of scrub inland of the frontal dunes. Farther inland are extensive areas of pine plantation, home to the English mainland's most southerly Red Squirrel population. Smaller pockets of deciduous woodland and dune heathland are interspersed with several golf courses.

The dune coast is divided by the estuary of the River Alt, which flows into the sea at Hightown. South of the Alt the band of suitable habitat is much narrower than in the north, but there is little ornithological difference between the two sections.

The Sefton Coast is used extensively for recreation, but most of it is managed primarily for nature conservation by the main landowners, Sefton Council, Natural England and the National Trust. It is easy to avoid the crowds except at the height of summer. The main sites are under separate ownership – Ainsdale and Birkdale Hills and Ravenmeols Local Nature Reserves (Sefton Council), Ainsdale and Cabin Hill National Nature Reserves (Natural England) and Formby Point (National Trust) – but management is co-ordinated through the Sefton Coast Partnership. Footpaths connect the sites and access is largely unrestricted, except at Altcar Rifle Ranges at Hightown. Permits are required from Natural England for full access to the National Nature Reserves, but public paths cross each of them.

Habitat and Species

At high tide Formby Point provides good seawatching, especially during late summer and autumn when gales may produce Leach's and European Storm-petrels, Gannet, Kittiwake, terns, shearwaters, skuas and auks. In calm winter weather sea ducks, grebes and divers may be seen. It is the only site in Lanca-shire to consistently produce seabirds normally associated with deeper waters. The greatest prize was a Fea's/Zino's Petrel in 1995. Other notable finds have included Cory's, Sooty and Balearic Shearwaters and Forster's Tern. In winter, several thousand Common Scoters sometimes come within sight of land, together with smaller numbers of Red-throated Diver and auks.

The sandy shores throughout the area are frequented by waders and gulls, the latter sometimes occurring in tens of thousands after a winter shellfish wreck. At such times a search for the scarcer gulls such as Glaucous and Iceland can be rewarding. High tide wader roosts form along the Ainsdale and Birkdale shores and to the south of Formby Point on Taylor's Bank by Cabin Hill. From September to March, Knot is present in tens of thousands, Bar-tailed Godwit and Dunlin in thousands and Oystercatcher, Grey Plover, Redshank and Sanderling in hundreds. Smaller numbers of other species are also expected: Sanderling and Ringed Plover are more numerous on spring and autumn passage in May and August to September.

At low tide waders scatter over the flats, with some flying to feed along the North Wirral Shore or in the Dee estuary. Common Tern fish in the Formby Channel on spring passage in May, often joined by a few Little and Sandwich Terns. From July to September there are regularly several hundred Common Terns with smaller numbers of Sandwich and Little and, rarely, Arctic and Roseate Terns. A large roost of Pink-footed Geese gathers on Taylor's Bank on winter evenings. Breeding Ringed Plovers are now restricted to the least disturbed areas, mainly at Birkdale, where the Green Beach – a site of outstanding botanical interest – holds large numbers of wintering Common and Jack Snipes. Nearby, Sands Lake at Ainsdale is a notable winter haunt of Tufted Duck.

The dunes support a limited range of breeding birds, scrub species such as Stonechat, Common Whitethroat, Linnet and Reed Bunting. Grasshopper Warbler is a frequent breeder; the dunes south of Hightown are a reliable site for seeing them. Relatively few birds winter, but increasing numbers of Blackcap and Chiffchaff are found in sea-buckthorn scrub.

Firecrest

In spring, White and Yellow Wagtails, Willow and Sedge Warblers, Common Whitethroat, Northern Wheatear and a few Whinchat are staple birds. Other warblers, chats and flycatchers visit in smaller numbers. A similar range of species to those in spring migrates through the area in autumn, but there is an increased chance of rarities. Despite its proximity to Liverpool the dune coast is relatively under-worked by birdwatchers during migration periods. Rare and scarce species turn up regularly. These have included Wryneck, Barred Warbler, Firecrest, Great Grey Shrike, Bearded Tit, Red-breasted Flycatcher, Subalpine and Pallas's Warblers, Lancashire's only Sardinian Warbler and the first British Eleonora's Falcon in 1977.

The pine woodlands are of little interest, although Woodcock and Siskin are regular breeders and substantial numbers of Common Crossbill visit during irruption years, occasionally staying on the nest.

Access

The whole of the coast is readily accessible at many points and a network of footpaths connects the main sites. Car parking (charges usually apply) is

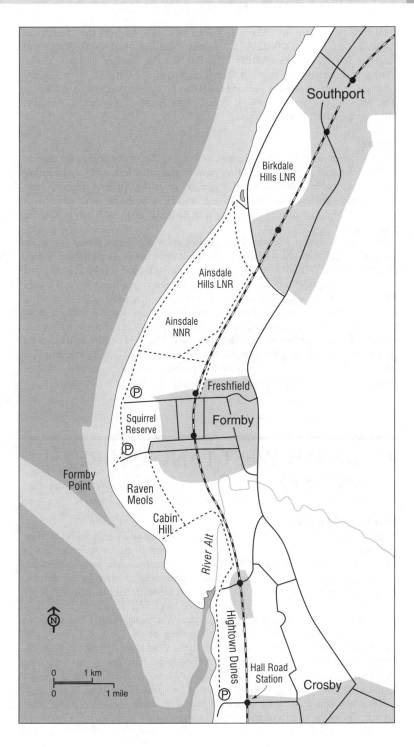

available at Southport Marine Lake (SD331179), on the beach at Ainsdale–Birkdale (SD296129), at Formby National Trust (SD275083) and Lifeboat Road, Formby (SD275066). For the Alt Estuary and Hightown Dunes, park either in Lower Alt Road, Hightown (SD296032), or at Crosby Coastguard Station (SD298004) at Hall Road on the northern edge of Crosby. The most convenient access by train is via Ainsdale, Freshfield, Formby, Hightown or Hall Road Stations.

Timing

During the summer months the coast is very popular with trippers. Its interest is then primarily in plants and other aspects of natural history. Early morning visits are advisable at passage times, especially in spring. Autumn migrants may linger longer in less busy areas. To see waders or seabirds, time your visits around the high tide. Wader roosts begin to gather a couple of hours before the tide peaks.

Seawatchers favour Formby Point, either from the dunes about 440 yards (400 m) south of the National Trust car park or at the end of Lifeboat Road, about 1.3 miles (2 km) to the south. Seawatching from Formby Point is best on an incoming tide; movements generally drop off very quickly on the ebb. Morning tides are usually more productive than afternoon ones. Any wind direction with west in it is fine, and any wind above force 4 is potentially productive. Winter seawatching can be good here over a calm sea, with a fair chance of divers, grebes and sea ducks. Seawatching at Formby Point can be productive in onshore gales, but the site is very exposed. In dry conditions a strong wind can produce a sand blow. Watching is possible in greater comfort from the Crosby Coastguard car park, although the setting is not ideal.

46 SOUTH-WEST LANCASHIRE MOSSES
OS Landranger Map 108

Habitat and Species

Inland of the dunes and estuaries the Lancashire Coastal Plain is dominated by peat mossland, virtually all of which has been reclaimed for intensive arable agriculture and horticulture. The mosses are most well known for the wintering flocks of Pink-footed Goose and associated rarer goose species. Fields are large and hedgerows rare, but there are scattered plantations, largely retained as game cover. These hold some breeding birds, including a few Long-eared Owls and the seriously declining Willow Tit. Sadly, Turtle Dove seems to be facing extinction here, but the jingling song of the Corn Bunting is still heard quite commonly on the mosslands. Barn Owl is doing particularly well, encouraged by the provision of nest boxes on farms. The largest surviving area of active bog and heathland, at Simonswood Moss near Kirkby, was destroyed in the early 1980s, taking with it the last of Lancashire's breeding Nightjars.

Keen watchers using a car as a hide may find other goose species in small numbers amongst the Pink-footed flocks, particularly Russian and Greenland

White-fronted, Barnacle, Bean, Brent and Snow Geese. Raptors in winter include Merlin, Peregrine, Hen Harrier and Common Buzzard, the latter an increasing nester in recent years. Marsh Harriers regularly summer and have bred. Northern Lapwings and Grey Partridges breed in good numbers, the latter encouraged by the provision of conservation headlands around fields.

A few mossland sites are traditional stopovers for small trips of Dotterel in May, but several years have passed with no records. Passage flocks of 50 or more Whimbrel can be found in late April. A fairly recent addition to the agricultural landscape are irrigation reservoirs, one such on Downholland Moss attracts a variety of species including raptors and waterfowl.

Access
The following are probably the best areas to check: Formby Moss, Altcar (SD325064), Downholland Moss (SD335085) and Plex Moss (SD340097). As with the similar habitat in the north Fylde, the best strategy is to drive the roads inter-linking these sites, especially when searching for wintering goose flocks. The area to work is the rectangle between the A5147 in the east and A565 in the west, and the A570 in the north and B5195 in the south.

46A   RIMROSE VALLEY COUNTRY PARK   OS Ref: SD329982

This is a site managed by Sefton Council. It provides a direct link between the mosslands and the coast. Winter sightings include good numbers of Snipe and Jack Snipe, a few Water Rail and Woodcock and regular Barn and Short-eared Owls. Hobby has been seen regularly and rarities have included Red-rumped Swallow.

46B   MARTIN MERE

Martin Mere was the largest of several freshwater meres that punctuated the south-west Lancashire mosslands. It was drained from the late 17th century onwards with the loss of most of its spectacular wildlife. In 1973, the Wildfowl and Wetlands Trust established a 370-acre (150 ha) reserve at Martin Mere and effectively recreated some of the habitats associated with the historic landscape. The reserve has become internationally important for wildfowl such as Whooper Swan, Common Teal and Pink-footed Goose, while Pintail, Pochard and Shelduck occur in nationally significant numbers. Birds of prey in winter and on passage include regular Merlin, Peregrine Falcon and Marsh Harrier. Wintering Common Buzzards are a recent feature. The reserve also regularly holds 100 or more Ruff, several hundred Common Snipe and several thousand Northern Lapwings. Martin Mere is one of the most reliable sites in the county to see Barn Owl.

Important breeding species include Northern Lapwing, Common Snipe, Redshank and Tree Sparrow. An extension of the reserve into a former carrot field created a new wetland. This holds a breeding population of Avocets, following the first three pairs in 2004. Farmland in the Martin Mere area is one of the few remaining Lancashire breeding sites for Yellow Wagtail.

An impressive list of rare and scarce birds has visited the reserve over the years, including Blue-winged Teal, Cattle and Great White Egrets, Kentish Plover, Collared and Black-winged Pratincoles, Wilson's Phalarope, Franklin's Gull and Red-backed Shrike. Temminck's Stint, Pectoral Sandpiper and Green-winged Teal have been annual in recent years. A pair of Black-winged Stilts attempted to breed in 2006.

Timing

Maximum Pink-footed Goose numbers of around 21,000 usually occur during a six-week period from mid-September to late October. A shorter influx in late January and very early February produces similar numbers to autumn. There are also smaller arrivals and departures during midwinter, with a population of 4,000–5,000. This pattern is due to many of the birds spending midwinter in Norfolk. Whooper Swans tend to peak in December and January. The site record count is 1,900 in January 2005.

The winter months are the best time to see wildfowl, including regular Green-winged Teal, but visits during May to early June and July to August are probably best for the chance of rare waders, although later in the autumn has also been productive.

Access

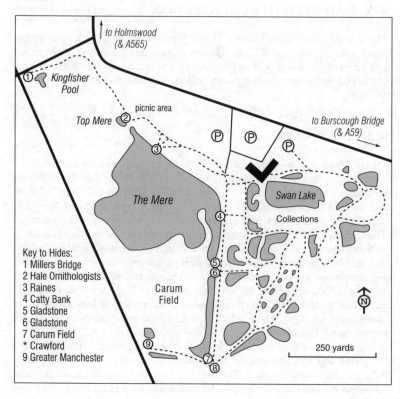

Key to Hides:
1 Millers Bridge
2 Hale Ornithologists
3 Raines
4 Catty Bank
5 Gladstone
6 Gladstone
7 Carum Field
* Crawford
9 Greater Manchester

47 WEST PENNINE MOORS

OS Explorer
Map 287

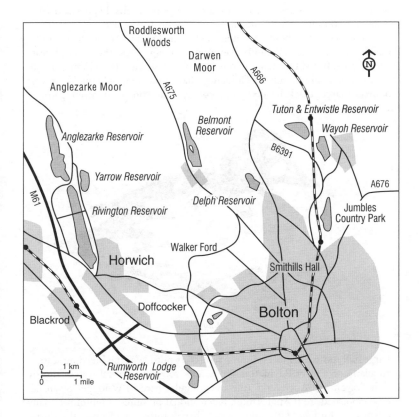

Habitat

The area to the north of Bolton consists largely of pasture rising to grass moorland with some heather moor on the highest ground. There are areas of young conifer plantations on the moors, and more mature conifers around the margins of the many reservoirs that lie within the steep-sided Pennine valleys. Tracts of old oak woodland add to the diversity. Sheep farming predominates on the moors with cattle pasture on the moorland edge; some heather moors are managed for grouse shooting.

Species

A good range of birds breeds on the moors, including Red Grouse, Merlin, European Golden Plover, Dunlin, Curlew, Short-eared Owl, Cuckoo, Stonechat, Whinchat, Northern Wheatear and Linnet. Only a relict population of Twite remains and Ring Ouzel is now only a very occasional breeder. Yellowhammer was recently lost from the moorland edge. Peregrine Falcon, Raven, Stock Dove, Kestrel and colonies of Jackdaws breed in some abandoned quarries. Hen Harriers winter and pairs regularly linger into spring. In midwinter the high moors are occupied by Red Grouse, parties of Reed Buntings and the occasional Snow Bunting. European Golden Plovers often start to return to the tops in January.

Most of the valleys are now dammed to create reservoirs. Dipper and Grey Wagtail are common on the upland streams with Kingfisher in places lower down. The reservoirs hold breeding waders including Oystercatcher, Little Ringed Plover, Redshank and Common Sandpiper, together with Great-crested Grebe, Tufted Duck, numerous Canada Geese and a few Common Teal. Pintail has bred and Common Goldeneye has summered. Belmont Reservoir supports a large Black-headed Gull colony that contained seven pairs of Mediterranean Gull in 2007.

Goldeneye

Large gull roosts assemble on some reservoirs outside of the breeding season, particularly on Lower Rivington. Goosander roosts on several waters, mostly Delph, Wayoh and Anglezarke (the once regular herd of Whooper Swan has now disappeared from Anglezarke). Recreational pressures compromise many reservoirs for birding, with sailing and other disturbance affecting the distribution and numbers of winter wildfowl and breeding waders.

In-bye pastures surround upland farmsteads; many now degraded as rush cover increases. Very few hay meadows remain and improved pastures are now mostly cut for silage, although many in-bye fields retain breeding Northern Lapwing, Redshank, Common Snipe and Reed Bunting, often in good numbers. Grey Partridge is still widely distributed. Numbers of Grasshopper Warblers are increasing as they take advantage of the rush-beds, farm buildings often hold large colonies of Swallows and Barn Owls have re-colonised recently.

Many steep-sided upland valleys are clothed with natural woodlands, typically oak, ash, birch, rowan and holly, often with wet woodland of alder and willow. Many have been supplemented by introduced beech, sycamore and rhododendron. Upland woodlands, particularly in the Rivington, Anglezarke and Roddlesworth areas, hold species such as Pied Flycatcher, Redstart, Tree Pipit, Spotted Flycatcher, Woodcock, Nuthatch, Green Woodpecker and Wood Warbler. Lesser Spotted Woodpecker, Willow Tit and Tree Sparrow are declining towards extinction, but there are signs that Common Buzzard, Goshawk and Hobby are colonising the area.

Extensive conifer and mixed plantations associated mainly with reservoir surrounds hold breeding Long-eared Owl, Siskin and Lesser Redpoll, with Common Crossbill in most years. There is a large heronry in a larch plantation at Entwistle. Woodcock winters in good numbers in plantations and rhododendron thickets. Several massive roosts of crows (mostly Carrion Crow) form in the plantations in midwinter. There is a Magpie roost on the county border at Egerton. Finch roosts also occur; the largest roosts of Brambling have been in rhododendron thickets at Belmont.

Visible migration is often evident through the valleys and along the moor edges (for example, Darwen Moor). Northern Wheatears and Ring Ouzels commonly linger on the in-bye land. Ospreys are annual on the reservoirs and, if reservoir levels are low, passage waders can be notable both in number and variety. County rarities are infrequent but have included Lancashire's first Whiskered Tern and Dartford Warbler, and the only Golden Eagle to be photographed in the county.

A large part of the area is covered by a countryside warden service. The wardens can advise on quiet areas to visit. Public footpaths are well maintained and signposted. Some of the better sites are detailed below, but there is plenty of scope for exploration.

Selected sites

Most of these sites have a rather repetitive species list comprising common wildfowl, common breeding waders and woodland passerines, including those associated with conifers such as Siskin in winter. These are sites where local patch observers may turn up only three or four sightings per year worthy of individual documentation in the county bird report. A classic example is Black Tern during south-easterly winds in late April or May. Unsettled weather, especially if there is low water level and muddy edges, is more likely to be productive for wader species than a sunny day.

47A   RIVINGTON, ANGLEZARKE AND
YARROW RESERVOIRS   OS Ref: SD6213

The large winter gull roost on Lower Rivington Reservoir may include one or two Mediterranean Gulls. There have been intermittent visits by a returning Ring-necked Duck in recent winters, mainly on the upper reservoir.

Access

The best vantage points for wildfowl and roosting gulls are from the A675 Bolton-Chorley Road just west of Horwich (SD626127) or from a minor road in the vicinity of the castle (SD628130). Other vantage points include the causeway roads.

47B   BELMONT RESERVOIR   OS Ref: SD675167

This reservoir hosts a Black-headed Gull colony which reached 3,450 pairs in 2007 (2.8% of the British population). As has been the case with most colonies this size, Mediterranean Gulls have been detected and bred for the first time in

2005 increasing to at least ten pairs in 2007. The edges of the reservoir are favoured by breeding waders and passage birds. The nearby streams contain Dipper.

Access

Parking is difficult along the A675 clearway, but a minor road crosses the dam (SD675164) and a footpath climbs the eastern shore.

47C   JUMBLES COUNTRY PARK RESERVOIR   OS Ref: SD734145

This is a multipurpose recreational site with some quiet areas that provide refuge for common wildfowl species. You might strike lucky with passage Black Tern and Little Gull during late April and early May. Vagrants have included Spotted Sandpiper and Pomarine Skua.

Access

The Country Park is signposted off the A676 Bolton to Ramsbottom Road (take the left turn at SD 737133). There is a second car park at Ousel's Nest off the B6391 on the west bank that gives a more circuitous walk. Footpaths encircle the reservoir and connect with Wayoh and Entwistle Reservoirs.

47D   WAYOH RESERVOIR   OS Ref: SD733166

Access

From Edgeworth crossroads (SD741169) take the minor road to the northwest. After half a mile (0.8 km) take the very narrow road at SD736175 – the turn off is easily missed; look out for the little church on the left to Entwistle station – and park beyond the causeway that crosses the tip of the reservoir. A path leads around the reservoir and connects with Turton and Entwistle Reservoir. The path passes through woodland and scrub habitats, with a good chance of Siskin in winter, and excellent views across two wildfowl refuges.

48E   TURTON AND ENTWHISTLE RESERVOIR   OS Ref: SD720175

Access

A car park below the dam is accessible off the B6391; turn right at SD 724168. A public footpath skirts the north shore.

GREATER MANCHESTER

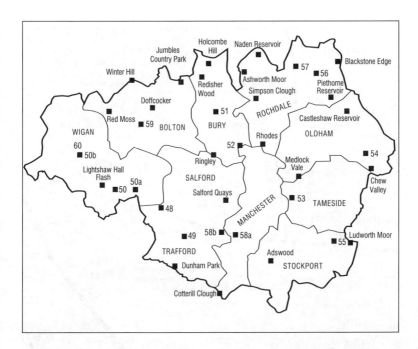

48 Chat Moss
49 Carrington Moss, Shell Pool and
Sinderland
50 Pennington Flash
    50A   Hope Car Reserve
    50B   Abram Flashes
51 Elton Reservoir
52 Heaton Park Reservoir
53 Audenshaw Reservoirs
54 Dovestones and Saddleworth Moor
55 Etherow Country Park
56 Hollingworth Lake
57 Watergrove Reservoir
    57A   Piethorne Valley

57B   Light Hazzles, White Holme
      and Warland Reservoirs
58 Mersey Valley
    58A   Chorlton Water Park
    58B   Sale Water Park and Broad
        Ees Dole
59 Rumworth Lodge
    59A   Smithills Moor
    59B   Red Moss
60 Wigan Flashes
    60A   Scotman's Flash
    60B   Horrocks' Flash and Turner's
      Flash

48 CHAT MOSS

OS Landranger Map 109
Explorer 276
Map ref: SJ7096

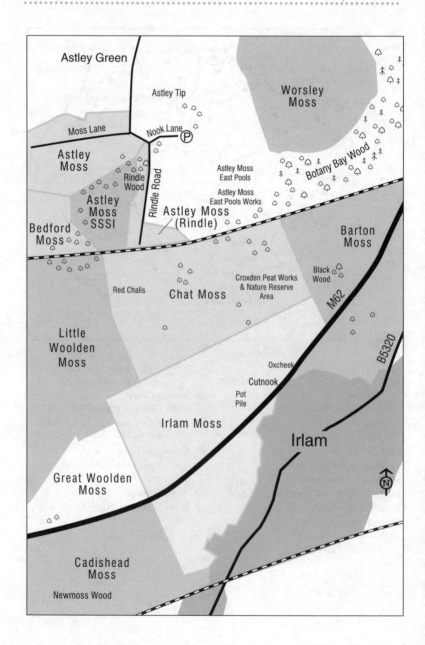

The name Chat Moss is a collective term encompassing a number of smaller mosslands – Astley Moss, Worsley Moss, Barton Moss, Irlam Moss, Little Woolden Moss and Cadishead Moss – as well as Chat Moss itself, which is at the heart of the area. These are remnants of a huge impassable peat bog that helped to isolate parts of North-West England in medieval times. Today, the area effectively separates Salford and Wigan and acts as a huge green lung for Manchester. The area is bisected by the M62 and the Liverpool to Manchester railway line, and is bounded by Astley village and the A580 to the north, the River Glaze to the west, the town of Irlam to the south and the M60 to the east. The area is under major threat as there is a plan to build a racecourse with associated leisure facilities in the NE sector.

Habitat

There is a wide variety of habitat in the area, including the county's largest wood, Botany Bay Wood (private), arable farmland, vegetable fields, grasslands (increasingly turned over to keeping horses and turf growing), virgin mosslands (mostly covered by the Manchester Mosslands SPA, parts of which are private and managed for shooting) and peat workings and associated pools. A flat landscape is common to all these areas. Even areas of intensive agriculture contain shrubby drainage ditches that can hold plenty of birds.

CALENDAR

Breeding: Oystercatcher, Redshank, Curlew, Little Ringed and Ringed Plovers, Corn Bunting, Yellowhammer, Lesser Redpoll, Tree Sparrow, Yellow Wagtail, Cuckoo, Barn, Little, Tawny and Long-eared Owls, Kestrel, Common Buzzard, Grey Partridge, Spotted Flycatcher, Tree Pipit, Willow Tit, Reed Bunting, Hobby (now regular) and Woodcock. Quail sing here in most summers.

Winter: Pink-footed Goose, Hen Harrier, Merlin, Peregrine Falcon, Short-eared Owl, large flocks of Skylark and finches, Jack Snipe and Common Snipe and Stonechat.

Passage: Northern Wheatear, Whinchat and Ring Ouzel. Wader passage on Astley Moss East peat pools includes Wood and Green Sandpipers, Greenshank, Ruff, Dunlin, Whimbrel, godwits and Little Stint.

Recent rarities: Greater Flamingo, Bean Goose, Bufflehead, Red-footed Falcon, Desert Wheatear and Nightjar (former breeder; habitat now destroyed).

Access

From Irlam via Astley Road, which runs north across the moss (unsurfaced and rough in places). Twelve Yards Road runs east from Astley Road at SJ704956 and provides views over the arable fields.

49 CARRINGTON MOSS, SHELL POOL AND SINDERLAND

SJ 7491

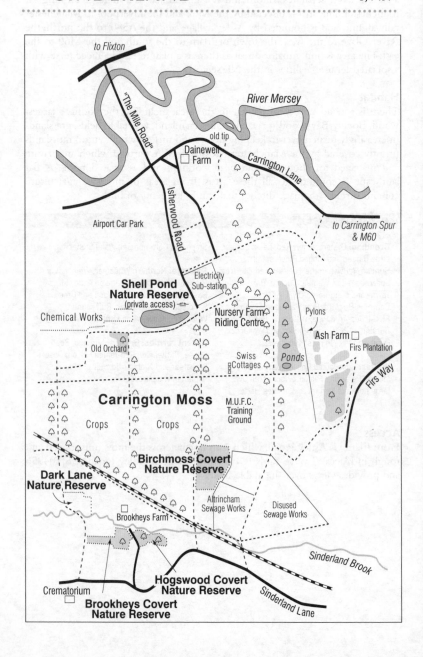

This area is bounded by Partington in the west, the A6144 to the north, Sale and Altrincham in the east and the Bridgewater Canal in the south. The habitat is arable and pastoral farmland with Shell Pool Reserve (private) on the north edge within the chemical works complex, but no peatland, and partly taken over for training grounds by Manchester United FC. Some of the large arable fields just south of the chemical works can hold very large numbers of Skylark and finches in winter; breeding birds include Corn Bunting, Yellowhammer, Quail, Tree Sparrow, Yellow Wagtail, Buzzard, Grey Partridge. Access from Sinderland Road in the south or from Isherwood Road, off the A6144, in the north. Shell Pool holds a wide variety of breeding waterfowl (enquire on 0161 436 7551 for permits).

50 PENNINGTON FLASH

OS Landranger Maps 109 and 276
OS ref: SJ640990

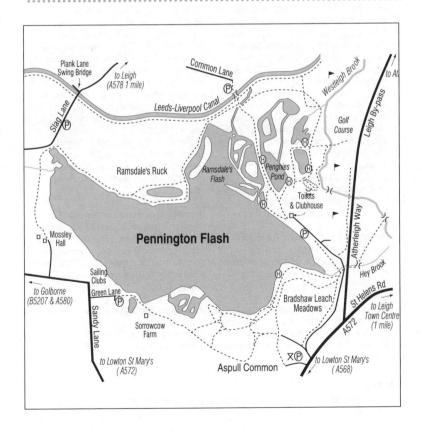

Habitat and facilities

A large colliery subsidence flash 1 mile (1.75 km) long, south west of Leigh off St Helens Road (A572). Wigan council developed Pennington as a 500-acre (200 ha) nature reserve in the early 1980s. A network of lagoons and pools with scrapes lies on the north-east side of the flash, cleverly planned to cope with large numbers of visitors without disturbance to birds. Woodland planted in the 1980s on the south side is now maturing and attracting suitable species. Mining spoil heaps (rucks) on the north side have recently been landscaped, which has reduced off-road biking. There is some disturbance from sailing at weekends. A mobile café is usually stationed in the main car park. Facilities include a notice board with sightings, information leaflets, excellent hides and a toilet block.

Species

Up to December 2005, 237 species had been recorded. The site is famous for the discovery of the first Black-faced Bunting in Britain in 1994.

CALENDAR

Winter: Regular waterbirds include Great Crested and Little Grebe, Mute Swan, Mallard, Gadwall, Common Teal, Shoveler, Pochard, Tufted Duck, Common Goldeneye, Goosander and sometimes Eurasian Wigeon. Northern Lapwing flocks on spit. Cormorant roost. A winter gull roost includes around 5,000 Black-headed Gulls and is worth checking for Mediterranean Gull and, in midwinter, occasional white-winged gulls. Occasional visits from divers and rarer grebes, Whooper Swan, Bittern, Smew, Common Scoter and Scaup. Pintail is regular in small numbers. Birds of prey include Peregrine Falcon, Buzzard, Merlin and sometimes Short-eared Owl. A feeding station at Bunting Hide provides reliable and excellent views of Willow Tit, Bullfinch and Water Rail. Siskins and Bramblings are usually present in the same area.

Passage: Large numbers of Tufted Duck in August and September are worth scanning for rarities and hybrids. Black-necked Grebes are frequent in spring and autumn. Little Egret is becoming annual, mostly in August. Garganey is present in autumn, when flocks of Eurasian Wigeon on passage to the west coast call in. Reliable for most of the commoner passage waders (often on the spit and seen from Horrocks Hide): Dunlin, Ruff, Common Snipe, Black-tailed Godwit, Greenshank, Green Sandpiper, Redshank and Common Sandpiper. Turnstone and Sanderling are most common in May. Grey Plover, Knot, Bar-tailed Godwit and Wood Sandpiper are annual but rare. Little Stint, Curlew Sandpiper and Spotted Redshank visit occasionally. Little Gull is often present in May. Sandwich and Little Terns are annual but rare, and Arctic Tern is often seen in late April or early May. Black Tern numbers are variable, but most likely in late April and late August to September. Osprey is rare but annual. White Wagtail passes through in good numbers in spring. Swift and hirundine flocks feeding over the water can reach thousands, especially in spring.

Breeding species: Black-headed Gull, Common Tern, Gadwall, Tufted Duck, Ringed and Little Ringed Plovers. Passerines include Reed, Sedge and Grasshopper Warblers and Reed Bunting. Up to three pairs of Mute Swan breed and there is a summer moult flock of around 100 birds.

Recent rarities: Whiskered Tern, Spotted Crake, Canvasback, Lesser Scaup, Temminck's Stint and Pectoral Sandpiper, Red-necked Phalarope.

Timing

There is usually something of interest throughout the year.

Access

From junction 23 of the M6 take the A580 East Lancs Road east towards Manchester. After a little less than 4 miles (6 km), take the A579 Atherleigh Way to the left. Pennington Flash is signposted. Turn left at the first set of lights onto the A572. After about 100 yards (100 m) turn right into the Pennington Flash entrance. Visitors with disabilities have excellent access to all hides and there is a disabled toilet. There is a fee for parking at the main car park, but free parking is available in three areas: at the entrance on the A572; at the end of Common Lane (SJ 640997, access over canal bridge); and on Plank Lane just before the swing bridge at the west end of the flash (SJ 630995). It is possible to walk all round the flash, although about half of the south side is in private ownership.

Contact

Pennington Flash Rangers' Office (01942 605253)

Nearby sites

50A   HOPE CARR RESERVE, LEIGH   OS Ref: SJ 667985

These purpose-built lagoons at the south end of Leigh sewage works attract a wide variety of wildfowl and waders in good numbers. The adjoining working sludge lagoons can attract rare waders when conditions are right. Passage and overwintering Green Sandpipers (up to 10 can be present) are a feature of the site. Shoveler, Gadwall, Tufted Duck, Little Grebe, Oystercatcher, Grasshopper Warbler and Willow Tit all breed. Recent rarities include Temminck's Stint and Wood, Pectoral and Curlew Sandpipers and Grey Phalarope.

Access

From the A580 and A574 roundabout turn north towards Leigh and at the first set of lights just over the river turn left onto the industrial estate. Turn left at next mini-roundabout (signed to the environmental centre). Park on the spare land just past the cottages or, in office hours, continue left to the environmental centre car park.

50B   ABRAM FLASHES SSSI   OS Ref: SD615000

A series of subsidence flashes and marshes that follow the west side (towpath side) of the Leigh branch of the Leeds to Liverpool Canal, commencing just over half a mile (1 km) west from Plank Lane swing bridge near Pennington Flash. The canal is raised above the level of the surrounding land enabling good oversight. Lightshaw Flashes are about 200 yards (200 m) from the canal; a telescope is recommended. Farther along is Dover Basin, which is alongside the canal, and then marshland.

After crossing under the A573 there is a further marsh and wetland before Coffin Brook Flash, and yet more wetlands following the towpath to the A58. Crossing on to the other side of the canal here, the towpath continues about 440 yards (400 m) to the start of the Wigan Flashes at the West Coast Mainline railway bridge.

Designated for breeding birds, this SSSI has a number of landowners and management has been neglected over the last 10 years, leading to a decline in its value for breeding birds. Recently this trend has begun to be addressed and the future looks brighter for this important breeding area linking Pennington Flash and the Wigan Flashes. The Hey Brook, running parallel with the canal, floods regularly and, unfortunately, washes out nests. The area is heavily shot over in autumn and winter, so expect very few birds at this time.

Breeding birds include Redshank, Shelduck, Common Snipe, Water Rail, Sedge, Reed and Grasshopper Warblers and Reed Bunting. Common Teal, Tufted Duck, Shoveler and Gadwall have begun to breed in recent years. Passage waders include Black-tailed Godwit (often flocks of up to 40), Ruff and Greenshank.

Access
Park at or near the Dover pub on the A573 bridge at Abram (SD607007) and walk in either direction along the towpath on the south side.

51 ELTON RESERVOIR

OS Landranger Map 109
OS Explorer 277
SD 788094

Habitat
Originally built in 1803 to feed the now-disused Manchester, Bury and Bolton Canal, which runs below it on its east side, this 0.6-mile (1 km) -long reservoir in the Irwell valley is the major birdwatching site in Bury and the only water of any size in the area. The east side consists of a stone retaining wall, but the land below Old Hall Farm on the south-east bank is of interest and is currently not farmed. On the west side of the reservoir, there are gently shelving banks, which can hold waders. There is a lot of disturbance from anglers, dog walkers and sailing. An arm of the reservoir known as The Creek can often hold visiting ducks. Variable water levels due to the demands of the canal can sometimes militate against waders.

There is excellent habitat on all sides of the reservoir. Tall hedgerows, scrub and pasture on the north, south and west sides attract winter thrushes, summer visitors and passage birds. The river and canal on the east side provide alternate water environments. To the north east, behind the sailing clubhouse, are the pools known locally as The Dip.

Species
The site list stands currently at 201. This is a remarkable total for such a disturbed site, and is due largely to a dedicated band of recorders.

Timing
Disturbance from anglers, sailors and walkers make it essential to visit very early in the morning.

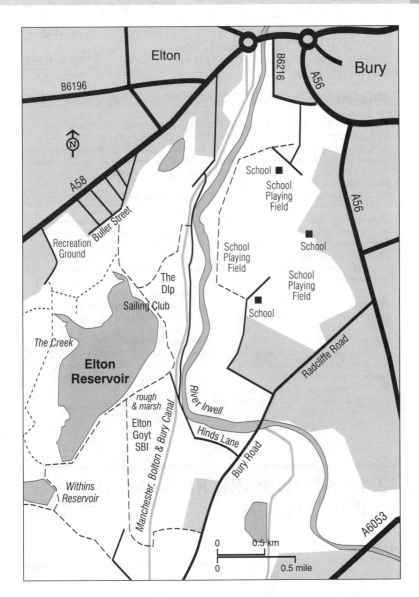

Access

There is free parking next to the sailing club on the north side. It is signposted from the A58 Bolton Road (Kitchener Street) 1.2 miles (2 km) from Bury town centre, opposite the Wellington pub. Follow the narrow road across the old bridge, then turn abruptly right at the hospital and follow the track to the sailing club. There is also access from Radcliffe via Warth Road; after crossing the tramway and canal, park near the nightclub (currently not in use). There is no suitable access for disabled visitors beyond the car park, but there is a good overview from there.

Recent rarities include Red-backed Shrike, Little Egret, Gannet, Mediter-ranean Gull, Firecrest and Red-necked Grebe.

Reference: Elton Bird Report (annual) from Peter Baron, 17 Elton Brook Close, Bury, BL8 2SN.

CALENDAR

Winter: Waterbirds include up to 40 Great Crested Grebes and small numbers of Tufted Duck. In cold weather a large Goosander roost may relocate from Ashworth Moor Reservoir. Elton is a reliable site for divers, with both Great Northern and Red-throated occurring in two years of the last five. If disturbed, these can often be found on Withins Reservoir just to the south. The electricity pylon nearest the north end often holds Cormorants, and most winters a Peregrine Falcon hunts from here. Water Rail and Jack Snipe can be found near the outlet feeder on the east side, where Stonechat winters.

Passage: Small numbers of migrant ducks pass through annually, including Common Scoter, Scaup and Eurasian Wigeon. All the commoner terns are recorded. The Dip pool is reliable for Spotted Flycatcher on passage in August and September. The surrounding habitat attracts Common Redstart and Whinchat. Waders visiting (and perhaps breeding not far away) include Oystercatcher

and Little Ringed and Ringed Plovers. Dunlin, Common Sandpiper, Whimbrel, Curlew and Redshank are annual. Uncommon species such as Little Stint and Wood Sandpiper have turned up in recent years.

Breeding: Little Grebe, Reed Warbler and probably Willow Tit breed on The Dip pool, and Great Crested Grebe at Withins Reservoir. Tufted Duck has bred in the last few years on the nearby canal and on the reservoir. There is a Sand Martin colony on the nearby River Irwell; Kingfisher also breeds in the vicinity. The hedges and associated scrubland near the feeder inlet provide habitat for Lesser Whitethroat, Sedge Warbler and Reed Bunting. The woods of the nearby hospital have Tawny Owl and Great Spotted Woodpecker, and Old Hall Farm has a Little Owl nest box scheme. Common Snipe and Northern Lapwing still breed in the damp marshy farmland between Old Hall Farm and Crow Trees Farm.

52 HEATON PARK RESERVOIR, PRESTWICH

OS Landranger Map 109
SD 826050

Habitat

Heaton Park Reservoir is a large stone-lined balancing reservoir on the north side of Manchester, adjacent to but separate from Heaton Park, a large parkland area. There is some scrub habitat at the water's edge on the north side.

Species

Hosts an important gull roost, particularly for large gulls and white-winged species that feed at Pilsworth Tip less than 2 miles (3 km) to the north. This tip and associated sand quarry has just been extended and will continue for the foreseeable future. Up to 500 Great Black-backed and 2,000 Herring and Lesser Black-backed Gulls roost in winter. Yellow-legged, Iceland and Glaucous Gulls are annual. About 5,000 Black-headed Gulls, occasional Mediterranean and small numbers of Common Gulls also use the roost. There is a notable Golden-

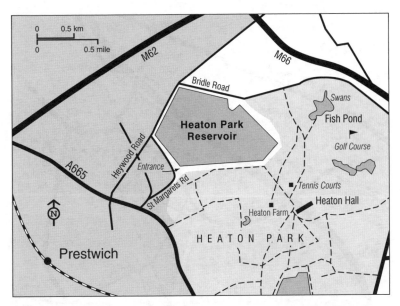

eye roost, too, of birds that feed mainly on the nearby River Irwell during the day; numbers can reach in excess of 140. A Goosander roost is also building up here. In some years large numbers of Tufted Duck visit in January. Late summer sees a post-breeding flock of around 20 Little Grebe. Breeding birds include Tufted Duck and – if water levels permit – Little Ringed Plover. Recent rarities include Lesser Scaup, Kumlien's Gull, Caspian Gull, Smew, Slavonian Grebe and Leach's Storm-petrel.

Access

There is no public access; a permit and key are required. Enter through the yard next to the former waterman's house on St Margaret's Road, Prestwich, on the bend just after park entrance. Permits are free from Conservation Officer, United Utilities, Bottoms Office, Woodhead Road, Tintwistle, Glossop SK13 1HS (Tel: 01457 864187), but limited in number.

53 AUDENSHAW RESERVOIRS, MANCHESTER

OS Landranger Map 109;
OS Explorer 277
SJ 915965

Habitat

Audenshaw comprises three late 19th century stone-lined balancing reservoirs with a total area, including verges, of around 250 acres (100 ha), with intersecting paths. It is easily the largest water area in the Greater Manchester,

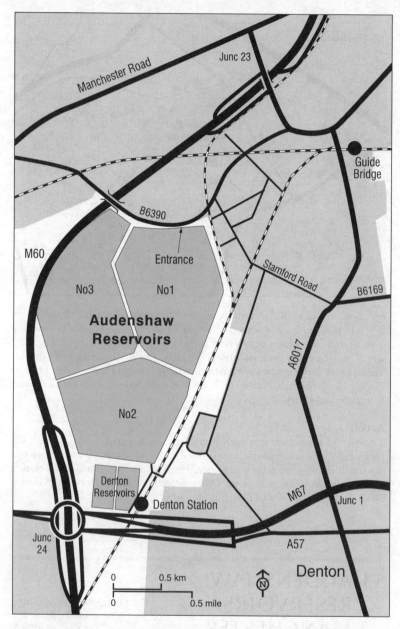

and is slightly elevated above the surrounding property, enhancing its visibility to migrant birds. Audenshaw's value lies as a passage stopover for migrants crossing the Pennines; there is little habitat to attract most species to stay. No. 3 bed is particularly attractive to waders as the refurbished bank is gently shelving. Audenshaw shares with Pennington Flash the position of premier site in Greater Manchester county. Its much larger water area rarely freezes. Gorton

Reservoirs at Debdale are only around a third of a mile (less than 1 km) away, with golf courses and parkland between the sites, but sailing, angling and walkers disturb these.

Species
The current list stands at 209, and has included four species of diver, five grebes, three skuas and 27 of waders. Certain species, such as Rock Pipit (including subspecies *littoralis*), are Audenshaw specialities. The gull roost is one of the best in the county.

CALENDAR

Winter: Variable numbers of *Aythya* duck sometimes include overwintering Scaup. A substantial Goosander roost – up to 100 birds – has developed over the last 10 years. The gull roost holds mostly Black-headed and Common Gulls, but often includes Mediterranean Gull. Large gulls usually roost in small numbers, but late winter brings white-winged species. Up to 30 European Golden Plover roost and Snow Bunting has wintered in recent years.

Passage: Audenshaw's major interest, particularly the last fortnight in April and first two weeks of May, for terns and waders, and July to September for return passage.

Practically any wader can turn up, albeit often for only a short time, and there is usually a good passage of Arctic Tern and Little Gull in spring. Storms can bring in skuas and storm-petrels. Rock Pipit is almost guaranteed in October. In spring, Yellow and Blue-headed Yellow Wagtails are regular, along with Northern Wheatears.

Recent rarities: Red-necked Grebe (overwintered), Great Northern Diver, Lapland Bunting, Leach's Storm-petrel, Sabine's Gull, Velvet Scoter, Spoonbill, Fulmar, Arctic and Great Skuas, Temminck's Stint, Grey Phalarope, Purple Sandpiper, Wryneck.

Timing
Passage periods are best, when unsettled weather can bring in rarities. Mornings visits are best in spring and summer, and afternoons in winter for roosting birds.

Access
A permit and key from United Utilities are required. This is free from Conservation Officer, United Utilitie, Bottoms Office, Woodhead Road, Tintwistle, Glossop, SK13 1 HS (Tel: 01457 864187), but numbers are limited.

From junction 23 on the M60 take the A635 east 550 yards (500 m) to the junction with the A6017. Turn right and follow signs to Audenshaw. After two-thirds of a mile (1 km) turn right at a roundabout onto Audenshaw Road (B6390) and continue until the bankings of reservoir appear on the left. There is ample parking on Audenshaw Road and nearby streets.

Enter the complex via the gate near the M60 bridge (SJ912972). Grassy paths intersect the reservoirs and encircle them. The site is not suitable for disabled visitors. A logbook is in the hide overlooking No. 2 bed (key required). This site is exposed, with only low walls providing protection from the elements. No facilities.

Reference: Audenshaw Bird Report (annual) from Roy Travis, 188 Smallshaw Lane, Ashton-under-Lyne, OL6 8RA.

54 DOVESTONES AND SADDLEWORTH MOOR

OS Landranger Map 110
SE020030

Habitat

The only area of Greater Manchester within the Peak District National Park, the Dovestones area comprises reservoirs, moorland with upland peat, and woodland. This is a high-altitude site ranging up to 1,804 feet (550 m).

Species

The reservoirs and Chew Brook hold breeding Common Sandpiper and Dipper, and the larch and pine woodlands at Binn Green (free car park off the A635) and elsewhere can have flocks of Common Crossbill (which may breed), Common Redstart and Pied and Spotted Flycatchers. Stonechat breeds regularly, and until very recently this was the only reliable site for Ring Ouzel in the area (they may still breed). Red Grouse and Northern Wheatear are fairly common, and Whinchat may still breed. European Golden Plover breeds on Saddleworth Moor, but the terrain is difficult. Raven and Peregrine Falcon are both resident. Red Kite is a recent rarity.

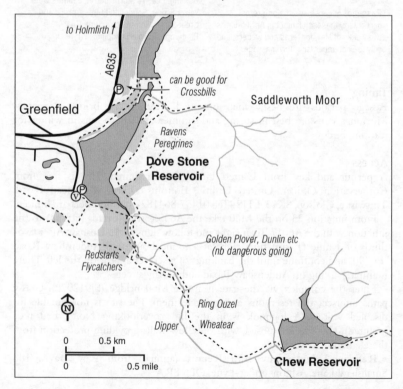

Access

From the A635, pass through Greenfield and look for the sign to Dovestone Reservoir on the right. Park at the bottom of the reservoir dam (charge at weekends); easy uphill paths pass in several directions. There are toilets at the Peak District National Park office and limited access for those with disabilities.

55 ETHEROW COUNTRY PARK, STOCKPORT

OS Landranger Map 109
SJ 9891

Once part of the estate of George Andrew, a 19th century cotton magnate, this local nature reserve consists of Compstall Lodges, riverine woodland, the Keg Pool and a number of mature woods. Greater Manchester has few woodlands, and this complex is probably the best in the area.

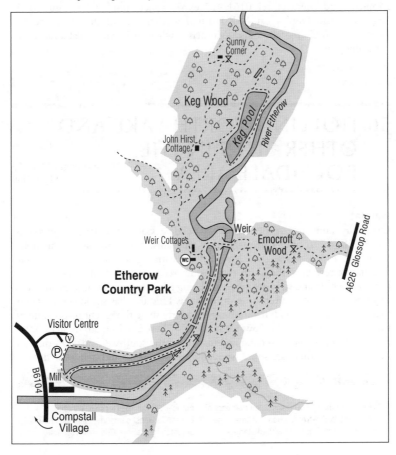

Species

The lodges were once a part of Compstall Mill and are now used for fishing. Mute Swan and Great Crested Grebe breed alongside introduced waterfowl, though Mandarin Duck has colonised naturally along the river valley. Beyond the lodges, a selection of paths leads into various mature woodlands alongside the River Etherow, where a large weir has breeding Dippers. The Keg Woodland is well known for breeding Pied Flycatcher. Ernocroft Wood has Wood Warbler and Common Redstart. Other breeding birds include Woodcock, Spotted Flycatcher (some years), Garden Warbler, Goldcrest and Lesser Spotted Woodpecker, as well as more common woodland species. From the hide by the river, just beyond the weir, Kingfisher can frequently be seen, and there is a Cormorant roost. The Keg Pool attracts Goosander and Tufted Duck. Common Buzzard, Raven and Sparrowhawk are relatively common, although breeding by the first two is not proven. Winter brings flocks of Siskin and Brambling.

Access

From Stockport or Marple take the B6104 to Compstall village. There is a small amount of free parking on George Street, where the visitor centre (closed Mondays and Tuesdays, tel. 0161 427 6937), toilets and cafe are situated. A larger Pay and Display car park is on the other side of the visitor centre fronting on to Compstall Lodges. Motorised wheelchairs are available; access is generally good.

56 HOLLINGWORTH LAKE AND OTHER SITES IN THE ROCHDALE AREA

OS Landranger Map 109
SD 937150

Habitat

Originally built as a feeder for the Rochdale Canal, this large reservoir is ideally placed to attract cross-country migrants, but is intensively used by sailors, sea cadets and anglers. Much of the banking is stone-lined and steep. The nature reserve at the south-east corner has been neglected in recent years, but it has a hide and steps are currently being taken to improve its attractiveness to birds and cut off waterborne disturbance. This area has shallower gradients that reveal exposed mud in autumn, particularly since the recent re-opening of the Rochdale Canal led to lower water levels. There is a footpath to Shaw Moss (SD 933139, a shallow wetland and marsh) on the southwest side. On the east side of the lake there are some wooded areas, scrubland and mature hedges.

CALENDAR

Winter: In the last 10 years small numbers of Greenland White-fronted Goose (some ringed in Iceland) have wintered with the large numbers of Canada Geese. A variable Goosander roost sometimes includes Red-breasted Merganser. Common Teal and

Common Snipe visit Shaw Moss, and the lake if water levels are low enough.

Passage: Kittiwake, terns, Common Scoter, Eurasian Wigeon. The woodland attracts Common Redstart and Spotted and Pied Flycatchers.

Breeding: Dipper on Longden End Brook.

Recent rarities: Hawfinch, Ring Ouzel and Shag. The site had the only county record of Black-winged Stilt in 1993.

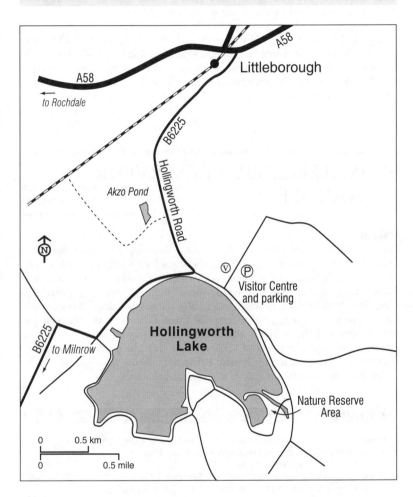

Access

From junction 21 of the M62, turn north following signs to Milnrow; turn right at the lights then left at a roundabout on to Kiln Lane (B6225). Look out for the sign to Hollingworth Lake (Wild House Lane) on the left after 330 yards (300 m). At a roundabout, turn right onto Lake Bank. Follow the edge of the lake, bearing right at the junction with Hollingworth Road and park at the visitor centre (fee). Walk round the edge of the lake to visit the nature reserve area. Suitable for disabled visitors.

Contact

Ranger service, 01706 373421.
Reference: Birds at Hollingworth Lake (annual report) from Simon Hitchen, 28 Shore Road, Littleborough OL15 9LG

Nearby site

Akzo Ponds, on the west side of Hollingworth Road, 550 yards (500 m) from the lake (SD 935155) often host any White-fronted Geese.

Clegg Hall Pools is reached by a rough track, Branch Road, off Wild House Lane on the north-west side of the railway and canal (SD920147). The pools are private but can be viewed from an elevated point on the railway bridge. Breeding species include Mute Swan and, occasionally, Common Sandpiper, Little Ringed Plover, Tufted Duck and Redshank depending on conditions.

57 WATERGROVE RESERVOIR, WARDLE

OS Landranger Map 109
SD910180

Habitat

Constructed between 1930 and 1938, this water supply reservoir lies in a south-facing valley at 790 feet (240 m) above sea level a little over half a mile (1 km) north of Wardle village. The southern edge consists of a dam wall, but the northern edge has exposed muddy islands and bays, and an arm reaching north into Higher Slack Brook Clough. Windsurfers and dogwalkers disturb the area, particularly along the eastern side where there are paths between the water's edge and the reservoir wall. Behind the reservoir to the north is a curving ridge of moors rising to 1,320 feet (400 m). The northern side of the reservoir was planted extensively with native trees during the 1980s and early 1990s, providing habitat for species not present previously.

CALENDAR

Winter: Small numbers of wintering wildfowl include Common Scoter, Common Goldeneye, Goosander and Red-breasted Merganser. Woodcock roosts in the new woodlands and double figures of Common Snipe are around the wetland pools. Stonechat.
Passage: Ringed Plover, Redshank, Spotted Redshank, Ruff, Whimbrel, Dunlin, European Golden Plover, Northern Lapwing, Oystercatcher, Greenshank and Common and Green Sandpipers. Ring Ouzel may join winter thrush flocks. There are occasional sightings of Hen Harrier, Peregrine Falcon, Merlin and Long-eared Owl.

Breeding: Little Ringed Plover, Great Crested Grebe, Northern Lapwing, Common Sandpiper, Common Snipe, Oystercatcher (all with varying degrees of success due to disturbance).

Recent rarities: Broad-billed Sandpiper, Gannet, Red-crested Pochard and Great Grey Shrike.

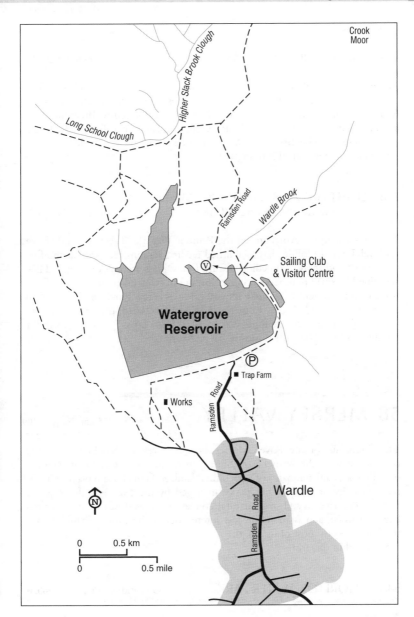

Access

From the A58 Halifax Road turn left to Wardle village at SD 911151; follow the road north through the village until it comes to a dead end in car park below the dam. There is a visitor centre and disabled access through much of site.

Contact: Ranger on 01706 379060.

Reference: Watergrove Reservoir and Valley: a site history 1993–2005 (Steve Atkins) in Birds in Greater Manchester: county report 2004.

Other sites

57A PIETHORNE VALLEY   OS Ref: SD9512

There is a series of three upland reservoirs in the Piethorne valley, with a
further three moorland waters to the east. Access along Ogden Lane from the
A640 about half a mile (1 km) east of Newhey; visitor centre. Breeding birds
include Stonechat and probably Twite, Common Sandpiper, Tufted Duck and
Great Crested Grebe. Brent and White-fronted Goose were recorded recently
  Contact: Ranger on 01706 881049.

57B LIGHT HAZZLES, WHITE HOLME
AND WARLAND RESERVOIRS   OS Ref: SD964197

These moorland reservoirs are on the Pennine Way 1,300 feet (400 m) above
sea level. United Utilities has established feeding stations for Twite at the first
two waters and there is breeding nearby. Many birds are colour ringed. They
are joined by small numbers of Snow Bunting in winter. Peregrine Falcon and
Raven visit frequently. Ringed Plover, Little Ringed Plover and Common
Sandpiper all breed. Access from the A58 Halifax Road, park at the White
House pub and take the Pennine Way by Blackstone Edge Reservoir north for
1 mile (1.5 km). The path is mostly flat and easy.

58 MERSEY VALLEY   OS Landranger 109

The floodplain of the River Mersey between western Stockport and the
confluence with the Manchester Ship Canal contains a variety of habitats:
mature woodland, remnants of agricultural land, golf courses and playing fields,
reclaimed tips and two water parks, managed by the Mersey Valley Ranger
Service. The river is still in its natural course in the west of this area, but has
been canalised, and is therefore less interesting, in the more urbanised east;
there is access to most of its length.
  Sites within the area:

58A CHORLTON WATER PARK   OS Landranger 109, SJ820920

Access
Enter Chorlton Water Park from the end of Maitland Avenue on the south side
of the A5145 Barlow Moor Road, Manchester. There is free parking, a visitor
centre, toilets and disabled access. The lake is used for water activities by
organised groups in the summer months and there is angling all year round.

Species
The main interest of this site is its wintering flock of *Aythya* ducks, with Tufted

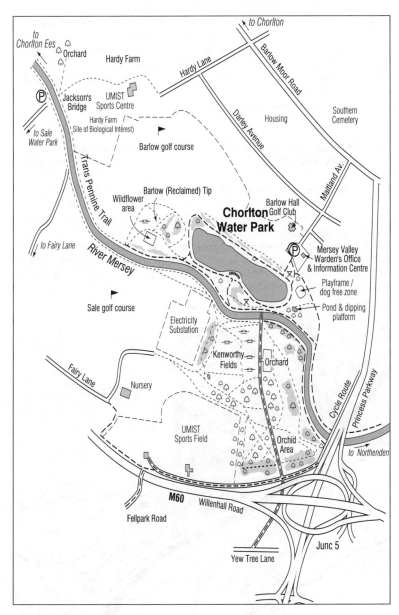

Duck and Pochard, occasional Scaup and, rarely, Ferruginous Duck (last recorded 2001, but hybrids appear most years). In common with many other sites in the UK, flocks here have shrunk notably in the last few years, from around 2,000 in a good season to around 200 in 2006 (Tufted); 330 in 2006 (Pochard). Other breeding species include one or two pairs of Grey Heron on the islands, Great Crested Grebe and Tufted Duck. Kingfisher, Goosander and Goldeneye visit in winter.

Flocks of Siskin, Goldfinch and Lesser Redpoll frequent the alder plantations around the lake in winter. Barlow Tip, a mature grassed-over reclaimed site at the west end, offers an excellent variety of birds with warblers in summer and Short-eared Owl, Jack Snipe, Stonechat and Woodcock in winter.

Recent rarities include Great White Egret, Firecrest, Ferruginous Duck, Long-tailed Duck and Smew.

Contact: Ranger Service on 0161 881 5639.

58B   SALE WATER PARK AND BROAD EES DOLE

OS Landranger Map 109
SJ800930

Access is from junction 6 of the M60; at the roundabout take the north-east exit onto Rifle Road, which ends at a free car park and the main visitor centre for the Mersey Valley with a restaurant, toilets and disabled access. Contact the Ranger Service on 0161 905 1100.

A network of paths leads from the visitor centre, where maps are available. The lake is used for water skiing and angling. Rarities can drop in, but the disturbance is considerable. At the nearby Broad Ees Dole a hide overlooks a marsh and swamp with shallow water.

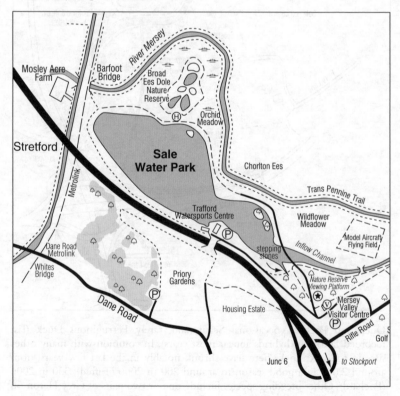

Species

The lake itself has a large flock of Canada Goose and breeding Mute Swan and Great Crested Grebe. There is a large daytime Cormorant roost on the pylons nearby. Broad Ees Dole has more variety, with dabbling ducks such as Shoveler, Common Teal and Gadwall, Little Grebe, Kingfisher, Common Snipe, Sedge and Reed Warblers and Reed Bunting.

Other sites: **Banky Meadow** (SJ766933), **Chorlton Ees** (SJ805932), **Loonts Lake** (SJ838934: ask for permission to enter, from Northenden Golf Clubhouse).

59 RUMWORTH LODGE, BOLTON

OS Landranger Map 109
OS Explorer 276, SD678078

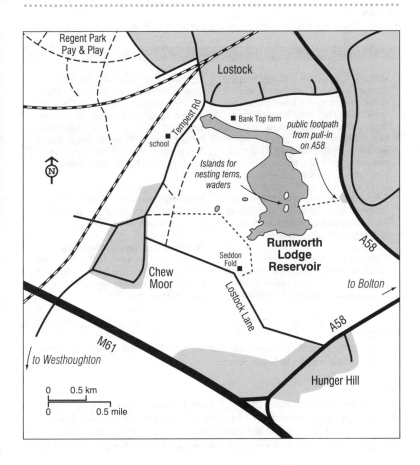

Habitat

A shallow eutrophic reservoir formed in 1849 by the damming of the Knutshaw Brook to provide water for mills along the River Croal. Most of the lodge has a gentle shore profile, although the northern end adjacent to the dam is deeper with steep wooded sides. The south end has a willow thicket and a decent reedbed. Despite its proximity to a large housing estate the site is surprisingly unfrequented. Damp meadows with small pools on the west side attract wintering ducks and Common Snipe, while fluctuating water levels allow large exposed mud areas in late summer that attract many species of passage waders. Two islands enable waders and terns to breed. Pasture surrounding the lodge encourages large flocks of Northern Lapwing and European Golden Plover, winter thrushes, and geese. This is probably the best lowland site in Bolton. Morning visits are best due to sun, if accessing from Beaumont Road. There is fishing along both sides of the lodge, but the southern end is an informal nature reserve. Hedges, the willow copse and a small mature wood at the north-west end of the site can hold Common Redstart, flycatchers, migrant warblers and chats.

Species

At least 160 species have been recorded in the last 15 years.

CALENDAR

Winter: The large flock of Canada Geese (control measures in force) attracts other congeners such as Pink-footed Goose (a few sometimes winter). Bar-headed, Barnacle, Greylag, White-fronted, Brent and Bean Geese have all been recorded. The site was once well known for Whooper Swan, but they are rare visitors these days, preferring Martin Mere. Up to 50 Common Teal, Great Crested Grebe, small numbers of Common Snipe, Tufted Duck, Pochard, Eurasian Wigeon and Goldeneye winter. Territorial Oystercatchers are normally back by January. Woodcock and Jack Snipe occur in small numbers.

Passage: From June, water levels are usually low enough to expose plenty of mud, attracting a wide range of waders. As well as breeding Little Ringed and Ringed Plovers, Redshank, Dunlin, Green and Common Sandpipers, Ruff, Curlew, Black-tailed Godwit and Greenshank are annual; Wood Sandpiper is nearly so. Rarer waders include Little Stint, Sanderling, Turnstone, Curlew Sandpiper and Purple Sandpiper. Occasional visits by Black Tern, Mediterranean Gull (becoming more common), Marsh Harrier and Common Buzzard.

Breeding: Oystercatcher, Common Tern, Little Ringed Plover, Tufted Duck and Great Crested and Little Grebes.

Recent rarities: Avocet, Bittern, Ring-necked Duck, Little Egret, Turtle Dove, Smew, Pectoral Sandpiper, Bewick's Swan, Richard's Pipit and the first county record of Marsh Warbler (1996).

Timing

Spring, summer and autumn are best to see breeding birds and passage migrants when water levels are down.

Access

About 2 miles (3 km) along the A676 from Bolton town centre turn right at ring road junction. From the M61 junction 5 take the A58 towards Bolton. At the first set of lights after about two-thirds of a mile (1 km) turn left by the Shell garage along the A58 ring road (Beaumont Road). Keep in the left hand lane and after about a third of a mile (600 m), at the crest of small rise by the cycle lane sign, look for the new tarmac pull-in on the left (easy to miss at SD681078). Park here and walk down the field (public footpath) to the lake edge. Alternatively there are public footpaths on the south-west side of the lodge through Seddon Fold Farm, Lock Lane, turn left from the A58 about a quarter of a mile (400 m) after M61 junction 5. The area is not generally suitable for disabled visitors, although reasonable views can be obtained from Beaumont Road.

Nearby sites

59A SMITHILLS MOOR, INCLUDING BURNT EDGE, HOLDEN'S CLOUGH AND MONTCLIFFE

This area of moorland is surmounted by the television masts at Winter Hill. It has several excellent birding areas and stretches from Horwich in the west to Barrow Bridge in the east. The western slopes of Winter Hill are reached via Georges Lane from Chorley Old Road (B6226) at SD 659114. Turn up Mast Road at the isolated row of houses. These moors hold Stonechat, Red Grouse, Northern Wheatear and Raven. The area is an excellent migration watch site in the autumn. Flocks of winter thrushes often include Ring Ouzel.

Farther east along Chorley Old Road, at SD 679110, Walker Fold Road leads to Walker Fold Woods (SD675124). From its continuation, Colliers Row Road, turn off along Coal Pit Road to access Holden's Clough. This valley has held Red-footed Falcon in two years since 2000. Little Owl hunts from dry stone walls. Peregrine Falcon and wintering Hen Harriers can be seen virtually anywhere in this area, and Crossbills may breed.

59B RED MOSS SSSI, HORWICH   SD6310

A peat bog partly occupied by a tree-planted tip, where restoration work is being carried out to protect remnant mossland and sphagnum species. Species depend to an extent on water levels in the various beds, but include Common Snipe, Jack Snipe, Common Teal, Green Sandpiper, Grasshopper Warbler, Barn Owl, Long-eared Owl, Stonechat and Willow Tit. Access from Moss Lane, off the B5238 between Horwich and Blackrod, just west of the M61.

60 WIGAN FLASHES
OS Landranger Map 108
OS Explorer 276, SD5803

Habitat and access

A large area of colliery subsidence flashes, covering about 640 acres (260 hectares), commencing two-thirds of a mile (1 km) south of Wigan town centre and connected by the Leigh branch of the Leeds to Liverpool Canal. Since the 1980s, the eight flashes have been developed for nature conservation.

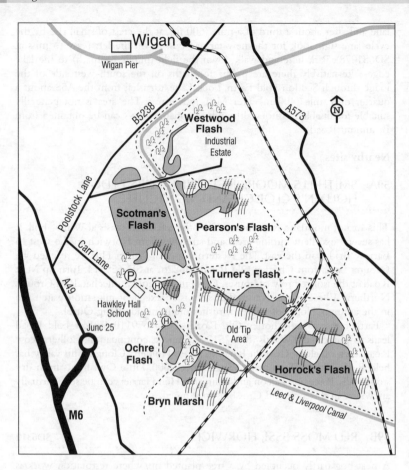

Two of the flashes – Horrocks' Flash and Bryn Marsh – have SSSI status, and all fall within the Wigan Flashes Local Nature Reserve. There is a wide variety of wildlife habitats, including open water, reedbed – the largest in the county – willow carr, scrub and rough grassland. The area is too large to cover in one day for most people, and can be conveniently divided into two sections:

60A   SCOTMAN'S FLASH, PEARSON'S FLASH, WESTWOOD FLASH, OCHRE FLASH AND BRYN MARSH   SD579032

Scotman's Flash and Pearson's Flash are separated only by the canal; when sailing disrupts birds on the former they relocate to the latter, which is undisturbed and has a reedbed at the east end. Good views of both flashes can be had from the canal, and there are crossing points at the lock at Westwood Flash and at Moss Bridge at the south end of Scotman's Flash. Hawkley reedbed is situated on the south side of Scotman's Flash. There is a viewing screen and feeding station near Hawkley school. Footpaths connect Scotman's Flash to Ochre Flash, where there are mature hedges and medium-age woodland. Beyond Ochre Flash, footpaths lead to Bryn Marsh, which has recently undergone major habitat work under the European Life Project for Bitterns, the object being to increase the amount of reedbed and prevent succession. It is possible to follow a circular route to return to Scotman's Flash. On the west side of the canal, there is a former landfill site, now planted with trees, but with some rough grassland, between Pearson's Flash and Turner's Flash.

Access is best from Welham Road, by Hawkley School at the end of Carr Lane (parking and site map: SD579032). From junction 25 (northbound exit only) of the M6, take the A49 towards Wigan. Turning right at Marus Bridge roundabout onto the B5238. At the first set of traffic lights by a modern church, turn right onto Carr Lane and proceed towards the school; just before the school turn left onto Welham Road.

60B   HORROCKS' FLASH AND TURNER'S FLASH

Horrocks' Flash is bounded by railway lines on two sides and the canal on the third side, but there is a circular path which gives good views of the various pools and reedbeds that make up this site. A track across the level crossing on the loop line leads through some fishing ponds and under a railway bridge, immediately left to Turner's Flash, negotiate the barrier that prevents vehicles and a good view of this water can be obtained from its east end. Alternatively, this water can be accessed from Moss Bridge on the canal. A large reedbed runs the whole length of the site. Both flashes have small peaty islets which are used both by passage waders and breeding terns and gulls.

Access the area from Stratton Drive. From the A573 Warrington Road, going north towards Wigan, turn left into Miller's Lane at Platt Bridge, just after the roundabout. Turn left again into Victoria Road almost immediately: this becomes Stratton Drive. After a playing field on right, the road bends and there is a stile on the right. Park here and take the track from the stile to the canal. Turn right on the towpath under the railway bridge to access Horrocks' Flash. After about 100 yards (100 m), it is possible to either turn right into woodland to begin an anticlockwise circular walk round the flash or continue along towpath to do the same walk clockwise. On both routes, turn off along the level crossing to access Turner's Flash. Alternatively, having viewed part of Horrocks' Flash from the towpath, continue under the Liverpool to Wigan railway bridge about two-thirds of a mile (1 km) to Moss Bridge and the rest of the complex.

NB Parking elsewhere in the Wigan Flashes may not be safe, particularly at weekends. Personal safety is a consideration anywhere in this complex, although the paths along either side of the canal at Scotman's and Pearson's Flashes are well frequented and have an open aspect. Please also note that habitat work is ongoing on several flashes for the foreseeable future. It is possible to walk about 3 miles (5 km) along the canal to Pennington Flash, through the Abram Flashes SSSI.

Species
The site is more important for breeding birds than passage species, as it is not within a river valley, but there is always plenty of interest. Horrocks' Flash and particularly the Westwood scrubland (near the lock) are interesting for wild flowers due to industrial alkaline content in the soil. Rare helleborines, viper's

bugloss, mulleins, toadflaxes, evening primrose, yellow bird's nest and orchids are found here. There is also a wide variety of dragonflies, butterflies and bats.

CALENDAR

Winter: Bittern can occur in any reedbed (in recent years Hawkley reedbed, the south end of Scotman's Flash and Bryn Marsh have been preferred), but is not easy to see. In total there can be up to 1,000 Coot, three-figure numbers of Tufted Ducks and good numbers of Common Goldeneye (congregate on Scotman's Flash at dusk) and Ruddy Duck. There is a Cormorant roost on Horrocks' Flash. Small numbers of Eurasian Wigeon, Shoveler, Pochard, Gadwall and Common Teal winter. The Mute Swan herd is sometimes joined by Whoopers on Horrocks' Flash. In some years there is a spectacular Starling roost in Turner's Flash reedbed. There are large numbers of wintering and resident Water Rails. Willow Tit is guaranteed at the feeding hide at Hawkley reedbed near Hawkley School, along with a dozen or so Reed Buntings. Scotman's Flash has a pre-roost assembly of gulls that depart at dusk to Pennington Flash.

Spring and summer: About 30 pairs of Common Tern and around 100 pairs of Black-headed Gull nest on Horrocks' and Turner's Flashes. There is a small heronry on Horrocks' Flash. Several hundred pairs of Reed Warbler breed. Other breeders include: Great Crested and Little Grebes, Greylag Goose, Sedge Warbler, Common Whitethroat, Grasshopper Warbler, Reed Bunting, Willow Tit, Lesser Redpoll, Tufted Duck, Gadwall, Mute Swan (up to 12 pairs), and Pochard. Waders breeding regularly or occasionally include Redshank, Little Ringed and Ringed Plovers, Northern Lapwing, Common Snipe, Oystercatcher and Common Sandpiper. Longeared Owl is present and possibly breeds. More than 20 pairs of Water Rail breed.

Passage: in late summer and early autumn the site can be nationally important for Gadwall and Shoveler, and large flocks of Eurasian Wigeon pass through. In autumn, Common Snipe numbers can pass 100, although numbers are difficult to quantify. Horrocks' Flash is best for the rarer passage waders, with Black-tailed Godwit, Dunlin, Greenshank, Curlew and Ruff all annual. Black-necked Grebe often lingers, especially on Scotman's Flash.

Recent rarities: Red-necked Phalarope, Long-tailed Duck, Velvet Scoter, Smew, Spoonbill, Little Egret, Hobby and Marsh Harrier, Yellow-browed Warbler.

Timing

There is usually something of interest here at any time of the year, but spring and summer are best. In late summer and autumn Pearson's Flash is usually best for duck congregations; afternoon visits have the best light conditions.

Access

See above. No facilities; not suitable for disabled away from main paths and tow-path at Scotman's Flash. Some viewing screens, but hides cannot be installed due to vandalism. There are seats on the towpath at Scotman's Flash, Horrocks Flash, Pearson's Flash, Bryn Marsh, and also at Ochre Flash.

Contact: Wigan Flashes Project Officer at The Grange Community Centre, Highfield Grange Ave, Wigan WN3 6SU (01942 233976).

CHESHIRE AND WIRRAL

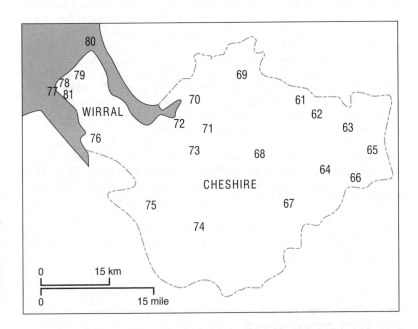

61 Rostherne Mere
62 Tatton Park and Knutsford Moor
63 Alderley Woods
64 Rudheath Sand Quarries
   64A Newplatt Wood Sand Quarry
   64B Rudheath Woods Nature Reserve
65 Macclesfield Forest, Langley
   Reservoirs and Teggs Nose
   Country Park
66 River Dane Valley
67 Sandbach Flashes
68 Marbury Country Park and Witton
   Lime Beds
   68A Witton Flashes and Butterfinch
   Bridge
   68B Budworth (Marbury) Mere and
   Pick Mere
69 Woolston Eyes
70 Moore Nature Reserve
71 Lower Weaver Valley: Acton Bridge
   to Kingsley
72 Frodsham Marsh and the Weaver
   Bend
   72A Hale Head

73 Delamere Forest
   73A Delamere Switchback
   73B Blakemere
   73C Hogshead Wood
   73D Nunsmere
   73E Abbots Moss
   73F Petty Pool and Pettypool Wood
   73G Newchurch Common
74 Beeston Castle and Peckforton Hills
75 The River Dee
76 Gayton Sands and the Inner Dee
   Marshes
77 Hilbre Island the Dee Mouth
78 Red Rocks, Hoylake
79 North Wirral Shore
   79A Dove Point, Meols
   79B Meols through Leasowe
   Lighthouse
79C Gun Site Car Park (Leasowe)
80 New Brighton and the Outer Mersey
   Estuary
   80A Woodlands on the Wirral
81 Wirral Way

Cheshire and Wirral contains a very broad spectrum of habitats. The majority of the mid-Cheshire Plain comprises farmland with hedgerows, but is particularly noted for its numerous fresh water meres and flashes. Many of the meres were formed by glacial action. The flashes are more recent floods following subsidence as a result of industrial pumping of brine from underground salt fields. Additional wetland habitat was created as a result of dredging of the Manchester Ship Canal and the River Weaver Navigation canal, which created large wet sludge beds that are extremely attractive to birds in general and waders in particular.

To the east, where Cheshire leads into the Peak District, there is an area of upland moors, dales and Macclesfield Forest. Little moorland survives on the eastern hills, where sheep farming has altered the habitat. However, this area remains attractive to birds and ramblers alike and contains specialised habitats providing further diversity to the county's avifauna.

In the west lies the Wirral Peninsula with its 40 miles (65 km) of coastline forming a continuation of the vast tract of sand dunes and mudflats that extend around the whole of Liverpool Bay. Wirral is bordered on either side by two of the most important estuaries for wintering wildfowl and waders in Britain: the Dee and the Mersey. Both estuaries provide superb habitat for birds and for watching birds.

Cheshire and Wirral still hold some ancient woodlands that are accessible to birdwatchers. Many typical woodland species breed in the county and can be located with relative ease.

61 ROSTHERNE MERE   OS Landranger Map 109

Habitat

Rostherne Mere (SJ743843) lies in a deep natural hollow formed partly by subsidence due to salt strata below. The mere covers 119 acres (48 ha) and has a maximum depth of around 100 feet (30 m). Its size and depth mean it rarely freezes. The banks shelve steeply for the most part and although much of the mere is fringed by narrow reedbeds, there is little submerged vegetation and few wildfowl breed. There is limited habitat for passing waders. Mixed woodlands run down to the mere edge for more than half of its circumference. Elsewhere it is bordered by pasture. The mere, woods and pastures together comprise the Rostherne Mere National Nature Reserve, which comprises 193 acres (around 80 ha) of mere, woodland and willow beds together with 177 acres (around 70 ha) of farmland around the mere farmed by tenant farmers. Access is restricted to the public allowing wildlife to thrive in the area. The mere is best known as a winter haunt of wildfowl. The birds can be watched in relative comfort from the A. W. Boyd Memorial Observatory run by the Cheshire & Wirral Ornithological Society.

Species

During the winter months hundreds of ducks line the edges of the mere, roosting among the reedbeds. Mallard predominate in the autumn, but in

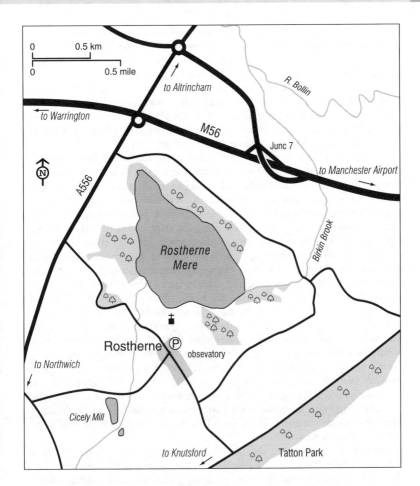

winter Common Teal outnumbers its larger cousin by several hundred. Eurasian Wigeon, Coot and Canada Geese graze the pastures. Up to 300 of these feral geese may be present. Other geese also occur; the proliferation of wildfowl collections has led to an increase in sightings of escaped birds and it is now not unusual to find one or two Barnacle Geese among the Canadas. Snow, Lesser White-fronted and Bar-headed Geese have all turned up from time to time, and hybrid birds of questionable parentage also occur. Shoveler is most common in autumn, and a few remain through the winter. In recent years flocks of 100 or more Gadwall frequent the mere in late autumn. Pintail is a scarce winter visitor. Pochard forms the bulk of the diving duck population throughout the winter. In recent winters a large flock of more than 1,000 birds has based itself on the Mersey valley, spending some of the time at Rostherne. Several dozen Tufted Ducks mingle with the Pochard and a few Scaup occur sporadically. With careful searching a Ferruginous Duck or a hybrid diving duck might be found; the former is now very rare, but assorted hybrids are seen in most winters. In midwinter 20 or more Common Goldeneye spread out across the back of the mere to feed. Rostherne is as good a place as any in

Cheshire to see Smew and Ruddy Duck has been as common here as elsewhere in the region. Scarcer waterbirds, such as Goosander and the rarer grebes, turn up from time to time. There have been records of Green-winged Teal and American Wigeon (1973, 1979 and 1995).

Severe weather concentrates wildfowl on the mere because Rostherne remains open long after other meres and flashes have frozen. When prolonged frosts cause the Baltic Sea to freeze over, and when alternative duck roosts in Greater Manchester are ice-bound, numbers of Pochard and Tufted Duck may run into thousands. This is a rare weather event these days.

Great Crested Grebe numbers reach a peak in late summer. A few remain on the mere during the winter, when Little Grebe may sometimes be seen. Bewick's Swans visit occasionally and Whooper Swans more rarely. A Bittern is reported in most winters, but even when present this species is notoriously elusive. A particular feature of Rostherne is the roost of Cormorants, occupied from September to April, in poplars along the edge of Harpers Bank Wood. Up to 300 of these birds leave the mere by day to feed in the rivers, meres and flashes of eastern Cheshire and parts of Greater Manchester. From mid afternoon onwards, parties of Cormorants come gliding back into the Rostherne hollow. Towards dusk they take up their positions in the trees. Look out for birds with coloured plastic leg rings. These can sometimes be read through a telescope and should be noted in the observatory logbook.

The elevated position of the observatory makes it ideally situated for watching diurnal cold-weather movements. With the onset of severe frosts Northern Lapwings may be seen flying west, sometimes being overtaken by faster, more pointed-winged, Golden Plovers. Skylarks and thrushes also move south or west. At any time during the winter, but especially after frost and snow, skeins of Pink-footed Goose pass over particularly to the north of the mere, heading either from the south Lancashire mosslands east to The Wash or northwest on their return journey from East Anglia. Only rarely do wild geese alight on the reserve.

Towards dusk in winter the number of birds on and around the mere increases rapidly. Woodpigeons line the treetops in enormous numbers when there is a good acorn crop. Corvids – mainly Jackdaws, Rooks and to a lesser

Cormorants

extent Carrion Crows – also congregate in considerable numbers. Up to 10,000 Black-headed Gulls and a few hundred larger gulls roost on the mere. The larger species have become less numerous since the refuse tip closed at Lindow Moss, near Wilmslow. Glaucous and Iceland Gulls are increasingly rare. Common Gull numbers may reach 1,000 or more between January and March.

From late summer to early winter thousands of Starlings wheel over the mere at dusk before roosting in the reedbeds. The gathering roost is often harassed in spectacular fashion by a Peregrine Falcon or, more likely, Sparrowhawk. Hobby has been seen with increasing frequency in recent summers in line with the species' continued expansion northwards across the region.

Woodland birds move through the alder trees at the mere edge, giving views of Siskin, Goldfinch and woodpeckers. Nuthatches, Long-tailed and Coal Tits, and Jays take food from a bird table just below the observatory. The winter flocks of wildfowl disperse during March and the reserve then becomes relatively quiet for the summer months.

Stock Doves displaying in front of the observatory is one of the first signs of spring. In this season, Lesser Spotted Woodpeckers call and drum from mereside alders, Curlews visit the pastures by day, and at dusk in some years Woodcocks rode around the woodlands. Passage migration in April and May brings a few Common Sandpipers and other waders to the shoreline. Far more conspicuous are the swirling flocks of hirundines and swifts that feed over the mere. Parties of Common, Arctic or Black Terns may visit at this time.

Principal breeding species at Rostherne are Mallard, Coot, Moorhen and Reed Warbler. Other breeders include Kestrel, Sparrowhawk and Little Owl, and woodland passerines such as Blackcap, Nuthatch and Spotted Flycatcher. Common Buzzard is often present. A Grey Wagtail may frequent the inlet stream and a Kingfisher sometimes perches on posts by the old boathouse.

A well-studied population of Reed Warbler breeds in the reedbeds. Nests were formerly parasitised by Cuckoos, sadly this is now a much rarer event. A few pairs of Sedge Warbler breed. Nesting waterfowl include Great Crested Grebe, sometimes Little Grebe, and Tufted and Ruddy Ducks. Non-breeding Cormorants, Eurasian Wigeon and Shoveler may spend the summer on the mere. Scores of feral Greylag Geese arrive to moult with the Canada Geese.

Late summer and early autumn may see a build-up of Great Crested Grebes, resting in a flock out on the open water. Parties of drake Pochard may arrive in July from breeding waters, and Tufted Ducks may be more numerous than at any other season (except during severe winter weather). Shoveler numbers reach a peak in September or October. A few terns and waders pass through, and autumn gales may blow a shearwater or other seabird inland.

Migrants on spring or autumn passage include terns and a few waders. Seabirds seen at Rostherne include Kittiwake and Fulmar and one astonishing record of a Little Shearwater, an exceptionally rare bird in British seas, never mind inland. It was present from 29 June to 3 July 1977. Other rarities include Purple Heron (1977 and 1980) and Franklin's Gull (1987).

Timing

For general viewing of wildfowl visit at any time of day. During the winter months afternoon and dusk visits are recommended for roosting birds. Persistent frosts concentrate wildfowl driven off other waters. Westerly or northwesterly gales at any time of year may blow in a seabird.

Access

Leave the M56 at junction 7, turning south onto the A556(T). After 1 mile (1.6 km) take the second turning on the left. Continue along this winding road for three-quarters of a mile (1.2 km), past the church, and park on the left opposite a T-junction, outside the warden's house, 'Rowans' (SJ743837). Otherwise follow signs for the main, north entrance to Tatton Park (SJ748827) and take the minor road northwards directly opposite the park gate. Access to the mere is prohibited. Permits for the observatory are readily available at £7 per person, £10 for a family and £2 for OAPs, disabled and children under 16. Permits are valid from 1 January to 31 December and are available from D.A. Clarke, 1 Hart Avenue, Sale, Cheshire, M33 2JY on submission of a stamped, addressed envelope. Cheques should be made payable to the Cheshire & Wirral Ornithological Society. Postal orders are accepted. Directions from Rostherne village to the Observatory are given on the back of the permit. Day permits are available for £1 per person. Limited viewing of the mere is possible from the churchyard.

CALENDAR

All year: Great Crested Grebe, Cormorant, Canada Goose, Tufted Duck, Sparrowhawk, Kestrel, Common Buzzard, Stock Dove, Little Owl, all three woodpeckers, Nuthatch, Jay.

December–February: Cormorant, Eurasian Wigeon, Common Teal, Pochard, Tufted Duck, Common Goldeneye, Ruddy Duck and perhaps Gadwall, Smew and other wildfowl. Gulls and crows roost. Siskin below the observatory.

March–May: Gull roost vacated and wildfowl disperse. Occasional Curlew and Common Sandpiper and possibility of other waders;

Swift, hirundines and occasional terns fly over the mere.

June–July: Non-breeding waterbirds may include Eurasian Wigeon, Shoveler and Cormorant. Few wildfowl breed but Greylag Geese join the Canada Geese in June to moult. Pochard and Tufted Duck increase in July. Reed Warbler is numerous in the reedbeds.

August–November: Great Crested Grebe, Shoveler and Tufted Duck are numerous. Occasional terns or waders.

62 TATTON PARK AND KNUTSFORD MOOR   OS Landranger Map 109, 118

Habitat

In 1958, after the death of the last Baron Egerton, Tatton Park passed to the National Trust. Its 2,000 acres (810 ha) are now largely accessible to all being run on behalf of the National Trust by Cheshire County Council. About one third of the park is still farmed; less than a third is woodland and water. The remainder is open parkland. The main attractions for birdwatching are Tatton Mere and the smaller Melchett Mere, and the woodlands surrounding them. All areas are worth a look on a day out.

The larger area of woodlands comprises mixed oak, chestnut, beech and pine. Grazing by sheep, cattle and both Red and Fallow Deer has prevented the

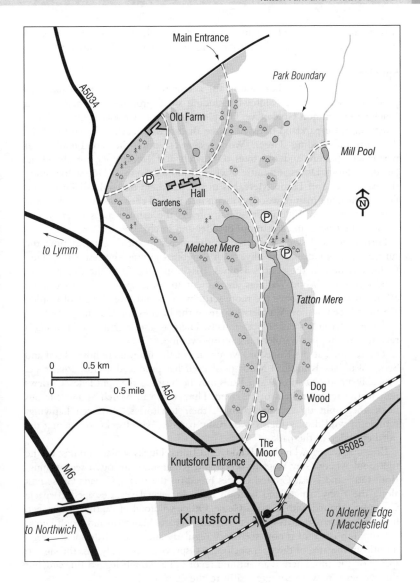

development of a scrub layer in all but a few fenced woods. Tatton Mere was dammed by the monks of Mobberley Priory in medieval times and has little marginal vegetation. The mere extends to become Knutsford Moor to the south where the River Lilley enters. An extensive reedbed separates the mere from Knutsford Moor pool, which lies outside the park.

Tatton Mere is often heavily disturbed by water sports. The smaller of the two meres, Melchett Mere, has boggy areas of rushes along its banks and acts as a refuge for wildfowl when boats and windsurfers force them from the main mere. At the northeast corner of the park is a mill pool backed by a large bed of sedges. The fast-flowing brook downstream from the mill attracts riparian species. To the north of the mill is the deer enclosure, a secluded area of grassland with scattered old trees standing on ancient field boundaries.

Species

Winter is arguably the best season for a visit to the meres, and is likely to produce a selection of wildfowl including small groups of Pochard, Tufted Duck and Common Goldeneye. The plentiful mature woodland makes Tatton outstanding for parkland birds. All three British woodpeckers breed regularly. The ground-feeding Green Woodpecker favours the combination of permanent pasture and old trees. Nuthatch and Treecreeper are abundant. Jackdaws, Stock Doves and Little Owls nest in holes in trees. Dog Wood, along the eastern side of Tatton Mere, has in the past held both Marsh Tit (which favours the drier mature woodland with its oaks and chestnuts and has become scarce of late) and Willow Tit (which prefers the damper areas where it can excavate nest holes in soft stumps of alder and birch).

Hirundines and swifts appear over the meres in spring. At this time the surrounding woodlands are alive with songbirds joining the resident species. Goldcrests nest in the scattered pines. Blackcaps sing from the canopy over rhododendrons. Wood Warblers are present in some springs and have bred. Whitethroats dance above the more scrubby areas and several pairs of Garden Warblers breed. Willow Warblers sing from the birches and Common Redstart and Pied Flycatcher occur occasionally. There is also a chance of hearing a reeling Grasshopper Warbler on a spring evening.

The reedbed at the Knutsford Moor end of the main mere hosts Reed and Sedge Warblers. Knutsford Moor pool itself has produced a Grey Phalarope. Probably a pair or two of Water Rails may be heard as the light fades. Curlews nest in the remoter areas of parkland. They arrive in March as a vociferous flock, then split up as pairs establish their territories. Northern Lapwings tumble in wild display flights over rushy patches. Woodcocks rode along the northern edge of the park.

Breeding waterfowl include Ruddy and Tufted Ducks, which also nest on the mill pool where Grey Wagtails breed and Kingfishers are often seen fishing. Both Little and Great Crested Grebes breed on the meres. Canada Geese nest along the rushy fringes and beneath trees. In several years escaped Barnacle Geese have paired with Canada Geese. Other wildfowl of captive origin seen here with some regularity are Red-crested Pochard, Mandarin and Wood Duck.

Common Buzzard is now seen very regularly and a Red Kite spent several months in the area of the deer enclosure. Ospreys occasionally pass through in spring or autumn. There is an autumn record of a Rough-legged Buzzard, but this species is now a very rare visitor to the county.

Winter wildfowl include Common Teal, Pochard and Common Goldeneye. There is a chance of a Smew, although it is not as regular as it once was. Tufted Duck is always present. Movements between here and Rostherne Mere occur, so the likely species are similar. Rarer birds such as Black-necked Grebe and Ferruginous Duck have commuted between Rostherne Mere and Tatton Park in the past. Winter brings an increase in Great Crested Grebe numbers. Occasionally these are joined by a Slavonian, Black-necked or even Red-necked Grebe. Black-throated and Great Northern Divers have occurred. As spring approaches, Common Goldeneyes display here regularly and numbers increase as passage to the northeast commences.

Common Snipe creep around the edges of Melchett Mere and the occasional Jack Snipe is flushed from this area. Water Rail is often present. Rails are more easily seen around the Knutsford Moor reedbed, where Bearded Tit has occurred. In autumn the reedbed holds roosts of Pied Wagtail and Swallow. In winter Redwings and Blackbirds roost in birch scrub and rhododendrons nearby. Also in winter Siskins and Redpolls feed in mereside alder and birch trees. Greenfinches and Chaffinches gather in the stubble fields around the park, and Brambling often appears either there or under beeches.

March brings the first passerine migrants to the mereside, when parties of Meadow Pipits, Pied Wagtails and Reed Buntings comb the short turf, and Wheatears sometimes flit along the shoreline. During showery weather in April the flocks are joined by White and Yellow Wagtails and perhaps a Water or Rock Pipit. Common Sandpipers rise from the water's edge and fly away low across the mere. The first Sand Martins are seen in late March, to be joined by Swallows and then House Martins during April, and swifts by the end of that month.

Terns are recorded annually on either passage, with Black, Common and Arctic possible. There is a chance of a Little Gull in the autumn. Migrant parties of hirundines appear over the meres in September and October, when their numbers may change markedly from hour to hour as flocks arrive in dribs and drabs from the north, feed for a while as they reassemble, then depart en masse to the south.

Tatton is not without its rarities. Records from the past have included Common Crane on a couple of occasions, a Red-breasted Flycatcher in November 1983 and even more rare a Nutcracker in October 1968.

Timing

The park is open during the low season (October to March) from 11am until 5pm (last admission 4pm; gates locked at 5pm) Tuesday to Sunday. During the high season (April to September) the park is open daily from 10am to 7pm (last admission 6pm; gates locked at 7pm). Sunny weekends, bank holidays and special events days are best avoided. Morning visits are best as disturbance increases during the day and waterfowl may then leave the park and fly to Rostherne. Evening visits in spring can be rewarding. Showery weather at passage times produces most migrants, particularly when the wind is from a southerly quarter in spring. Admission is free for pedestrians and cyclists. There is a £4.20 admission charge for cars.

Access

Three entrances allow access to Tatton. The park is well signposted on all approach roads to Knutsford, but most birdwatchers enter through Dog Lodge. Take the B5085 from the A537 out of Knutsford, pass a brick church, then pull into a loop behind a grass verge on the left and park (SD 754786). Continue walking in the same direction and turn left into Teal Avenue. Take the first left into Mallard Close and cross the railway bridge. The stile into the park will then be obvious. Knutsford Moor and scrub areas are visible to the left.

For another way in, park in the car park below the lower shopping street in Knutsford, from where the Moor with its hungry ducks can be seen. Cross the Moor, keeping the railings on the left, and follow a rough track to the left through the scrub. This track eventually leads through to Dog Wood. On a short visit it is customary to walk up the east side of the mere inspecting the wildfowl and any migrants, then continue to Melchett Mere which can be scanned from the southeast corner. It is then possible to complete the circuit of the mere, perhaps following an avenue of mature beeches down the west side of the park to the Knutsford gate. On evening visits this gate may be locked, so it is advisable to retrace one's steps.

CALENDAR

All year: Little Grebe, Great Crested Grebe, Canada Goose, Tufted Duck, Ruddy Duck, Common Buzzard, Woodcock, Stock Dove, Little Owl, all three woodpeckers, woodland species.

December–February: Cormorant, Common Teal, Pochard and Common Goldeneye on the meres; Water Rail, Common and Jack Snipes in marshy ground; Brambling under beeches, Lesser Redpoll in birches and Siskin in alders. Thrushes roost at the Moor.

March–May: Common Goldeneye displays conspicuously; Shoveler frequents the reedbeds; flocks of pipits, wagtails and Reed Bunting should be checked for Water Pipit and White Wagtail; Northern Wheatear and Sand Martin appear from late March; other hirundines in April and Swifts around the end of that month. Terns may visit from late April.

June–July: Broods of ducklings, Canada Goose and grebes; Curlews may have young; Reed, Sedge and Garden Warblers nest on the Moor; Willow Warbler and Whitethroat; Blackcap and Chiffchaff in woodlands; Tree Sparrow in the parkland.

August–November: Hirundines sometimes plentiful; terns and perhaps Little Gull occasional over the meres; Pied Wagtails and Swallows roost on the Moor; wildfowl numbers increase sharply from October.

---

63 ALDERLEY WOODS
OS Landranger Map 118
SJ87

Habitat

The Edge at Alderley is an escarpment of red sandstone that contains veins of copper ore, mined from prehistoric times until early last century. Evidence of these mining activities is widespread in the form of square-sided cuttings and tunnels. On a fine day the escarpment offers impressive views of the surrounding countryside across Cheshire towards the Peak District. The mature, planted woodland that covers much of the edge consists principally of oak, Scots pine and birch, with some chestnut and beech on the thinner soils overlying rocky outcrops, and larch. Ground flora is rather sparse, with wavy hair grass, bracken and brambles dominant. An extensive network of paths and bare, eroded areas around mine entrances give the woodland an open character. On the site of the old west mine, where a spoil tip stood into the 1960s, an area of open ground is developing birch scrub that is attractive to small finches and warblers.

Species

During the winter months the woods contain large flocks of tits, generally accompanied by a few Goldcrests, Nuthatches, Treecreepers and sometimes

Lesser Spotted Woodpecker. Marsh and Willow Tits are scarce. Coal and Great Tits in particular feed on beech mast; both species may outnumber Blue Tits in winter. In years with a good mast crop Chaffinches and Bramblings gather under the beeches. Parties of Lesser Redpoll feed in the birches, a food source also used by small groups of Bullfinch. Siskins also feed here, but move into larches towards spring.

Redwings visit to feed on holly berries so long as these are available. Green Woodpeckers are seen each winter, often remaining into April. As spring approaches their ringing "yaffle" echoes through the woods with increasing frequency, but the birds usually disappear without nesting. Great Spotted Woodpecker nest commonly in the less accessible reaches of the woods; Lesser Spotted Woodpecker nests in very small numbers.

In spring, Wood Warbler is the chief attraction at Alderley and is easily located by its song: a shivering trill sometimes replaced or preceded by a series of three or four clear "peu" notes on a descending scale. The first Wood Warblers arrive in late April and soon after engage in their breathtaking display flight, in which the bird flies rapidly through the branches, changing direction with such speed and frequency that its flight is very difficult to follow. Common Redstart and Pied Flycatcher also breed in some years. Tree Pipit may also nest, finding the numerous clearings to their liking. Treecreeper and

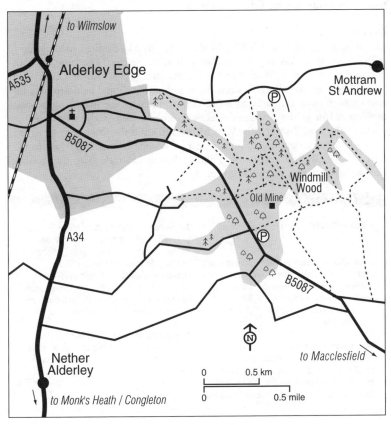

Nuthatch are both plentiful breeders, the latter even occasionally plastering up fissures in the exposed rock faces to nest. From the middle of May Spotted Flycatchers stammer their weak song while Chiffchaffs, which arrived in early April, are still singing vigorously. Coal Tits nest in mouse holes beneath the pines where the numerous Goldcrests hang their flimsy nest structures.

The heath and scrubland area at the West Mine site supports breeding Common Whitethroats, Garden Warblers, Linnets and Lesser Redpolls. Lesser Whitethroat and Grasshopper Warbler have occurred. Yellowhammers were once plentiful, but have undergone a rapid decline here and elsewhere in eastern Cheshire. Adjacent pastures support a few pairs of Northern Lapwing. A Kestrel often hunts the area. Although Alderley is not often noted as a Woodcock site, one or two birds rode over the woods in spring, occasionally passing over the main car park. In May young Tawny Owls may be heard.

Timing

The woods are owned mostly by the National Trust and attract many visitors. At times, particularly at weekend and on sunny evenings in spring and summer, the area becomes a little crowded with visitors. As with all woodland birding, early morning visits are preferable. In spring birdsong is at its best early in the day, although evening visits generally give sufficient time to locate most species. In winter timing is less important.

Access

The woods straddle the B5087 Alderley Edge to Macclesfield road about 1 mile (2 km) from Alderley. Several laybys border the road. The large car park just to the east of the "Wizard of Edge" restaurant (SJ860773) may be locked at dusk. Numerous paths criss-cross the woods and it should be no trouble for visitors to remain on paths to avoid contributing to the increasing erosion problem. Most of the woodland species can be located in the woods to the north of the road. To reach the West Mine area, enter the southern part of the woods by a track opposite an unmade car park some 200 yards (200 m) to the west of the Wizard restaurant. Follow this main track past the conifer plantations until you reach the gorse.

CALENDAR

All year: Good variety of common woodland birds.

December–February: Large flocks of mixed tits roam the woods; other woodland species; Green Woodpecker; Redwings in holly; Bullfinch, Lesser Redpoll and Siskin in birches; Bramblings may join Chaffinches under beeches.

March–May: Summer visitors arrive during April and by early May most warblers will be present; Lesser Spotted Woodpeckers may be conspicuous in March or April; roding Woodcocks; by May young Tawny Owls call to be fed.

June–July: Residents and summer visitors busy with nesting duties; unmated Wood Warblers continue to sing regularly; Common Redstart, Spotted and perhaps Pied Flycatcher, possibly Tree Pipit, present in woods with Chiffchaffs and Blackcaps; Lesser Redpoll and Linnet; Common Whitethroat and Garden Warbler nest on the heathland.

August–November: Wood Warbler slips away unnoticed; other migrants depart to be replaced by finches and thrushes for the winter.

64 RUDHEATH SAND QUARRIES

OS Landranger Map 118

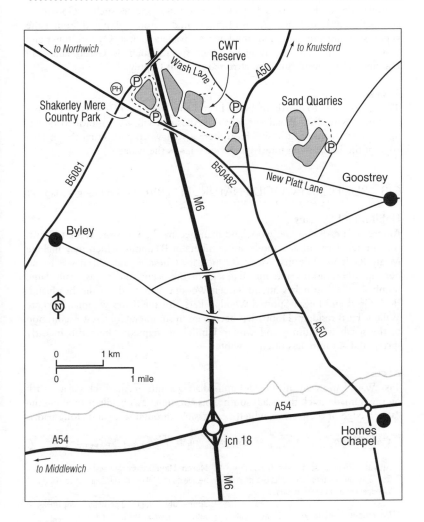

Habitat

Rudheath, north of Holmes Chapel, was once an extensive heathland. Most of the land has been turned over to agriculture, but small areas of heath, birch woodland and pine plantations remain. Several flooded sand quarries add to the diversity of the area. It is an area of wet and dry heath, scrub and grassland.

64A   NEWPLATT WOOD SAND QUARRY   OS Landranger Map 118

This is a large, shallow flooded sand quarry used for angling. A flock of Canada Goose is resident, and small numbers of several wildfowl species are usually present, especially between autumn and spring. These include Common Teal, Shoveler, Pochards and Tufted Duck. Less common species such as Goosander and Garganey have visited. Areas of sandy mud are often exposed around the gently shelving shoreline. This mud attracts waders such as Oystercatcher and Common Snipe, and occasionally other species such as Greenshank and Dunlin. The plentiful fish have attracted migrant Ospreys.

Access

The quarry lies to north of New Platt Lane and east of the A50 Holmes Chapel to Knutsford Road just south of Allostock village. A minor road runs up the eastern side of the site. From here a well-worn path skirts the eastern edge of the lake, giving interrupted views across the water.

64B   RUDHEATH WOODS NATURE RESERVE OS Landranger Map 118

Habitat and Species

An area of heath and wet woodland managed by the Cheshire Wildlife Trust, this site regularly attracts moderate numbers of Redpolls, which may include Mealy Redpolls. The first Arctic Redpoll for Cheshire and Wirral was found here in 1995. Siskins and mixed flocks of tits occur, and occasionally large numbers of Chaffinches attend. Green Woodpeckers feed on the heathland. Both Great and Lesser Spotted Woodpeckers visit the damp woodland, where Willow Tit is resident. Hobby has been seen in summer. Goldcrest is common in the scrub in autumn and winter. Chiffchaff frequents the scrub in early spring and autumn, less often in winter.

Access

Take Wash Lane west off the A50 immediately south of Allostock village. Park on the unmade track that leads south. This continues as a bridle path along the eastern edge of the reserve, which is accessible through stiles and along paths.

CALENDAR

All year: Great Crested Grebe, Canada Goose; woodland birds including Green Woodpecker and Lesser Redpoll.

December–February: Waterfowl including Common Teal and Tufted Duck; Common Snipe on exposed mud; Siskin in Alders; tit and Lesser Redpoll flocks in birch woods and mixed finch flocks in the area.

March–May: Occasional passage waders beside quarry lakes; warblers in scrub.

June–July: Tufted and perhaps Ruddy Ducks with young; woodland birds nesting.

August–November: Few passage waders may include Greenshank, Green Sandpiper; returning migrants include Goldcrest, Chiffchaff, finches.

65 MACCLESFIELD FOREST, LANGLEY RESERVOIRS AND TEGGS NOSE COUNTRY PARK   OS Landranger Map 108

Habitat

Lying just three miles south-east of the town of Macclesfield, this is an area of conifer plantations on the slopes of the Pennines, planted following the construction of Trentabank Reservoir in 1929. The other reservoir in the forest is Ridgegate, which is a long, narrow lake formed when an embankment dammed the valley in 1840. Farther down the valley just outside the forest area are two smaller reservoirs near the village of Langley. The whole area is home to a limited and specialised community of birds. The area is popular with ramblers.

Pine, spruce and larch are the principal trees, with some sycamore and a few other broadleaved trees, notably beech, along the roadsides. The plantations should improve for birds as the first generation of trees matures, when felling

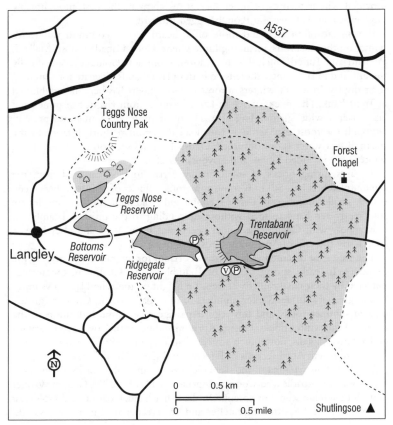

and replanting will become more prevalent. The forest is surrounded by upland pasture and rough sheep-grazed moorland. Red Deer frequent the plantations, emerging into the open by night. The reservoirs are steep sided with rocky shores. As the water level fluctuates markedly in summer, little marginal vegetation has developed. Trentabank, the topmost reservoir, is out of bounds to anglers but seldom holds many waterfowl.

Teggs Nose Country Park includes an area of mixed broadleaved woodland with oak, ash, beech and other trees, and plentiful dead wood. Cattle graze among the trees, but there is nonetheless a considerable scrub layer of brambles and other undergrowth. At the bottom of the steep hillside the woodland changes to alder carr. At higher altitudes the woodland peters out and is replaced by stands of bracken and some heather.

Species

Despite an overall impression of quiet, the forest does have some specialities and unusual birds turn up with surprising frequency. During the winter months flocks of Goldcrest and Coal and Long-tailed Tits roam the plantations, their thin calls breaking the misty silence. With perseverance Common Crossbill is quite likely to be seen in flight across the valley, and they sometimes alight in roadside trees. Siskin, Jay and Sparrowhawk are regular. The area has provided winter records of other species of raptor in the past, most notably Goshawk, Hen Harrier and Rough-legged Buzzard.

Ravens are often seen and more often heard. A few common waterbirds winter on the reservoirs, including Little Grebe, Coot, Canada Goose, Mallard, Pochard and Tufted Duck. Up to a dozen Common Goldeneye are usually present, and in late winter there is no better place than Ridgegate for watching their display. In recent winters, a roost of Goosanders has become established at Trentabank. The ducks arrive in late afternoon from rivers, fish ponds and lakes over a wide surrounding area. Thirty or more are sometimes present, although the roost may settle at Lamaload Reservoir, a short distance to the north, if that water is not disturbed. Unusual species seen on the reservoirs in winter have included Smew and Slavonian Grebe.

Towards spring flocks of small finches arrive to feed on seed from the opening larch cones. Siskin is most numerous – flocks of 150 have been seen – with smaller numbers of Lesser Redpoll and Goldfinch. All these species are sufficiently acrobatic to feed without descending to the ground. Bramblings may appear with Chaffinches under beeches at Teggs Nose and elsewhere in March. By the end of April most birds have departed.

The west–east oriented valley forms a corridor for migrant birds crossing the Pennines. In early spring parties of Brambling and Chaffinch, the former detected by their nasal calls, fly at tree-top height up the valley. Jackdaws move east at greater altitude. Winter numbers of this small crow in Cheshire greatly exceed summer totals, and this regular passage gives some indication of the origin of the winter flocks. During April hirundines gather over the reservoirs and Yellow Wagtails, now much scarcer than formerly, return to the pastures. There are recent April records of Firecrest and Great Grey Shrike.

The breeding avifauna of the plantations is as remarkable for its absentees as for its variety. Broadleaved woodland species such as Blue Tit, Garden Warbler and Nuthatch are scarce or absent. On the other hand, Coal Tit and Goldcrest are plentiful, and Spotted Flycatcher and Treecreeper nest in mature stands, where a few pairs of Siskin also sometimes breed. Lesser Redpoll and Willow Warbler frequent the younger plantations and Tree Pipit occupies the clearings.

Crepuscular and nocturnal species include roding Woodcock, best seen from the road by Trentabank. Their curious display flight begins in the last few days of February in mild springs, but is better witnessed in May or June when, with the hours of darkness restricted, the performance begins while the light is still good. At a distance the only call to be heard is a sharp squeak, but as the birds pass overhead with deep, slow wingbeats listen for a series of three or four deep grunts.

Tawny Owl is common and makes use of old crow nests due to the lack of cavities in trees that provide the usual nest site. Long-eared Owl no doubt breeds in the area and hunts the moors above the forest, but is very difficult to locate. By day, Kestrels hover above the ridges. The spring can produce sightings of Goshawk and Peregrine Falcon, but Kestrel and Sparrowhawk are more frequent. Osprey is an occasional visitor at this time over the reservoirs. Cleared areas appear suitable for Nightjar, but this bird is now very scarce in Cheshire – perhaps with the expansion in nearby areas it might recolonise the county. The east Cheshire hills are sadly no longer the haunt of Black Grouse.

A few waterfowl breed on the reservoirs. Great Crested and Little Grebes may nest on Bottoms Reservoir, and Tufted Duck may rear ducklings on Ridgegate. Canada Geese sit conspicuously on nests beneath trees near the water. Common Sandpipers, which feed along the shoreline, evade the anglers by nesting inside the plantations. As the young hatch the adults perch on roadside walls, bobbing and calling anxiously. Of particular interest is the heronry in trees beside Trentabank. Renovation of old nests may start in February, with new nests still being built in April. The Grey Herons fly out to fish in brooks, pools and rivers in the surrounding hills. Returning birds are greeted with much bill clattering by their mates. During May and June the growing young birds gabble and squawk noisily.

The woodlands at Teggs Nose come alive during the summer. Wood Warblers trill beneath the oaks and are more easily located than the pair or two in the forest proper. Common Redstarts flit in and out of tree holes or warble from the cover of a thorn bush. Pied Flycatcher has bred in recent summers.

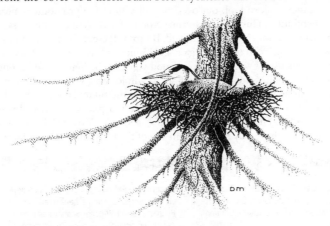

Grey Heron

All three woodpeckers are seen, although Lesser Spotted is scarce. Nuthatch and Tree Pipit also nest, as do lowland birds such as Garden Warbler.

Autumn passage brings the occasional rarity to the forest – Honey Buzzard, Wryneck and Firecrest have been noted – but the area is known best for heavy movements of commoner species. The area is good for migration with thrushes, larks, pipits, wagtails, finches and Wood Pigeons passing overhead between September and November.

Migrant Bramblings are often recorded here even when they appear to be absent elsewhere in the county. Easterly winds in October or November bring the largest movements, with thousands of Redwings and Fieldfares, hundreds of Blackbirds and dozens of Song Thrushes on the best days. Starling and Jackdaw are important passage species. Tired migrant thrushes and finches will often settle in the scrub and woodland at Teggs Nose, where they make easy pickings for the resident Sparrowhawks.

Timing

Evening visits are advisable for watching roosting and crepuscular species. Clear mornings are best for raptors. On cloudy days mist may obscure the valley, although on cold winter days when fog blankets the lowlands the sun may well be shining on the hills. Diurnal passage over ridges above the forest is heaviest on autumn days with mist, hazy cloud or when it is totally overcast, although very large movements have occurred with a clear sky and light wind from the east. Passage stops abruptly in heavy or persistent rain or in high winds. On bright sunny days migrants fly too high to be seen, detected only by a few calls. Teggs Nose and Trentabank can be crowded at weekends, particularly in summer, but few people wander far from the roads into the forest.

Access

The forest lies east of Langley village south-east of Macclesfield. Immediately through Langley village a left turn, Holehouse Lane, leads to a car park at the foot of Teggs Nose (SD946717). Follow the path up the hill and explore the scrubby areas to the right. A larger car park at the summit of Teggs Nose (SD949731) is signposted off the A537 Macclesfield to Buxton road, and provides an easier walk to look out over the valley from the promontory near the quarry exhibition. This is a good vantage point for Ravens and on passage days. Otherwise continue up the main road. Bottoms Reservoir appears on the left. Carry on up the road for Ridgegate and Trentabank Reservoirs. A lay-by alongside Trentabank (SD963713) allows good views of the heronry and is one of the best viewpoints for the forest as a whole. For watching autumn migration continue up the road past Trentabank to the hilltop, then walk right along the footpath on the ridge and wait. If there is a passage, birds will pass low over this ridge. The Forest Chapel road is generally most productive for Crossbill, although these may be seen from any of the tracks through the forest.

CALENDAR

All year: Tufted Duck, Common Buzzard, Sparrowhawk, Kestrel, Tawny Owl, Goldcrest, Long-tailed and Coal Tits, Raven, Common Crossbill.

December–February: Common Goldeneye on the reservoirs, with perhaps a few Pochard, Teal or Wigeon; Goshawk and other raptors occasionally; Carrion Crows roost in large numbers; Goosanders roost either here or at Lamaload Reservoir.

March–May: Common Goldeneye display by March when Canada Geese take up territory and Grey Herons renovate nests; Woodcocks start to rode and Common Crossbills may be nesting; passing migrants in March include Jackdaw, Chaffinch and Brambling. Finch flocks in early spring include Siskin, Lesser Redpoll and Goldfinch; in April hirundines and Yellow Wagtail pass through; summer visitors arrive including Common Sandpiper, Pied Flycatcher and Tree Pipit.

June–July: Grey Herons fledge; Great Crested Grebes, Tufted Ducks and Common Sandpipers may have young; Common

Redstart, Wood Warbler and Pied Flycatcher at Teggs Nose; possibility of Siskin in the conifers.

August–November: Summer visitors depart; Goldeneye may return from August, more likely in October; diurnal passage includes Meadow and Tree Pipits and White Wagtails in August and September, with Meadow Pipits continuing to pass through in October; Pied Wagtails are more numerous in October and a few Grey Wagtails likely; Siskin from mid-September; Chaffinch and Brambling in October. Large-scale thrush movements in October to November include Redwing, Fieldfare, Blackbird and Song Thrush. Goosander numbers may build up at Trentabank.

66 RIVER DANE VALLEY   OS Landranger Maps 118, 119

Habitat

The River Dane is a clean trout stream forming the boundary between Cheshire and Staffordshire. Its waters are rich in invertebrates (look for Banded Agrion Damselflies in the lower reaches) that provide food for a good number of riparian birds. Danebower is a gritstone hill topped with peat moorland.

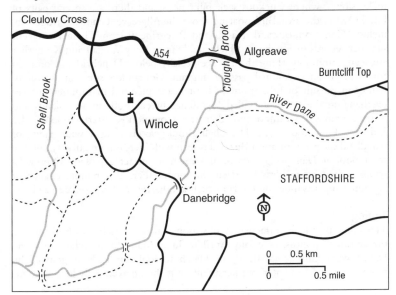

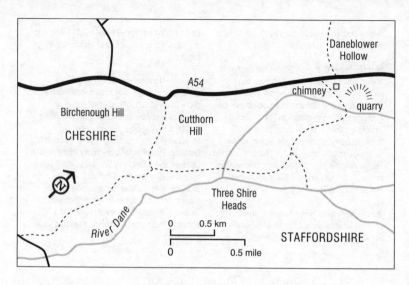

Rocky slopes and mixed woodlands, including those at Shell Brook, support a diverse range of breeding species. There are Red Deer in the woods.

Species

European Golden Plover still breeds on the Danebower moors in small numbers, but is increasingly disturbed by ramblers. Red Grouse is easy to see, and there is a chance of a Twite or a passing Merlin. Curlew nests on moorland and rough pastures. The Ring Ouzels that used to feed in the pastures around the quarry chimney have become scarce transient visitors, although they showed well in Spring 2007. Northern Wheatears still nest commonly along rocky slopes, where Cuckoos seek pipit nests, and there are several pairs of Little Owl in the area. Birds soaring above the Allgreave–Gradbach ridge may include Common Buzzard, Raven and Peregrine Falcon. There are recent summer records of Hobby and Fieldfare. Dipper, Grey Wagtail and Kingfisher are seen commonly along the river, especially below Danebridge. Common Sandpiper is an occasional passage migrant. Goosanders sometimes visit in winter in pursuit of fish. Spotted Flycatcher is plentiful in summer in trees overhanging the river, and Pied Flycatcher breeds both in woodlands and scattered stands of sycamore and other trees. Common Redstart, Wood Warbler and Tree Pipit also occur. The Shell Brook woods hold a wide range of woodland species. Common Buzzard is seen with increasing regularity, and the trout pool at Danebridge has been known to attract a passage Osprey. In winter, when many birds have left the moors, there is a remote chance of encountering a wandering predator such as a harrier or Short-eared Owl.

Timing

The valley is visually attractive at all seasons, but is far richer in birds during the summer months, especially April to June. Many birdwatchers visit the Danebower chimney (SK0170) in March to look for early migrants. The moors are quiet in winter, but persistent visits should eventually be rewarded.

Access

For the upper Dane valley, the public footpath northwards from Danebower to the Cat and Fiddle (SK009700 to SK000719) offers a good chance of moorland species in early spring before the rambling season intensifies. Look for Cheshire's only wild thyme on the roadside verges at the northern end. The lane below Cutthorn Hill (starting at SJ999686) and its continuation as a footpath up the brook is a good place for moorland edge species, as is the rocky slope alongside the minor road running eastward from the Rose and Crown at Allgreave (SJ973669). Access to the valley farther west is easy from Danebridge (SJ964651): a footpath follows the river downstream for 1 mile (1.6 km) before crossing into Staffordshire (SJ955641). The Shell Brook woods (SJ9463–SJ9466) are accessible by footpaths in places.

CALENDAR

All year: Red Grouse, Little Owl, Dipper, Grey Wagtail, Kingfisher, Common Buzzard, Sparrowhawk, woodland birds.

Spring–summer: European Golden Plover, Curlew, Meadow Pipit and Skylark return to the moors in March; Ring Ouzel and Northern Wheatear appear on scree slopes, where Cuckoos often perch in May; Wood Warbler, Common Redstart and Pied and Spotted Flycatchers sing in woods from late April.

67 SANDBACH FLASHES OS Landranger Map 118

Habitat

Sandbach Flashes is the name given to a series of 15 or so shallow pools formed during the last century as a result of salt mining. The flashes lie in a triangle between Sandbach, Middlewich and Crewe. The main flashes are in an area designated as an SSSI. The more than 230 species of birds recorded in the area make it one of Cheshire's premier birding areas. The larger flashes Watch Lane, Pump House, Elton Hall and the old lime settling beds, commonly known as the "salt pan", have muddy margins that are attractive to wading birds. Elton Hall Flashes are a diurnal roost for wildfowl. Watch Lane and several of the smaller flashes have marginal stands of reedmace (*Typha*) or reed-grass. *Phragmites* is spreading at Watch Lane. The most important *Typha* bed is at Fodens Flash, a small pool backed by a carr of alder and willow – the only woodland of consequence in the area. Across the road from Fodens Flash a partly derelict market garden is a useful cover of willow and hawthorn scrub. This site, and industrial wasteland in the area, furnishes a good supply of weed seed for winter finches and other birds. Sunken rushy areas in pastures and tall thorn hedges form further valuable habitats.

Despite rapid siltation of the Elton Hall flashes, intensification of agriculture in the surrounding fields and the drainage of Railway Farm Flash (done in spite of its SSSI status) the area remains one of the best in Cheshire for birdwatching.

Species

With over 230 species recorded to date, the flashes form one of the best-known birdwatching sites in Cheshire. Passage waders are perhaps fewer than formerly, but a good variety of winter wildfowl remain.

Spring passage begins in March. Little Ringed Plover is one of the first arrivals. Northern Wheatear passage traditionally starts around mid March, and birds linger long enough around rabbit burrows to give rise to suspicions of breeding. In late March and April, southwesterly winds and showers may bring large movements of Meadow Pipit. Feeding flocks spread out across the short turf bordering Watch Lane and other flashes in company with Reed Buntings, Pied, White and, later, Yellow Wagtails and, rarely, Water Pipits. Common Sandpipers, en route to their Pennine nesting streams, also mingle with these flocks, snapping at Yellow Dung Flies on cow pats. If the wind blows from the east in mid April, there is just a chance of a migrant Osprey.

Wader passage picks up gradually during April and May when more than a dozen species can be present. Most of the typical autumn species occur in small numbers. Arctic Ringed Plovers in May or early June may be accompanied by Sanderlings. Whimbrel, Greenshank, Black-tailed Godwit and Ruff pass through each spring. Recent rarities have included Temminck's Stint and Spotted Sandpiper. Approximately 30 species of wader have been recorded at Elton Hall Flash alone. Terns are also seen occasionally at this time.

Fodens Flash comes into its own during the summer months with Reed Buntings and Sedge and Reed Warblers nesting in the marsh; Great Crested Grebe, perhaps Ruddy Duck and Little Grebe breed on the flash; and Willow Tit, Treecreeper, Spotted Flycatcher, sometimes Lesser Spotted Woodpecker and possibly Water Rail frequent the carr. The adjacent market gardens are alive with Common Whitethroats in the nettle beds and Willow Warblers in the scrub. Bullfinch is common here, their presence betrayed by a thin whistle or a white rump glimpsed as a bird flies into a thorn bush.

The area of the flashes as a whole supports important breeding populations of several wetland species. Little Grebe is present on several of the smaller pools. Throughout the spring Great Crested Grebe can be seen displaying from the end of Watch Lane, at times very close to the car park. A pair of grebes will

Ruddy Duck

face each other so that they are almost touching, and shake their heads vigorously from side to side. In more advanced versions of this display the birds may rear up out of the water and shake limp waterweeds or algae in their bill. One other aquatic species nesting on all pools is the Coot. Throughout the breeding season territorial Coots may be seen rearing up out of the water and thrashing away with their legs and beak at any intruding rival, while non-breeders of the same species swim meekly in a sociable flock.

Shelduck nests annually. Birds return from the moult from December onwards and by spring they too are displaying aggressively. By the time the ducks are sitting on eggs, the drakes will be busy driving ducks of all species, and even Grey Herons, off their adopted flash. Few waders now breed, although Little Ringed Plover still nests in the area. Ringed Plover has also attempted to nest. Redshanks may be seen displaying from December onwards, but rarely settle at Sandbach.

Lesser Whitethroat nests in overgrown hedges at Watch Lane, Elton Hall and elsewhere, but is more often heard than seen. Little Owl breeds in hedgerow trees throughout the area. Its yelping calls are often heard by day, especially in showery weather. Corn Bunting and Yellow Wagtail are present around arable fields, but have become rather scarce recently. The local population of Yellow Wagtail is of particular interest since aberrant birds resembling Sykes' and Blue-headed Wagtails occur from time to time, and have been seen feeding young on several occasions. Summer can be quiet but June or July has produced rarities including Stilt Sandpiper, Spotted Sandpiper, White-winged Black Tern and Night Heron.

Return wader passage may begin by the end of June with the first Green Sandpiper, or perhaps a Greenshank or black-plumaged Spotted Redshank. Common Sandpiper passage peaks in July when a Turnstone or Sanderling may also occur and Green Sandpiper increases, its liquid calls carrying on the twilight air. Green Sandpipers have become a feature of autumn passage. Ruff, Green-shank and Spotted Redshank, and possibly a Wood Sandpiper may appear in August. Little Stints or Curlew Sandpipers may latch on to parties of Dunlin, and a godwit or Grey Plover may turn up, even quite late in the autumn. The flashes have provided several records of rare waders during the autumn including Pectoral Sandpiper, Wilson's Phalarope, Upland Sandpiper and Lesser Yellowlegs.

Autumn migrant passerines include Whinchat perched on fenceposts around Watch Lane (although numbers have decreased) and Common Redstart flickering along the hedgerows. The line of crack willows at Elton Hall provides rich pickings for passing warblers. A small but regular passage of Water and Rock Pipits is most obvious during the first few days of October when birds comb the edge of Watch Lane Flash, picking freshwater shrimps from among the debris. In some years Garganey is present among the Common Teal, but may often escape detection through its habit of sleeping for much of the day.

In winter Elton Hall Flashes is an excellent locality in which to see all the common dabbling duck species, with over 1,000 birds present at one time including Common Teal, Eurasian Wigeon, Pintail, Shoveler and Gadwall. Of particular interest is the flock of Pintail, which has visited the site annually since the 1960s. Numbers vary between 25 and 60 from year to year. Common Teal is the most numerous duck, with several hundred present at times. Eurasian Wigeon numbers up to 400 or more and is occasionally joined by an American Wigeon. Many Coots graze the pastures around the flash. In severe

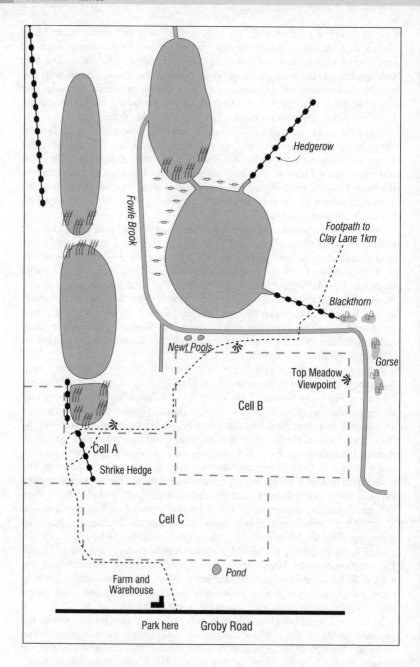

Hedgerow

Fowle Brook

*Footpath to
Clay Lane 1km*

Blackthorn

Newt Pools

Gorse

Top Meadow
Viewpoint

Cell B

Cell A

Shrike Hedge

Cell C

Pond

Farm and
Warehouse

Park here   Groby Road

weather less usual fowl appear, perhaps a family party of Bewick's or Whooper Swans or a small flock of White-fronted Geese.

So long as the weather remains mild large numbers of Northern Lapwing (up to 3,000 or more) feed on surrounding pastures and roost on the sludge bed at

Elton Hall. Snipe conceal themselves in the marshes and Jack Snipe occurs. Dunlin may be present through the winter, and a few Redshanks, Ruff, Curlews and European Golden Plovers wander down from their haunts around Northwich and Middlewich. The sloping field to the north of Pumphouse Flash regularly supports several dozen Moorhens. A flock of Skylark winters on the stubble fields between Elton Hall and Railway Flash – this species is remarkably local hereabouts at this season. Fieldfare and Redwing strip berries from the hedges and may fall prey to a Peregrine Falcon sallying out from a perch on a nearby electricity pylon. Great Grey Shrike has occurred in the past.

At Elton Hall as elsewhere, the behaviour of the large flocks of birds often gives warning of the presence of predators. A hovering Kestrel may elicit only local consternation among the smaller waders and Starlings. A passing Merlin or soaring Sparrowhawk will cause the Northern Lapwing flocks to scramble. The impending arrival of a Peregrine Falcon or migrant harrier (rare here) causes panic among the ducks as well.

Rare species that have occurred at Elton Hall Flash in past winters include Common Crane, Great White Egret and Lesser Scaup.

Watch Lane holds a few diving ducks in winter, but it freezes over rapidly. Ducks and Great Crested Grebes are then displaced to the coast. A few Jack Snipe winter in the *Typha* beds along with Water Rail. A Green Sandpiper may feed in the northeastern corner of the flash. The pool below the canal sometimes attracts a Kingfisher. Stonechat is a regular winter resident in the area when its population is at a high level, and can be seen perched on thistle stems and fence posts.

In winter Fodens Flash is a good place to see Water Rail. This shy bird performs particularly well in frosty weather, when they feed by open puddles or ditches in the willow carr. Willow Tit is resident, providing as good a place as any to get to know this species because Marsh Tit is almost unknown here. A long-established roost of Magpies in scrub behind the flash has held over 470 birds. Long-eared Owl has been recorded in at least three winters roosting in scrub.

Timing

In spring, showery weather from a southerly quarter or misty days are more likely to bring down migrants, as is wet or stormy weather in the autumn. Winter duck numbers tend to increase during the day as feeding birds are flushed off field ponds and minor flashes back to the roosts. Prolonged frosts concentrate waterfowl at Elton Hall where the River Wheelock provides some open water.

Access

Turn south off the A533 Middlewich to Sandbach road by The Fox public house just north of Sandbach station. Continue around the perimeter of the lorry works until you reach a narrow humpback bridge over the canal (SJ733611). For Fodens Flash turn right immediately at this bridge and park at the roadside by the flash shortly after the first corner. A bridle path runs westward through the carr just beyond the flash. For Watch Lane Flash return to the canal bridge and take the other fork. Turn left by the telephone box into Red Lane and continue round until Watch Lane appears as a minor road joining from the right. Car parking at the end of Watch Lane (SJ727606) allows good views of the flash. To reach Elton Hall take roads around the eastern side of the flash, viewing at intervals over the hedges. Turn right at the main road past the chemical works, then left after two-thirds of a mile (1 km) at the first crossroads. This road runs between Elton Hall Flash to the east (SJ725595) and Pumphouse Flash. Visitors should not wander off the roads at Elton Hall or Watch Lane.

CALENDAR

All year: Great Crested and Little Grebes, Mute Swan, Shelduck, Northern Lapwing, Dunlin (not breeding); Little Owl along hedgerows; Willow Tit and Bullfinch are common at Fodens Flash.

December–February: Eurasian Wigeon, Common Teal and Pintail at Elton Hall; Water Rail at Fodens; Northern Lapwing and Common Snipe widespread; a few Ruff and perhaps a Jack Snipe or Green Sandpiper; Sparrowhawk and sometimes Peregrine Falcon hunt the area; a few Stonechats in mild winters. Magpies form a huge roost at Fodens Flash.

March–May: Breeding waders appear in March and April, followed by passage birds in April and May – Little Ringed Plover, Ringed Plover, Oystercatcher, Common Sandpiper and other species. White and Yellow Wagtails may join flocks of Meadow Pipit and Reed Bunting. Northern Wheatear from late March. Wildfowl depart and summer visitors arrive.

June–July: Breeding species include Little and Great Crested Grebes and Ruddy Duck, Little Ringed Plover by flashes and on waste ground, Reed and Sedge Warblers, Common Whitethroat and Spotted Flycatcher at Fodens Flash; Lesser Whitethroat and Reed Bunting widespread. Wader passage resumes in July.

August–November: Autumn duck flocks may include one or two Garganey sleeping among the Common Teal; a sprinkling of passage waders; in October, winter visitors arrive including Water Rail; duck flocks build up in late autumn.

---

68 MARBURY COUNTRY PARK AND WITTON LIME BEDS
OS Landranger Map 118

Habitat

The cluster of sites lying to the north of Northwich offer a considerable diversity of habitats, encompassing woodland, fresh water, reedbeds and industrial sludge tanks. Access has been improved greatly in recent years as part of the Mersey Forest initiative. A number of threats to develop the area, most recently for a proposed national angling centre, would destroy much of the ornithological interest, but have so far been resisted.

Northwich lies at the heart of the Cheshire salt and chemical industry. Consequently a great deal of land has been left in a rough state, with plentiful scrub and coarse grassland. Flashes and subsidence pools formed as a consequence of underground brine pumping have been used as sludge beds for lime-rich waste. They may contain pools of shallow water following rain and are then attractive to waders and wildfowl. Budworth Mere and Pickmere may also have formed as a consequence of the dissolution of rock salt, but by natural means and much longer ago.

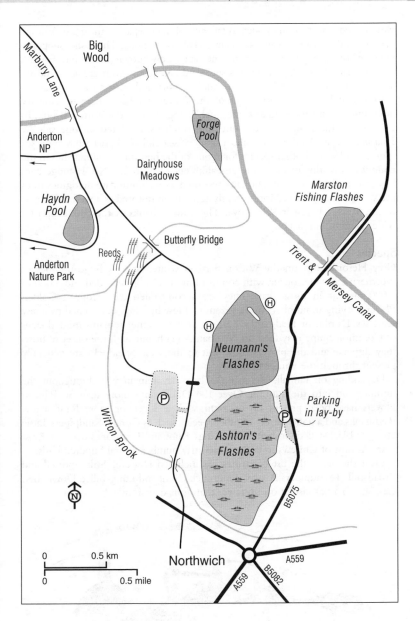

68A WITTON FLASHES AND BUTTERFINCH BRIDGE
OS ref: SJ665750 and SJ661753

. . . .

Habitat
The huge Witton Flashes (SJ665750 and SJ661753) have been filled with alkali
waste and now resemble sludge beds. Shallow rainwater pools form in wet

weather and attract passing waders. A tall embankment separates the grassy Ashton's Flash from the relatively bare Neumann's Flash to the north. The flashes support a range of lime-loving flowers that are otherwise hardly known in Cheshire: fragrant orchid, hoary mustard, ploughman's spikenard and yellow-wort are all abundant. The area in general is well endowed with hawthorn and other scrub.

Immediately to the north-west of the Witton Flashes a narrow tributary flows underneath the road at Butterfinch Bridge to join the Witton Brook. To the west of the road it widens out onto mudflats, bordered on one side by *Phragmites* reeds. To the other side a stand of sea club-rush, sea aster, lesser sea spurrey and several other species form one of the best inland saltmarshes in the county. Above this marsh is the embankment of Marbury No. 1 sludge bed, now called Haydons pool. This tank was used to accommodate dredgings from the Weaver Navigation. More recently it has been restored as a wetland as part of the Mersey Forest in Vale Royal. The flowery banks of the tank support a wide range of butterflies.

Species

Grey Herons roost on the Witton flats on winter days. A huge number of Northern Lapwings occur, with counts of up to 11,000 recorded and 3,000 to 5,000 present in most years. They are accompanied by European Golden Plover, varying in numbers from dozens to a few hundred, and joined by a few Curlews, Dunlin or Redshanks. So long as the weather remains mild, dozens of Common Snipe may feed on Neumann's Flash, but with the onset of frosts they disperse and the plovers move out to the west. Shelducks are generally present through the winter months.

Depending on rainfall, Neumann's Flash may remain wet throughout the summer and into the autumn. Over 100 Dunlin and more than 50 Ringed Plovers have been present on occasion, with a dozen or more Ruff, a few Redshanks and a good variety of other species, such as Curlew Sandpipers, Little Stints or Black-tailed Godwits. Sanderlings, Knot and Turnstones occur in most years. A roost of Curlews in late summer may number several hundred birds.

Over the years, the list of rarities has included Dotterel, Stilt, Spotted and Broad-billed Sandpipers, Avocet, Temminck's Stint and Long-billed Dowitcher. Caspian Tern has visited on no fewer than four occasions.

Curlew

Both Ringed and Little Ringed Plovers breed, and Shelduck does so in the vicinity. In winter, small parties of ducks of various species may dabble by flood pools at Witton. Water Rail lurks in the Butterfinch Bridge reedbed.

Scrubland species nesting locally include Common and Lesser Whitethroats and Garden Warbler, with a few pairs of Grasshopper Warbler in bramble thickets and Reed Warbler beside Witton Brook. Long-tailed and Willow Tits are common. A few pairs of Meadow Pipit nest among rough grass at the sides of the sludge tanks – the species is absent in summer from much of the Cheshire plain. Northern Wheatear occurs along the embankments on passage.

In winter a Blackcap or Chiffchaff may be found in the scrub, and towards dusk Pied Wagtails may gather on the mud at Witton before flying off west at sunset towards Winnington. Two scarce visitors have been Great Grey Shrike (seen in several winters) and Long-eared Owl roosting in thorn scrub. Woodcocks often roost beneath the scrub, favouring the insulation of ever-green species such as holly.

Haydons Pool (formerly Marbury No. 1 Bed) regularly attracts small numbers of Common Teal, Common Snipe and other waders and ducks. Wood Sandpiper has been seen in several recent autumns. Common Teal numbers increase into the hundreds in winter, when Green Sandpipers are often present.

Timing

Plover flocks are at their largest around full moon in autumn and early winter. Severe weather soon drives them westwards. Wader passage is best in wet weather in May to June and August to October. Visits at any time of day may be rewarding. Dusk visits are advisable to hear Grasshopper Warbler in summer and to see the wagtail flocks in winter.

Access

From a roundabout on the A559 to the east of Northwich town centre take Leicester Street westward towards the waste disposal site and supermarkets. The flashes are visible behind an embankment to the north. Take the first turning to the right, called Old Warrington Road at its southern end, but renamed Marbury Lane beyond the tip entrance. Continue across the metal bridge and look for a gateway on the right, from which a stile leads to a path up the embankment. View from this point through a telescope, or walk north along the embankment until reaching an opening through the fence, which leads to two screens overlooking Neumann's Flash. Do not venture onto either of the flashes. Butterfinch Bridge and Marbury No. 1 Bed lie a third of a mile (0.5 km) to the north along this same road. Limited parking is sometimes possible in a wide seldom-used gateway to the east of the road. All gateways are used by tenant farmers and rangers and should not be blocked, nor should the roadside passing places.

A footpath has been constructed alongside Witton Brook and reedbed. This continues through scrub towards Anderton Nature Park. A path leads up the eastern side of Marbury No.1 Tank to the Haydon Hide from which wildfowl and waders may be viewed. A silent approach is recommended.

CALENDAR

All year: Grey Herons roost at Neumann's Flash; scrubland species include Long-tailed and Willow Tits.

December–February: Flocks of Northern Lapwing, European Golden Plover and Common Snipe roost by day; a few Redshank and Ruff may winter; Pied Wagtails gather in large numbers at dusk prior to roosting; Water Rail at Butterfinch Bridge; possibility of Long-eared Owl, Blackcap or Chiffchaff.

March–May: Gull and plover flocks disperse; light wader passage; Redshank and Ringed and Little Ringed Plovers display; scrubland comes to life as warblers arrive and take up territory.

June–July: Breeding waders and Shelducks may have young; warblers – Grasshopper, Reed and Garden Warblers, Common and Lesser Whitethroats among others – continue to sing well into June; Northern Lapwing flocks start to gather by the end of June; the first passage waders appear in July.

August–November: Wader passage at its most varied and plover flocks increase in size; juvenile warblers roam the scrub, sometimes with mixed flocks of tits, and in September taking berries from elder and other bushes, and perhaps utter subdued practice songs before departing. Lesser Black-backed Gulls may gather in a diurnal roost at Neumann's.

68B BUDWORTH (MARBURY) MERE AND PICK MERE

OS ref: SJ 655768 and 683772

Habitat

The country park lies within the grounds of the now-demolished Marbury Hall. It consists for the most part of dog-walking grassland. The scrub that provided much ornithological interest has now largely been cleared away, but there a mature planted woodland of mixed broadleaved trees with some conifers encircles the park.

The mere, referred to as Budworth Mere to distinguish it from Marbury Mere near Whitchurch, is fringed by a narrow belt of *Phragmites* reeds for much of its perimeter. In places these reeds thicken out to form substantial beds, notably at the western end where a small woodland reserve has been set aside as a memorial to T. A. Coward, the great Cheshire naturalist. Other parts of the shoreline are subject to grazing and trampling by cattle. A sandy spit by the mouth of the Kid Brook on the north bank attracts bathing gulls and sometimes waders. The mere is subject to heavy disturbance from a sailing club based at the eastern end and by members of the public visiting the park.

Species

The mere seldom supports large numbers of wildfowl, but most of the common species occur regularly in winter. Frequent counting has produced occasional totals of more than 100 Eurasian Wigeon and 200 each of Pochard and Tufted Duck. A few Common Goldeneye are usually present, and Cormorants fly in from Rostherne. The mere attracts more than its fair share of divers and the rarer grebes, with one or two in most winters. Canada Goose is becoming more frequent and skeins of Pink-footed Goose pass over occasionally in midwinter. Bittern is seen regularly in winter or spring.

The reedbeds attract a good variety of waterbirds in spring. Gadwall and Shoveler have displayed in recent years, and the latter species has bred successfully. Tufted Ducks nest annually, as do Little and Great Crested Grebes.

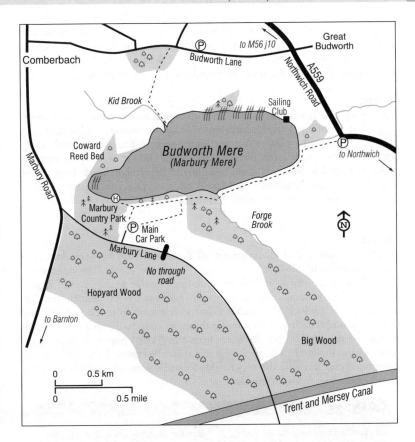

Ruddy Ducks may be present through the summer. Reed Warblers visit from late April, by which time the wintering Water Rails have departed. Kingfisher and Grey Wagtail nest in the vicinity. When Kingfisher numbers are high following mild winters, birds are often seen dashing low over the water within a few feet of the mereside footpath, their approach being heralded by a ringing "chee" call. A heronry held 80 nests in 1994.

Spring passage over and by the mere involves essentially the same species as at Tatton Mere (site 52), but Sand Martins tend to arrive here even earlier in March and Common Sandpipers are generally better represented. Oystercatcher may occur at this time. Other passage waders are more likely to be seen in autumn, when Dunlin, Green Sandpiper or Redshank may feed at the mouth of Kid Brook. Terns visit Budworth more regularly and in better numbers than at any other inland site in the county. Black Terns are more likely to appear in the autumn, but Common and Arctic Terns usually appear on both migrations. Little Gull is seen occasionally and Common Scoters may drop in.

All three species of woodpeckers nest locally. The woodlands fringing the park hold a good variety of birds including plentiful Long-tailed Tit and Nuthatch, with Blackcap, Spotted Flycatcher and Chiffchaff in summer. Marsh Tit still occurs, but is now rare. The first Chiffchaff often sings at the mereside well before the end of March.

Pick Mere, a little over 1 mile (2 km) to the east of Budworth Mere, attracts a similar range of species in winter and on passage, but lacks the woodland species. Its margins support Sedge and Reed Warblers and Reed Bunting. Damp fields alongside the mere are popular with migrant pipits and wagtails.

Timing

The sailing club is active on most days with even remotely favourable weather. The presence of boats concentrates waterfowl in the western end, where they may be disturbed by visitors to the country park: in fine weather only early morning visits are advisable. Tern passage is most likely in wet, windy weather from mid April to June and again from July to September. Black Terns arrive especially on easterly winds. Pick Mere is often worth a visit at passage times, especially during showery weather in spring. Winter visits may turn up unusual waterfowl.

Access

Marbury Country Park is signposted off the minor road between Anderton and Comberbach (SJ648763). Otherwise it may be reached by continuing northward up the private road from Butterfinch Bridge to the pay and display car park. There is open access to the southwestern shores of the mere through the park. To reach Pick Mere either follow minor roads from the park, turning right in Comberbach and continuing through Great Budworth to Pickmere village, or take the B5391 eastwards from the A559 Lostock to Warrington road. From Pickmere village follow signs for Pickmere Lake. Park at the fairground end and walk the very muddy footpath along the south bank of the mere, examining fields for migrants.

CALENDAR

All year: Woodland birds include Nuthatch, Treecreeper, Long-tailed and perhaps Marsh Tit, and all three woodpeckers; Great Crested and Little Grebes frequent the meres all year unless driven off by frosts; Grey Heron and Kingfisher seen daily.

December–February: Wildfowl include Pochard, Goldeneye, Eurasian Wigeon and Common Teal; Pink-footed Geese fly overhead occasionally and rare grebes or divers are seen most winters; Cormorants fish in the meres; Water Rail and Common Snipe frequent boggy parts of shoreline.

March–May: Sand Martin and Chiffchaff arrive by the end of March with other hirundines and Swift following in April;

Common Sandpiper and occasionally other waders pass through in April and May; waterfowl take up residence by reedbeds; terns and sometimes a Little Gull may feed over meres.

June–July: Residents and summer visitors busy feeding young, including Reed Warbler, Blackcap and Spotted Flycatcher; Common Tern, and perhaps other tern species, visits occasionally.

August–November: Terns pass through in appropriate conditions until September; a few waders such as Dunlin, Redshank and Green Sandpiper until October, when winter wildfowl return.

Contact: Friends of Anderton and Marbury, Alan Garner c/o Marbury Country Park, Comberbach, Cheshire Cottage, London Road, Allostock, Knutsford, Cheshire, WA16 9LT.

69 WOOLSTON EYES

OS Landranger Map 109
SJ68

Habitat

The Eyes Conservation Group in agreement with the Manchester Ship Canal Company manages the huge sludge tanks at the Woolston Deposit Grounds SSSI in part as a nature reserve. Part of the site is still used to accommodate dredgings from the Ship Canal. The site has been altered extensively in recent years. No. 3 Bed is a large area of water with reedy fringes. It holds a large colony of Black-headed Gulls and up to 35 Black-necked Grebes, which use the gull colony as protection from predators such as larger gulls.

Species

More than 200 species have been recorded at the Eyes, including all five European grebes, the three woodpeckers, and four species of owl. The principal interest lies in the huge populations of breeding warblers and in the waterfowl that favour the shallow pools.

Lying next to the Mersey, the flooded tanks attract large numbers of dabbling ducks that move inland from the estuary. The Mersey valley Pochard flock also spends time here in winter. Up to 1,000 or more Common Teal are present at this season, with dozens of Mallard, Shoveler, Tufted Duck and Pintail. Other ducks occur less frequently or in smaller numbers, and scarce or rare species such as Ferruginous and Long-tailed Ducks, Green-winged Teal, Common Scoter and Smew have been noted. In late autumn and winter Pink-footed Geese occasionally fly over and have been known to alight briefly.

The extensive shallow marshes form excellent nesting habitat for wildfowl. Common Teal, Shoveler, Mallard, Pochard, Tufted Duck and Ruddy Duck are all present through the summer. Gadwall nests here in increasing numbers. Pintail, Eurasian Wigeon and Garganey have lingered in some years. Broods of Tufted and Ruddy Ducks may appear in July and August respectively; young of the various dabbling ducks remain hidden in the marsh and are less easy to see. A few pairs of Little Grebe arrive in spring and stay to nest.

The Eyes support important nesting populations of several marshland birds. More than 200 singing Sedge Warblers and over 100 Reed Buntings are present in summer, with smaller numbers of Reed Warbler. A pair of Marsh Warblers bred in one recent summer, an occurrence that is unlikely to be repeated. Water Rail may be heard squealing at any time of the year and sometimes nest. Bearded Tit has now breed, as has Cetti's Warbler since the first arrival 20 years ago. Marsh Harrier is a regular spring and autumn passage migrant. Emergent tussocks provide nest sites for several hundred pairs of Black-headed Gull, whose presence may attract a migrant Little or Mediterranean Gull in spring. Hundreds of swifts often feed overhead.

Rank grass and brambles on the embankments contain Grasshopper Warbler and Common Whitethroat; Willow Warbler sings from taller scrub. Blackcap and Willow Tit nest along the more wooded stretches of riverbank, where Kingfishers are often seen. Sand Martins nest in the banks of the Ship Canal.

The scrub and *Typha* on No. 3 Bed hold large roosts of Starlings from spring to autumn, comprising thousands of birds at times. In some autumns Pied Wagtails roost. In most years there is a Swallow roost that may contain

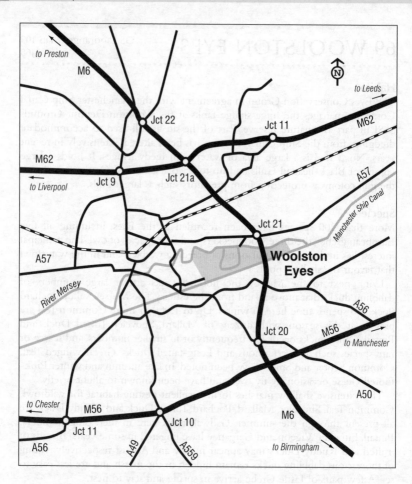

thousands of birds. A Hobby often attends the roost and has provided some spectacular performances. From October to early winter hundreds of Redwings and other thrushes may shelter by night. Mist netting by day has revealed significant passage of Reed Bunting and various other passerines through the Eyes. Warblers and Goldcrest pass through in moderate numbers. In winter, roosts dwindle as food supplies diminish, although Magpies seldom seem to go hungry and continue to roost in the scrub. One or two Chiffchaffs remain in the willow scrub during most winters. Merlin is seen annually in very small numbers and on occasion a Short-eared Owl hunts over grassy areas. A Peregrine Falcon may visit from time to time.

Changes in the pumping regime into the tanks mean that few waders now visit, but Common Snipe is regularly present in the marshes. Its numbers are notoriously difficult to estimate. Rarities recorded at the No. 1 Bed include a Chimney Swift seen on 5 November 2005 (accepted as the first Cheshire record). Other unusual sightings in recent years include a number of Great White Egrets, Bee-eater and a Blyth's Reed Warbler.

Timing

There is always something to be seen at Woolston Eyes. Even nocturnal visits might produce an array of surprising noises from species such as Water Rail and Spotted Crake. Morning visits are generally most productive for birdsong. Unwitting members of the public standing on the skyline may flush waterfowl from the tanks, so morning visits may also produce better views of waterfowl.

Access

Access is strictly limited to permit holders. There is no longer access to No. 1 Bed for security reasons (it lies directly under the viaduct). A public path skirts No. 2 Bed, but viewing other than from hides is likely to disturb the birds and should not be attempted. Permits are available at a cost of £8 per year (£16 for a family) from Brian Ankers, 9 Lynton Gardens, Appleton, Warrington, Cheshire WA4 5ED. A stamped addressed envelope (A5) should be enclosed and cheques made payable to the Eyes Conservation Group (WECG). There is an additional one-off payment of £10 for a key to the gate. A permit entitles the holder to visit the Eyes throughout the year and use the hides.

The Eyes is not an easy reserve to find. For visitors from outside the area the best approach is by leaving the M6 at Junction 21 and taking the A57 signposted to Warrington. After some 200 yards (200 m) turn left down Weir Lane and park by Woolston Weir (SJ654888) or in more secure settings close to houses. All permit holders receive a map of the reserve that gives details of the best viewing points and notice of which areas are out of bounds. Further information can be found at www.woolstoneyes.co.uk.

CALENDAR

All year: Common Teal, Shoveler, Pochard, Tufted Duck; Water Rail, Common Snipe, Black-headed Gull, Kingfisher, Willow Tit.

December–February: Wildfowl including Pintail and diving ducks; Pink-footed Goose occasional overhead; Short-eared Owl, Peregrine Falcon and Merlin occasionally hunt over reserve; Magpie roost in scrub where a few Chiffchaffs often winter.

March–May: Black-necked and Little Grebes return; Ruddy and other ducks take up territory; winter wildfowl may linger and show signs of nesting; Reed Buntings appear from March; warblers arrive in April and May.

June–July: Wildfowl broods include Tufted Duck and Gadwall; the gull colony bustles with activity; hundreds of Swifts may wheel overhead; warbler song tails off in July; Starling roosts in thousands.

August–November: Ruddy Duck broods still appearing in August; Shoveler increases in September and October; Common Snipe returns; warblers depart during August and September, when birds from outside the area pass through; Swallow roosts in early autumn are replaced by incoming thrushes in October; Goldcrest and Reed Bunting pass through in October; by November large numbers of Common Teal have usually returned.

70 MOORE NATURE RESERVE

OS Landranger Map 108 SJ 58

Habitat

Moore Nature Reserve includes alder woodland, rough grassland and two sizeable pools fringed by reeds. The gorse scrub that once housed many breeding birds has largely been cleared, but there are areas of sparsely vegetated sandy ground where gorse is beginning to re-grow. Between the reserve and the River Mersey there are areas of arable land and coarse grassland, some of this now being lost to Mersey Forest plantations. A large refuse dump has replaced a once excellent reedbed and has attracted a Black Kite. The mudflats of the River Mersey are a further interesting habitat, and the Manchester Ship Canal and flooded sand quarry to south of the reserve attract a few waterfowl.

Species

The alder woodlands have closed high canopies and attract a limited range of species including Willow Tit, Treecreeper and all three woodpeckers. In winter large flocks of Siskin are generally present in the woodlands. Reed Buntings feed on grass seeds in rough, open areas. Elusive Long-eared Owls favour areas of dense scrub.

In summer Common Whitethroat is plentiful where scrub and rank grassland meet, while Grasshopper Warbler favours stands of bramble and willow herb. The reedbeds around the pools shelter Sedge and Reed Warblers in summer. Several pairs of Little Grebe nest, as do a couple of pairs of Black-necked Grebe. Gadwall is seen with some regularity, but waterfowl are more varied in autumn and winter when small parties of Common Teal, Eurasian Wigeon and Shoveler visit. Pochard and Tufted and Ruddy Ducks are more likely to be seen on the deeper, western pool.

The sandpit south of the Ship Canal attracts Tufted Duck, Goldeneye and infrequent Scaup. To west of the reserve, a bend of the River Mersey approaches to within 65 feet (20 m) of the Ship Canal by Randell's Sluice. The river is estuarine here and low tide reveals areas of exposed mud. Flocks of up to 10,000 Northern Lapwings with up to several hundred European Golden Plovers are present through the winter. Other waders occur according to season and depending on tides elsewhere in the Mersey estuary. Up to 200 Dunlin and parties of Curlew visit; Redshank, Ruff and Black-tailed Godwit also visit. Less common species occur occasionally.

Predators such as Peregrine Falcon and Short-eared Owl sometimes wander by, attracted by the wader flocks along the river or small mammals in the rough grassland. Cormorants and Great Crested Grebes now fish in both the river and the Ship Canal – evidence of improving water quality from the industrial parts of the catchment area. Diving ducks occasionally visit from the lagoons of Fiddlers Ferry power station to north of the river. Gulls that feed on the rubbish dump visit the river to bathe. Glaucous, Iceland and Ring-billed Gulls are seen from time to time, and there is a single record of Franklin's Gull.

Arable fields attract Stock Dove, Tree Sparrow, Linnet, Yellowhammer and Corn Bunting. Fieldfare and Redwing feed on berries in the tall hedges.

Oystercatcher sometimes nests, and Shelduck can be seen prospecting for nest sites in spring.

Timing
The network of footpaths attracts many dog walkers, who tend to flush wary birds off the western lake. Morning visits are advisable. However, this is an extensive area and quiet places can always be found to watch birds in scrub, woodland or reedbeds, and on the mudflats at Randell's Sluice.

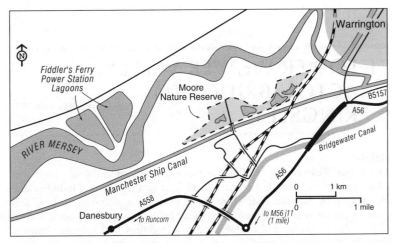

Access
From Moore village take Moore Lane in a northwesterly direction, signposted to various haulage firms. At the end of this road cross the swing bridge (SJ578853) over the ship canal into Lapwing Lane, taking the rough track which continues straight ahead, rather than following the surfaced road to the right. After a third of a mile (0.5 km) the track widens to form a parking space. From here paths lead westward along the bed of a dry canal – passing a screen from which 'Lapwing Lake' can be viewed – or eastward towards the reedbed pool a mile or so (2 km) distant. Alternatively, from the A56 at Lower Walton follow the main road north across the ship canal, taking the second turning on the left into Taylor Street then first right into Eastford Road. This continues as a track under the railway bridge from where it is a short walk westward to the reedbed pool (SJ5986).

From Lapwing Lane footpaths lead westward past the arable fields of reclaimed Norton Marsh and along a rough track parallel to the Ship Canal. After around a mile (1.5–2 km) view the Mersey mudbanks.

CALENDAR

All year: Common waterbirds including Little Grebe; resident woodland species including Willow Tit and woodpeckers.

December–February: Wildfowl include a few Gadwall, Common Teal, Eurasian Wigeon, Pochard and Tufted Duck; finch and sparrow flocks in weedy areas; possibility of Peregrine Falcon, Short-eared and Long-eared Owls; Cormorant, Northern Lapwing, European Golden Plover and loafing gulls (which may include rarer species) on the Mersey.

March–May: Sand Martins arrive along ship canal and Mersey; passage Northern Wheatears on sandy areas; breeding warblers arrive and passage birds visit the woodlands and scrub.

June–July: Breeding Reed, Sedge and Grasshopper Warblers, Common Whitethroat

and Willow Warbler; Little Grebe and other waterbirds with young.

August–November: Wildfowl return, including Shoveler; warblers mingle with tit flocks in scrub; Northern Lapwing flocks build up on the Mersey, where there may additional wader species.

71 LOWER WEAVER VALLEY: ACTON BRIDGE TO KINGSLEY

OS Landranger Map 117
SJ57

Habitat

The River Weaver was canalised to facilitate the export of salt from the Cheshire wiches. It is still used on a small scale by the chemical industry, and increasingly by pleasure craft. Continuous dredging is necessary to keep the canal open; silt is pumped into large riverside lagoons to drain. Such sludge tanks at Acton Bridge and Kingsley are both excellent bird habitats, showing quite different stages of vegetation succession. At Acton Bridge recent pumping has left areas of open mud and small pools with low, marshy vegetation, although nettles and coarse grasses are spreading rapidly. At Kingsley, where the lagoon has been unused for some years, a *Phragmites* reedbed has developed with scrubby margins and a sizeable, shallow pool. Reeds fringe the Weaver in places, notably by the side channel to Dutton locks. There are further reedy cut-off pools between here and Kingsley.

The valley bottom is farmed intensively (both arable and dairy) and there are a number of ancient woods on the steeper valley sides. Warburton's Wood at Kingsley is a particularly good example, and a Cheshire Wildlife Trust reserve. In May the blossom on the wild cherry trees can be spectacular. Small-leaved lime and wild service tree are present – both are rare in the county – and many unusual fungi appear in autumn.

Species

In winter small numbers of dabbling ducks feed at the sludge beds, but note that Kingsley is shot over on occasions. Reed Buntings pick seeds from flattened grasses at both sites, and Water Rails lurk in the Kingsley reeds. Tree Sparrows and Yellowhammers flock to stubble fields, where Corn Buntings may join them. A wintering Green Sandpiper may feed at Acton Bridge, or rise unexpectedly from the side of the Weaver. Common Snipe is regular in damp ground, along with a Jack Snipe or two. From mid afternoon parties of gulls drop in at Acton Bridge to bathe before roosting on the Mersey estuary.

April brings passage migrants to the valley. White and Yellow Wagtails dart around the pools at Acton Bridge. Common Whitethroats dance over the

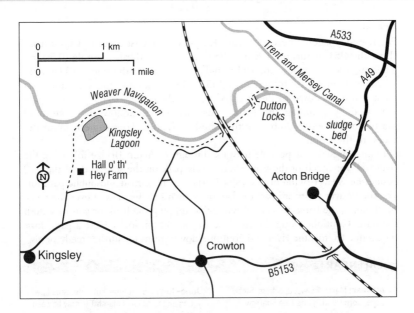

banks and Lesser Whitethroats rattle from cover. Depending on the state of the tanks, Sedge Warblers may settle, and Reed Warblers sing from the Dutton reeds. Common Sandpipers flicker along the river, and may hop over the bank on to the sludge bed perhaps to join a Green Sandpiper or two. In May, wader passage increases, provided that recent pumping has left an expanse of open mud. Dunlin, parties of arctic Ringed Plovers and other species, such as Greenshank, may drop in. Cuckoos sometimes occur in small migrant parties, calling noisily from the telephone wires above the riverbank and gliding down to snap up caterpillars.

At Kingsley, Reed and Sedge Warblers take up territories in the reedbed and a Grasshopper Warbler or two may reel in bramble patches. Cuckoos enter the reeds and may lay in Reed Warbler nests – an unusual occurrence these days. Towards dusk a Water Rail may start its eerie calling. Various scrubland birds breed around the lagoon. Look for broods of Mallards, Coots, Little Grebes and other waterbirds on the open water.

Great and Lesser Spotted Woodpeckers are resident in the woodlands, along with other typical woodland species. Marsh Tit remains numerous along the Weaver valley.

Autumn brings Shoveler, Common Teal and perhaps a Garganey to the sludge beds. Green Sandpiper is regular, and a few other waders visit. Small passerines feed in the muddy tanks following pumping, especially pipits, wagtails and Reed Bunting. Stock Doves join Yellowhammers in stubble fields.

Timing
Early morning visits are likely to be most productive at Acton Bridge, but any time of day will do provided that recent pumping has left muddy pools to attract wildfowl and waders. Unless shooting is taking place, the Kingsley lagoons are less prone to disturbance.

Access

For Kingsley lagoon, head east from Kingsley village (southeast of Frodsham) along the B5153, turning left into Ball Lane after a third of a mile (0.5 km). There is space to park at the right-angled bend where the track to Hall o'th' Hey farm branches off to the north (SJ557758). Walk up to the farm and a cart track continues down to the river. At the riverbank turn right for the lagoon – viewed by climbing the bank – or turn left to follow the bottom of Warburton's Wood. Members of the Cheshire Wildlife Trust can obtain further access to the wood.

From Kingsley it is possible to walk through to Acton Bridge following the riverbank for much of the way. Alternatively park on the side road off the A49 beside the Weaver swing bridge (SJ601761). A private road and public path follow the Weaver westward past the lagoon, which may be viewed over the fence by climbing the bank. Be careful when first topping the bank or you may flush the birds. Continue along the riverside to the Dutton locks. Here a path skirts the reedbed. Cross the river and continue downstream for further reedy pools.

CALENDAR

All year: Marsh Tit, woodpeckers, Stock Dove, Corn Bunting and Tree Sparrow.

December–February: Small numbers of waterfowl, Green Sandpiper, Water Rail and Reed Bunting.

March–May: Waders such as Ringed Plover, Little Ringed Plover, Green and Common Sandpipers and Dunlin may occur at Acton Bridge when the tank is wet; warblers here and at Kingsley include Reed, Sedge and Grasshopper; Cuckoo often conspicuous.

June–July: A quiet time, but waterbirds have young and families of Marsh Tits may be seen in the woodlands; wader passage resumes in July.

August–November: Wader passage continues; dabbling ducks gather in eclipse plumage; Stock Dove, buntings and other seed-eaters in stubble fields or weedy tanks.

72 FRODSHAM MARSH AND THE WEAVER BEND

OS Landranger Map 117
SJ47, 57

Habitat

The Mersey estuary supports internationally important wildfowl and wader populations but is inaccessible to the casual birdwatcher for the most part. An exception is Frodsham Marshes – a stretch of flat grazing marsh between the M56 motorway and Manchester Ship Canal – together with the 'estuary' of the River Weaver, which flows into the canal.

Frodsham Score lies to the north of Manchester Ship Canal and consists of an area of closely cropped turf bordering the tidal mudflats of the Mersey. Although the estuary is severely polluted by the various chemical works in the vicinity, considerable numbers of Shelduck and waders feed out on the mud.

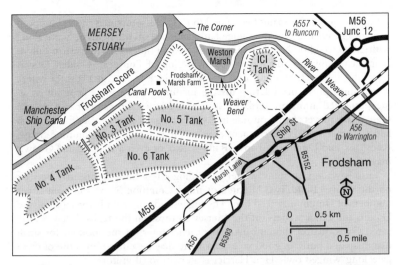

Much of Frodsham Marsh consists of huge sludge tanks into which dredgings from the Ship Canal are pumped to drain. The tanks ultimately revert to pasture, but while still wet they may form habitats of outstanding value for wildfowl and waders. The new No. 6 tank contains drowned hedgerows and stands of *Phragmites* reed that have grown out from the drainage ditches of the embanked former farmland. Bulldozing during construction work on the retaining banks of the tanks often results in a good crop of weed seed on the disturbed ground. Established banks develop a cover of scrub and rough grassland.

The low-lying fields on the remainder of the marsh are bordered by tall berry-bearing thorn hedges and drained by deep ditches that contain stands of reed. Some fields are devoted to cereal crops, the resultant stubble providing winter feed for many birds.

The Weaver Bend consists of a meander of the river Weaver extending 2 miles (3.2 km) between the motorway bridge and the Ship Canal, where it overflows into the estuary through the Weaver Sluice. The Bend contains extensive mudbanks, which may be exposed at low tide, depending on the operation of locks and sluices on the canal. These banks, and the riversides which are lined with marsh vegetation in places, attract wildfowl and waders.

Species

In winter a wide range of wildfowl visit Weaver Bend. Tufted Duck and Pochard feed near the junction with the Ship Canal and may be joined by a few Scaup, often brown immature birds. Common Goldeneye visits in small numbers and one or two redhead Smew are infrequent visitors. Ruddy Ducks arrive in severe weather when the flow of the river keeps the Bend open after meres have frozen. Cormorants and Great Crested Grebes are also likely to appear under such conditions. Scarcer diving ducks, including Long-tailed Duck and Ring-necked Duck, have been recorded. Numbers of surface-feeding ducks fluctuate widely, not least because of early morning visits of wildfowlers. A flock of Canada Geese has taken up residence. Bewick's and more rarely Whooper Swans are infrequent visitors. Small flocks of grey geese, usually either Pink-footed or White-fronted, occasionally alight on the marsh.

Many other birds inhabit the fields. Up to 1,000, sometimes more, European Golden Plovers roost on the sludge tanks and feed on the fields or Score along with 2,000 to 3,000 Northern Lapwings. Several times a day the alarm calls of Northern Lapwings and the excited whistling of European Golden Plovers signal the approach of a predator. The whole flock rises with a rush of wings, which must prove bewildering for the incoming Peregrine Falcon, often an inexperienced immature bird. A visit from a Merlin also causes panic, despite these heavy plovers being outside the typical range of prey species for the small falcon. Other waders attach themselves to the plover flocks: Common Snipe, Redshank and Dunlin, perhaps a Ruff or two, or even a Black-tailed Godwit may attend.

Various waders, in some winters including a few Little Stints, may be seen on the Weaver Bend. Two hundred or more Common Snipe and even larger numbers of Dunlin may feed here. The highest tides may flush several thousand Dunlin and other waders off the Mersey to roost on the tanks. A few Short-eared Owls quarter the embankments each winter on the lookout for small mammals and birds. In good vole years there may be a dozen or more of these pale, long-winged owls. Hen Harrier is an occasional visitors.

Stubble fields attract flocks of Wood Pigeon, Stock Dove and finches, including dozens to hundreds of Chaffinches, Bramblings and Greenfinches, with smaller numbers of Linnet and possibly a few Twite. In snowy weather hundreds of Skylarks from farther inland gather on the stubbles. Cold weather may drive in thousands of Fieldfares and other thrushes, which strip any remaining berries off the tall thorn hedges before being forced to feed on the ground. Coveys of Grey Partridge inhabit most fields. They are as common here as anywhere in the region south of the Mersey. Partridge shoots are held in most winters. A few Red-legged Partridge or hybrids are also seen.

Many of the winter bird flocks remain intact during March before dispersing as spring approaches. European Golden Plover may still be present in late April, by then showing the extensive black on the underparts that characterise the northern subspecies. Spring arrives late in high latitudes, and these birds time their departure accordingly. Many Wood Pigeons nest late, so there may still be 1,000 or more on the Marsh in early May.

Garganey is recorded in most springs, occasionally in March but more likely in April or May. Oystercatcher and Ringed and Little Ringed Plovers all breed locally in small numbers; by April they are back in territory. Common Sandpipers pipe as they fly beneath the riverbanks, and other passage waders such as Ruff and Greenshank may occur. Sanderling and northern Ringed Plover move through in May and early June, when there is a chance of a Curlew Sandpiper or perhaps a Temminck's Stint. Other rare waders at this season have included Dotterel, Collared Pratincole, Red-necked Phalarope and Broad-billed and Stilt Sandpipers. The flooded, reedy ditches and tanks have attracted such southern marshland species as Spoonbill, Little Egret, Marsh and Montagu's Harriers and Black-necked Stilt.

Common, Arctic and Black Terns may pass along the Weaver, sometimes flying straight on upstream without stopping. Passerine migrants include Northern Wheatear and Reed Bunting in late March, joined in April by Yellow Wagtail and perhaps a Rock or Water Pipit. Goldfinches and Linnets move through in parties, and may fall victim to a lingering Merlin. Short-eared Owls usually remain into April. Reed Warblers appear in stands of *Phragmites* and

Sedge Warblers chatter along the ditches. The thin reeling song of the Grasshopper Warbler emanates from bramble clumps on the sides of the tanks. Whinchat nested formerly, but is now an uncommon passage migrant. A small nesting population of Meadow Pipits shares the same embankments.

Return passage is already underway by July. Often a single adult Little Stint or brick-red Curlew Sandpiper portends the main passage which is due to follow a month later. These birds may have lost their eggs or perhaps not bred at all, hence their early arrival. Dusky-plumaged Spotted Redshanks may appear in late June, and Greenshank and Ruff are almost certain to arrive at some time in July. Redshank and Dunlin numbers increase, and Curlew numbers start to build up on the fields where they use their long bill to probe for earthworms. Swifts gather in hundreds over the Bend and Grey Herons roost on fields nearby.

Wader passage picks up during August and September. Several hundred Dunlins are often present. High tides may force other species off the Mersey estuary to roost on the sludge tanks. A thousand or more Ringed Plovers may appear there. Knot is more likely from September, and a few Sanderlings or Turnstones occur in either month. In August in some years a few Curlew Sandpipers appear on the Bend, and may increase to dozens in September. In other years almost none are seen. Redshanks gather in hundreds. Ruffs find the river to their liking and up to 50 may be present. Black-tailed Godwits are also frequent, if erratic in their occurrences. Little Stints are usually late in passing through. Small numbers in August may increase to 50 or more in September and October, with a few remaining later. One hundred and sixty were counted in September 1993. A small number of Little Stints now regularly winter here, particularly on No. 6 tank, a phenomenon not shared by any other Cheshire site. The Weaver bend was once a magnet for rare American waders. In the last decade records have reduced dramatically. Water levels appear to be permanently high, reducing the muddy edges and banks that are favoured by waders.

Green Sandpipers tend to stay farther up the Weaver towards the motorway bridge, where Snipe become more numerous in late autumn. By then the plover flocks have returned to the fields and several hundred Curlews may be present. Most waders that occur regularly in Britain are noted from time to time. Frodsham offers a better chance of seeing truly rare waders than anywhere else in the region: Buff-breasted, White-rumped, Pectoral, Baird's, Sharp-tailed and Stilt Sandpipers and Wilson's and Red-necked Phalaropes have all occurred. In August 1990 a Long-billed Dowitcher arrived in breeding plumage. During the late 1990s the No. 5 tank was the site to watch: American Wigeon, Lesser Yellowlegs and Terek and Broad-billed Sandpipers were all sighted. Today the tank drains quickly and holds little water, but after heavy rain large pools of transitory standing water form for a few days and are always worth a look.

From August increasing numbers of ducks feed on the marsh: Common Teal, Eurasian Wigeon and Shoveler gather in drab, eclipse plumages. Small numbers of Garganey often consort with the much more numerous Common Teal. Little Grebes pursue small fish beneath the algal blanket on the Weaver or flooded tanks. Terns pass through in autumn as well as spring. Black Terns and Little Gulls may linger for a few days, picking flies off the water. White-winged Black Tern has occurred several times. Swarms of House Martins gather over the river before leaving for the south, and hundreds or even thousands of Swallows roost with Sand Martins in reedbeds by the Ship Canal and elsewhere. A Hobby or two now appear annually, scything in at dusk and perhaps at dawn to cut down hirundines.

One rarity that turns up with some regularity is Spotted Crake, a short-billed relative of the more numerous Water Rail. During August and early September parties of Yellow Wagtail feed in damp fields, and loose groups of up to 20 Sedge Warblers move through the reedy ditches. Goldfinches and Linnets form noisy flocks, including many young birds, to feed on the ripening seed of thistles and ragwort. Many of these birds have moved on by October when Rock or scarcer Water Pipits appear briefly beside the Weaver. On overcast days with an easterly breeze southward passage of pipits and Skylarks may be heavy, and small parties alight to feed beside the tanks. Reed Buntings may also be prevalent at such times.

Timing

Dawn or dusk visits may coincide with wildfowlers' activities. Otherwise there are good birds to be seen at almost any time, and plenty of habitat to cover apart from the Bend itself and the No. 6 tank. The highest tides are likely to push waders off the Mersey, and at such times the sludge beds should be checked carefully. Consult tide tables for predicted high tides. In severe weather wildfowl may concentrate on the unfrozen river. Thrushes and larks also gather, having been driven west by snow.

Access

Leave the M56 at Junction 12 and follow signs into Frodsham. After passing beneath a footbridge the road descends towards a set of traffic lights. To reach the Weaver Bend, turn right shortly before the lights into Ship Street and follow this lane until a bridge over the motorway appears on the left (SJ520785). Turn left, pass over the bridge, and continue along the unmade road until a gate bars the way. A footpath continues from here up to the Bend. Once over the motorway, the roads on the marsh are private. Many visitors drive as close to the Bend as practicable: this is a potential cause of friction with landowners and tenants.

For the main marsh and sludge tanks, continue through the lights in Frodsham and pass along the main shopping street before turning right down Marsh Lane. This lane passes over the motorway where, now a private road, it forks (SJ512779). Take the right-hand fork to reach the Bend. This track runs alongside then climbs the bank of No. 5 tank. From here the path to the Bend is obvious. The left-hand fork leads along the southern side of the embankment of No. 5 Bed; another fork climbs the bank to the right and skirts the newer No. 6 tank. This is a single-track road with passing places. Take care not to cause obstructions.

CALENDAR

All year: Northern Lapwing, Redshank and Dunlin at almost any time; Grey Partridge; Peregrine Falcon; Little Grebe, Canada Goose and Shelduck usually present.

December–February: Eurasian Wigeon, Common Teal and perhaps Pintail; Pochard,

Tufted Duck and Common Goldeneye, perhaps Smew and Scaup; Ruddy Duck and scarcer waterfowl in frosty weather; wild geese and swans may visit. Peregrine Falcon, Merlin and Short-eared Owl hunt the marshes, with perhaps a Hen Harrier or Long-eared Owl; flocks of Northern Lapwing and European

Golden Plover are often joined by Ruff, Black-tailed Godwit and other waders; Common Snipe and Curlew on damper ground; stubble fields hold large numbers of pigeons, finches and, after snow, Skylarks, Fieldfares and Redwings in fields and hedgerows; Water Rail in reedbeds.

March–May: Winter flocks disperse and raptors move back to breeding haunts in March and April, when Northern Wheatears, pipits, wagtails and Reed Buntings appear with other incoming migrants; northern European Golden Plovers remain into May in breeding plumage; breeding Ringed and Little Ringed Plovers arrive; passage waders include more Ringed Plovers, Sanderlings, Common Sandpipers, Ruff, Greenshanks and others; terns move through quickly; Garganey likely from March onward.

June–July: Meadow Pipits and Grasshopper Warblers around tanks; Sedge and Reed Warblers in reeds; large concentrations of Swifts over river; return wader passage

begins in July, when Curlew Sandpipers, Spotted Redshanks, Greenshanks, Ruff, Dunlin, Redshanks and Curlews increase; day roost of Grey Herons.

August–November: Wader passage best August to early October, with Dunlin, Ruff, Redshank, Black-tailed Godwit, Curlew Sandpiper, Little Stint and occasional Turnstone, Sanderling or a rarer species; estuarine species such as Ringed Plover and Knot on tanks at high tides; Garganey regular among Common Teal and other ducks during August and September; Black and other terns pass through, perhaps Little Gull; Hobby likely at Swallow roosts in August–September; warblers and wagtails move out; Spotted Crake may lurk in reeds in September; Water Rail increases in October, when a small passage of Rock Pipits; passage of larks and Meadow Pipits may be heavy; winter thrushes and finches arrive October–November, followed by owls and raptors; plover flocks reassemble.

OS Landranger Map 108

72A   HALE HEAD

SJ 473809

Hale Head is a low sandstone bluff that juts out into the Mersey estuary from the north bank opposite Frodsham Marsh and offers an alternative viewing point for estuarine species. Approach by a minor road south from Hale Village. There is limited parking at the southern end. From here a track leads down to a disused lighthouse. As the tide rises, flocks of Dunlin and other waders may concentrate offshore, with attendant raptors and a range of wildfowl that includes Mersey specialities such as Teal, Wigeon and Pintail. Corn Buntings and Yellow Wagtails breed in the arable fields. Footpaths follow the shoreline to east and west. Pickerings Pasture, 1.5 miles (2.5 km) to the east, is a reclaimed rubbish tip landscaped to attract wildlife and boasting a wader scrape. To the west of Hale Head, Oglet Shore provides further viewing of estuary birds. More direct access is available down Dungeon Lane, which skirts Speke airfield.

73 DELAMERE FOREST

OS Landranger Map 117, 118
SJ56, 57

Habitat

Delamere Forest derives its name from the medieval hunting forest of Mara, this definition being legal rather than physical. Until recently the character of the forest was one of dry heath on sandy soils with boggy, sphagnum-filled hollows and stands of pine trees. Now much of the area has been ploughed for arable farming and almost all the heathland has been lost under conifers. Abbots Moss is a floating bog – a mat of sphagnum moss floating over several feet of liquid peat and water. It is noted for bog plants such as cranberry and bog rosemary, and for dragonflies, notably White-Faced Dragonfly and Downy Emerald. Green Hair-streak Butterflies and Orange Underwing Moths flutter around the birch trees; grass snakes and lizards are sometimes seen. The various sand quarries in the area are of some ornithological importance, and not only for aquatic and waterside species. Bulldozing of topsoil and 'overburden' allows the germination of arable weeds whose seeds attract finches and doves. These pits are worked wet, that is they are allowed to flood while still operational and sand is pumped out through hoses. Silt that drains back in from the stockpiles forms shallow beaches that attract gulls and waders and which eventually develop a covering of reed mace.

Species

The mature plantations support few species of birds. Common Crossbill is annual and breed in some years, but sizeable flocks are unusual. Siskin may breed in very small numbers but proof is seldom forthcoming. They are far more numerous in winter and especially in spring. The high-pitched squeaks of Goldcrests and Coal Tits, feeding in the tops of conifers, can be heard at all seasons. Wrens nest amongst the ferns beneath the pines, where Chaffinches

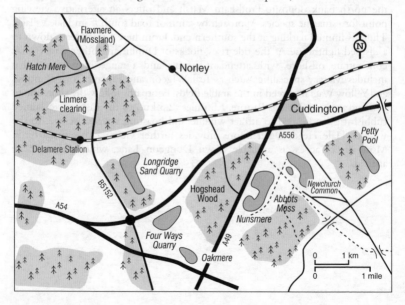

and Treecreepers sing. In summer they are joined by Blackcaps, Chiffchaffs and Spotted Flycatchers. A few pairs of Sparrowhawk are also present, and Kestrels hunt the cleared areas. Tawny Owl is common, but the smaller Long-eared Owl has become rare and elusive; it should be sought in winter roosting in willow scrub. Nightjar formerly bred in some numbers but there are no recent records, although much habitat remains apparently suitable. In some springs Bramblings extract seeds from ripening cones in the flat crowns of pines.

Green Woodpeckers seek out ants in open, sandy areas, and bound away on whirring wings when disturbed, their yellow rumps flashing. In June the noisy young of this species or Great Spotted Woodpeckers may be heard shouting for food from a nest in a shattered conifer or bog-side alder. Willow Tits frequent the alders and birches, and wander into the plantations to feed, as do the numerous Nuthatches that nest in roadside oaks and chestnuts. Other birds that favour broadleaved trees around the edges of the conifers include Common Redstarts, but the small numbers of Wood Warblers and Pied Flycatchers that bred here in the past have now gone and only single passage birds are now seen.

Recent plantations containing trees between 6 and 12 feet (2 to 4 m) tall are quiet in winter but come alive with nesting passerines in summer. Tree Pipit has become scarce recently, but a few sing from the tops of isolated birches or during their parachuting display flight. Common Whitethroats warble scratchy phrases during their briefer low-level display. The fluty cadences of Willow Warblers mingle with the ringing songs of Yellowhammers and the stammer of Reed Buntings, here nesting in unusually dry habitat. Redpolls and Linnets fly out into surrounding fields in small groups to feed, while Dunnocks and Long-tailed Tits are much less conspicuous. Toward dusk a Grasshopper Warbler may sing. Garden Warblers and Bullfinches favour taller, denser stands until the foresters remove the lower branches from the trees.

In spring, pairs of Black-headed Gulls take up territory by the quarry lakes and may display. They and the Common Terns that appear from time to time in summer might be encouraged to breed if rafts or islets were provided. A few waders occur on passage. Common Sandpipers and Dunlin are the most frequent species in both spring and autumn, with perhaps a Greenshank or Green Sandpiper at the latter season. Whimbrel pass through the area each May and sometimes alight in fields. With luck a small flock may be seen flying low to northward uttering their tittering multiple whistle, or even pausing to deliver the full bubbling song. Little Ringed Plovers have bred on the sandy beaches. In winter a few Snipe and Jack Snipe crouch among stands of reedmace. Little and Great Crested Grebes nest on the flooded quarries, and Black-necked Grebes have been seen. Shelducks display in April, but only Mallards and Tufted and Ruddy Ducks nest with any regularity. Up to 20 or 30 each of Pochard and Tufted Duck occur in winter, when up to a dozen Common Goldeneye and a few Common Teal are usually present.

Timing
The part of the forest closest to Delamere station attracts large numbers of day trippers, especially on sunny days, but there are always more remote areas that remain relatively free from disturbance. Morning or evening visits in spring are best for birdsong. Dusk visits in summer might reveal some of the nocturnal species. Evening visits to the sand quarries in winter may result in a sighting of an unusual gull attending a pre-roost gathering.

Access

The forest area straddles the A54 Chester to Winsford and A49 Warrington to Whitchurch roads. Access to the plantations is generally unrestricted along Forestry Commission rides. Some of the better sites are listed below.

73A DELAMERE SWITCHBACK   OS ref: SJ552713

Take the B5152 Frodsham road northward from the A556. Pass over the railway bridge and continue for almost a mile (1.5 km) before turning left onto a minor road just before Hatchmere (SJ552713). Tracks lead north and south from this road into the plantations. Explore this area for woodland birds: Nuthatch, Treecreeper, Green Woodpecker; Siskin in winter and spring, possibly summer; perhaps Common Crossbill; Common Redstart, Wood Warbler and Pied Flycatcher.

73B BLAKEMERE

A peaty area of wet heath land has now developed into a large lake that holds a sizable colony of Black-headed Gulls. Over the last few years an interesting development has occurred and the colony now holds at least four pairs of Mediterranean Gull, which have bred successfully. As yet the hoped-for returning Nightjar has not appeared, even though the area still looks good for this species.

73C HOGSHEAD WOOD   OS ref: SJ583690

This area of young plantations to the west of the A49 opposite Nunsmere tends to be less disturbed than other parts of the forest, and supports good numbers of scrubland species. Bulldozed areas are particularly attractive for butterflies. Part of the wood has been taken for a new quarry, which remains dry at the time of writing.

73D NUNSMERE   OS ref: SJ590690

A disused quarry adjacent to the A49 0.5 miles (0.8 km) to the south of the A556 crossroads. The banks are overgrown with birch scrub. Garden Warbler, Willow Tit, Bullfinch and Lesser Redpoll nest; Green Woodpeckers feed in more open areas. Breeding waterbirds include grebes and Tufted Duck, despite the occasional water-skiing. Winter wildfowl are few in number but have included Long-tailed Duck.

73E ABBOTS MOSS   OS ref: SJ587685

A forestry track runs eastward from the A49 immediately to the south of Nunsmere. Walk down the track, turn left at the end and then bear right where a striped pole bars the road. This ride leads through conifer plantations and between two floating bogs ringed with alder and birch trees. Green Woodpecker, Willow Tit and Tree Pipit nest; Common Redstart in some years. Common Crossbill, Siskin and Sparrowhawk are possible at any time of year. Hobby and Goshawk have been seen.

73F PETTY POOL AND PETTYPOOL WOOD   OS ref: SJ618701

Travel east along the A556 from A49 crossroads and turn right very shortly at another set of lights. After 1.25 miles (2 km), at the end of a line of large houses, a footpath leads into the plantations. Parking is not possible immediately by this entrance, so park elsewhere and walk back. Rides lead through the plantation to the pool. Breeding waterfowl include Ruddy Ducks. Siskin is plentiful in spring; plantation species and a few Wood Warblers appear in summer. Rhododendrons by the pool hold roosting finches, often including Brambling, in winter. Polecats reside in the vicinity.

73G NEWCHURCH COMMON   OS ref: SJ600688

Continue south along the minor road past Pettypool Wood and take the first right, signposted to Nova Scotia. Turn right at the end and park at the quarry entrance. A bridle path runs between the two quarries, which are now largely hidden by surrounding trees and scrub containing nesting Linnets and Yellowhammers. Goldeneye, Tufted Duck and Pochard favour these pools. There are a few Common Teal in winter, when Jack Snipe may occur in the reedmace. Large numbers of gulls may be present in winter. Scaup and Common Scoter have occurred. Stubble fields in the vicinity hold finch flocks. Green Woodpeckers feed in areas of short grass.

Follow Whitegate Way, which passes the southern end of the smaller pool, westward from Newchurch Common to view the Gull Pool: now devoid of nesting gulls, but supporting breeding Little Grebe, Tufted and Ruddy Ducks and rare dragonflies. From here it is possible to follow paths through to Abbots Moss and Nunsmere.

CALENDAR

All year: Sparrowhawk and Kestrel by day; Tawny and possibly Long-eared Owls by night. Woodland species include Green and Great Spotted Woodpeckers, Nuthatch, Treecreeper, Long-tailed and Willow Tit; Coal Tit and Goldcrest plentiful; Lesser Redpoll and often Bullfinch in birches; Common Crossbill and perhaps Siskin in pines; Stock Dove and Corn Bunting in arable areas; Little Grebe and Tufted Duck on quarries and pools.

December–February: Common Teal, Pochard and Common Goldeneye; Common Snipe and Jack Snipe by quarries; Common

Gull abundant; Bramblings may feed under beeches.

March–May: Shelduck visit; Ruddy Duck move to breeding pools; Brambling and plentiful Siskin in mature conifers; Common Crossbills may have young; breeding species, including warblers, move into young plantations.

June–July: Grebes and Tufted and Ruddy Ducks may have young; Little Ringed Plover and Sand Martin in quarries; Black-headed Gulls may summer and Common Terns appear at times; Turtle Doves feed along weedy banks; young plantations hold Common Whitethroat, possibly Grasshopper Warbler, Linnets, Lesser Redpoll, Reed Bunting and Yellowhammer; Nightjar formerly bred and might still occur; Common Crossbill numbers may be augmented by irrupting flocks from farther north; Tree Pipit, Common Redstart, Pied Flycatcher and Wood Warbler local.

August–November: Summer visitors depart and plantations become quiet; waders may drop in by quarries where Lesser Black-backed Gulls gather in hundreds.

74 BEESTON CASTLE AND PECKFORTON HILLS
OS Landranger Map 117
SJ55

Habitat

The Peckforton Hills form a ridge of sandstone standing isolated in the middle of the Cheshire Plain; Beeston Castle surmounts a solitary hill to the north. The tops of the hills contain heathy habitat, but most of the summit of Peckforton Hill has been planted with conifers. There are considerable tracts of oak woodland on the steeper slopes. Birch and bracken are spreading extensively across the remaining open areas. Cattle have been allowed to browse on Bickerton Hill to stem the loss of heathland to scrub. Bulkeley Hill has numbers of old chestnut and oak trees, but is largely covered by birch woodland. Climbing corydalis is a characteristic plant of the woodlands and cow-wheat is locally plentiful.

In summer, Purple Hairstreak butterflies dart around the sunlit crowns of oak trees. Bickerton Hill, and the Larkton Hill property of the National Trust, lie at the south end of the ridge, which is capped by probably the best remaining heathland area in Cheshire. In late summer, Oak Eggar moths fly over the heath, where bilberries fruit in profusion. The deep purple flowers of bell heather and pinker bells of cross-leaved heath grow in the damper areas, and later flowers of heather attract bees and butterflies to the rich source of nectar. The Iron Age ramparts of Maiden Castle at the highest point of the hill are now largely overrun by bracken.

Species

The older tracts of oak are particularly rich in woodland species, with a notable concentration of Pied Flycatchers, especially in the Burwardsley woods. Wood Warbler, Marsh Tit and a few Common Redstarts are also present. All three species of woodpecker breed. Pied Flycatcher and Wood Warbler may also be seen within the grounds of Beeston Castle, along with more common woodland species. The castle is infiltrated by Chiffchaffs each March. The hills would repay much closer attention as a focus for migrants than they have received to date.

Warblers often join mixed flocks of tits in autumn, but viewing can be difficult in the dense birch scrub. Siskin has nested in the conifers along the ridge and Common Crossbills visit. Bramblings sometimes work opening pine

Pied Flycatcher

cones during their northward passage in April and May. Bickerton Hill in particular supports a few pairs of Tree Pipits. Meadow Pipit has also nested recently. Nightjars continue to be reported on passage in May or June, and much suitable habitat remains for this species.

The isolated nature of the hills attracts migrant raptors. Peregrine Falcon and Raven both nest; Peregrines nested here in medieval times. Goshawks displayed in this area in spring 2007 and are believed also to be breeding. Hobbies occasionally soar along the ridges. Common Buzzards can usually be seen somewhere along the ridge. A few pairs of Little Owl are resident in hedgerow oaks on the farmland below the ridge, and may be heard yelping at dusk.

Timing

Trippers invade most accessible sites in Cheshire at weekends – especially Beeston Castle – but it is usually possible to find relatively quiet footpaths on the Peckforton Hills. Spring visits are optimal for woodland species, but there is exploratory work to be done here, with autumn and winter populations still poorly known.

Access

The hump of Beeston Castle (SJ537593) can be seen from afar, lying just to the west of the A49 south of Tarporley. Minor roads are well signposted and there are car parks at the foot of the outer wall. English Heritage manages the castle; there is an admission charge. The keep is very popular with day-trippers, but provides an excellent platform from which to view raptors. Minor roads skirt the Peckforton Hills on either side and there is a well-marked network of public footpaths. Burwardsley woods are best approached from the west. Follow signs for the Candle Workshops into the village, but turn left past the Pheasant Inn opposite a telephone box (SJ523565). This is a no-through road and parking is difficult. The lane deteriorates into a track that soon passes an area of old oak wood on the right. Explore the footpaths through the woods. Bickerton (Larkton) Hill is best approached from Bickerton village, just south of the A534. Take Goldford Lane, which runs beside the churchyard. There are signposted access

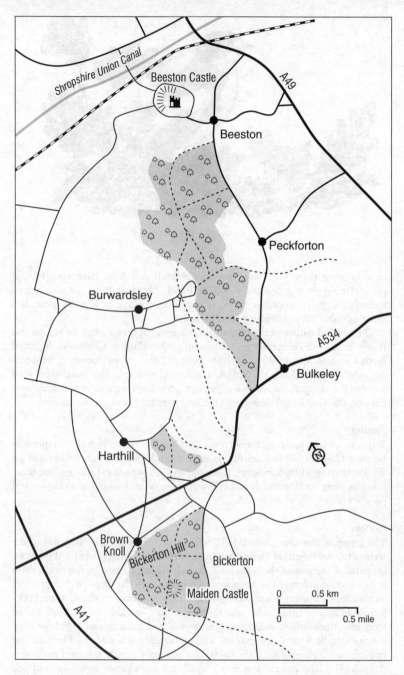

points at various points along the lane. A National Trust car park has its entrance beside a roadside pond. Foot- and bridle paths cross the heath and woods. An area of oak woodland at the southwest corner of the hill may be rewarding.

CALENDAR

All year: Common Buzzard, Peregrine Falcon, Raven, woodpeckers, Marsh Tit, Goldcrest, woodland birds; Lesser Redpoll and Bullfinch among other scrubland birds on the heaths.

December–February: Territorial Marsh Tits may join mobile flocks of resident woodland birds.

March–May: Siskin flocks in larches; Brambling may frequent pines; raptors display; spring migrants include Pied Flycatcher, Wood Warbler, Tree Pipit and Common Redstart.

June–July: Breeding species less conspicuous by July. Stock Dove and other birds feed on bilberries at Bickerton.

August–November: Woodland quiet; migrant warblers join tit flocks; Hobby more likely to appear early in season.

75 THE RIVER DEE

OS Landranger Map 117
SJ44, 45, 46

Habitat

The meandering River Dee forms the Wales–England border from the south-west corner of Cheshire at Shocklach north to Aldford, where the boundary swings west around Eaton Park. Willows overhang the river and exposed sandy banks on the inside of bends provide good areas for rare and scarce dragonflies and damselflies. This section of the river is prone to flooding and flooded arable land and pasture can attract wildfowl from the estuary. Eaton Park supports a feral population of Mandarin Duck. Small-leaved lime trees, a rarity in Cheshire, grow on the riverbanks between the Iron Bridge and Eccleston. The village of Eccleston lies on the west bank of the river Dee. It is characterised by lichen-rich sandstone walls and a mixture of mature evergreen and broadleaved trees. Historically Hawfinch frequented the village, moving both southward into Eaton Park and northward into the outskirts of suburban Chester. Sadly, the last reports of this stunning finch were as long ago as 1994.

Species

The mature timber of Eaton Park houses many hole-nesting birds: Stock Dove, Jackdaw and Little Owl at the larger end of the scale and Nuthatch, Marsh Tit and Tree Sparrow at the smaller end. A few pairs of Common Redstart used to nest in old ash trees in the southern part of the valley, but there have been no reports of successful breeding in the last decade. Of special interest in the area are several pairs of Mandarin that nest in hollow trees and, in some places, Barn Owl nest boxes.

From autumn until early spring the lakeside trees at Eaton hold one of the county's main inland Cormorant roosts. Several dozen birds are regularly present (93 in March 2004). A smaller roost is established in riverside trees near Churton. Many Cormorants fly out to the Dee estuary to feed and can be seen commuting over Chester, where tamer individuals fish on the weir. Winter waterfowl include small numbers of Common Goldeneye, parties of Common Teal and the occasional Goosander. Mandarin may be seen in winter on tree-lined stretches of river, particularly northwards from Farndon; an amazing 73 were counted at Eaton Hall in October 2001.

When the river floods following heavy rain or after a rapid thaw of snow on the Welsh hills, flocks of up to several hundred Pintail and other ducks fly in from the estuaries to flooded farmland upstream of Farndon or along Aldford Brook.

As the days lengthen, warblers and other migrants appear in riverside trees, and Common Sandpipers skim low across the river. In the early morning Nuthatches pipe from the treetops and woodpeckers drum on hollow branches. This area holds the scarce Lesser Spotted Woodpecker as well as the two more regular species. There is a large heronry in the secluded woods of Eaton Park. The birds radiate to feed in marl pits, by rivers, or beside the saltmarshes of the Dee estuary. Mandarins may be seen with ducklings along quieter reaches of the river. Kingfishers also breed locally and may be seen at any season.

Mandarin

Careful observation along the banks of the Dee, a large river with north–south orientation, might produce surprises at migration time. Common and Green Sandpipers follow the riverbanks, and with the onset of autumn parties of Siskin appear in the alders.

As with many areas of Cheshire, Common Buzzard is now a common resident, feeding on a flourishing population of rabbits. Ravens are also seen with increasing frequency and nested on Chester Town Hall in 1996. A Peregrine Falcon is sometimes seen roosting on electricity pylons in winter.

Timing

Historically, Hawfinch was most reliably present during March to April and June to August over Eccleston village or in the Overleigh cemetery, but there have been no reports for over a decade. The riverbank footpath at Eccleston attracts its share of human visitors, so Mandarins are most likely to be seen in the early morning before disturbance drives them away. This is a very pleasant walk at all seasons. The riverside path from Churton is best walked in frosty weather, especially when inland meres and flashes are frozen. Mandarins are often present here when the river downstream gets disturbed. Farmland is

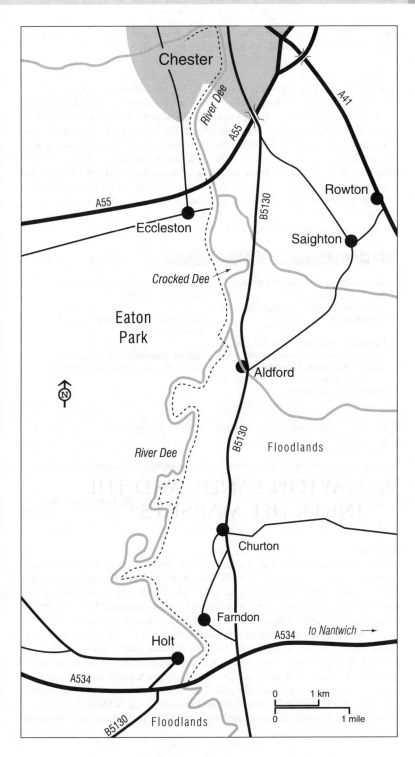

likely to flood at any time following heavy, prolonged rain, or when a quick thaw melts snow off the Welsh hills higher up the Dee catchment.

Access

Take the A483(T) southwards from the A55(T) roundabout (SJ390625). Turn left after 0.5 miles (0.8 km) onto a minor road signposted to Eccleston. Park in the village or on Ferry Lane, from which footpaths follow the riverbank in either direction. Eaton Park is strictly private, but interrupted views of the park lake can be obtained by following the path southwards for a little over a mile (2 km). Watching becomes more difficult when the trees are in full leaf. Geese may be visible at times from the Aldford to Huntington road (B5130) near the Crook of Dee (SJ425615). Hawfinches are most likely to be seen in the area around Eccleston Church. From Churton village take the lane beside the White Horse public house and walk down the farm track to the river. A footpath follows the meanders of the riverbank to north or south.

CALENDAR

All year: Grey Heron, Canada and Greylag Geese, Mandarin Duck, all three woodpeckers, Kingfisher, Nuthatch, Marsh Tit, Buzzard and perhaps Raven.

December–February: Cormorant roost reaches its peak, feral geese may attract wild relatives, Mandarin and Kingfisher on the river, floods may attract Pintail, Eurasian Wigeon and other wildfowl.

March–May: Woodpeckers drumming near river in early morning.

June–July: Mandarins may have young, geese now moulting.

August–November: Cormorant roost reassembles and geese become more mobile.

---

76 GAYTON SANDS AND THE INNER DEE MARSHES

OS Landranger Map 117
SJ27, 28

Habitat

The saltmarshes of the Dee estuary spread rapidly during the last century following the construction of embankments to reclaim the Sealand area and the diversion of the main river channel to the Welsh side (which was carried out in the eighteenth century). Their growth was accelerated by the arrival of common cord-grass, which stabilised mud banks throughout the inner estuary and now covers a stretch of beach from West Kirby to Red Rocks at the North West tip of the Wirral peninsula. Tidal creeks and gutters persist within the saltings. In places shallow brackish pools have formed. Sheep graze the upper parts of the marshes heavily, but elsewhere saltmarsh plants such as sea aster, scurvy-grass and sea purslane flourish. The marshes now extend from beyond the Cheshire border at Burton Point and seaward as far as Heswall.

Inner Marsh Farm was purchased by the RSPB in 1986 and now forms an outstanding area for birdwatching. In September 2006 the RSPB purchased a further 194 hectares of saltmarsh and adjacent farmland at Burton Marsh Farm. This purchase brings together the RSPB's existing land holdings of Gayton Sands and Inner Marsh Farm and allows access to manage a further 2,500 acres (1,000 ha) of saltmarsh. The new combined reserve is internationally important for waders and wildfowl and protects a large part of the estuary for future generations. The whole of the marsh from Burton Point to Gayton is now owned by the RSPB.

Pools in this vast marshland attract waders such as Redshank and Northern Lapwing to breed. These are joined by many waders and wildfowl in winter. From Neston northwards the character of the marsh changes because it is not grazed. The reserve straddles the England-Wales border and extends to over 12,000 acres (5,000 hectares). It includes an important reedbed at Neston and freshwater pools at Inner Marsh Farm.

The Wirral Way, a disused railway track, runs parallel to the coastline northwest from Neston. It is lined with scrub and passes through farmland, which includes stubble fields in winter. To the south of the Burton Marshes and separated from the estuary by the Bidston to Wrexham railway embankment is an area of flat fields. Formerly saltmarsh, Shotwick fields attract wintering geese and wild swans as well as waders such as Northern Lapwing and European Golden Plover.

Species

The Dee was once famous for its wild geese. Excessive disturbance early in the last century drove away the already dwindling remnants of the former flocks. Since the establishment of Gayton Sands RSPB reserve numbers of wildfowl wintering in the estuary have risen markedly. Pintail is well adapted to the open, estuarine environment, its long neck enabling it to detect approaching predators from considerable distances. Several thousand frequent the edge of the saltmarsh from October until February. Hundreds of Shelduck feed in the channel off Gayton; hundreds of Mallard and Common Teal, and thousands of Eurasian Wigeon frequent the outer edge of the marsh in the same area. Red-breasted Mergansers fish way out on the river channel. Common Teal and Eurasian Wigeon also feed in the wildfowl refuge off Denhall Lane. In recent winters small parties of Pink-footed and White-fronted Geese have been seen with some regularity on Burton Marsh. Family groups of Bewick's Swan may also take up winter residence and roost at Inner Marsh Farm. Whooper Swan is usually less numerous.

Farmland, marshland and estuarine waders meet in the inner Dee in winter. Several hundred European Golden Plovers and Northern Lapwings may feed on Shotwick fields or Burton Marsh. Spotted Redshank and Greenshank are occasionally present at the Decca pools or elsewhere. At high tide estuarine species gather to roost on the marshes. A roost on the pasture at Burton can hold several thousand birds: Oystercatcher, Knot and Dunlin, Curlews and Redshank.

The saltmarsh plants produce vast quantities of seeds that float up the various creeks on the tide and are deposited in masses along the tideline. This abundance of seed draws vast flocks of finches to the edge of the marsh. Between Parkgate and Gayton the top outer edge of the sandstone seawall is yellow with lichens that are nourished by the droppings of the winter finches. These may include hundreds of Chaffinches and Greenfinches, although they have been less numerous of late. Bramblings are more erratic in their appearances. Linnets are most numerous in autumn, but dozens remain in winter. A couple of flocks of Twite winter farther out on the marsh. At times they move to the landward edge, particularly at Neston. Thistles in the rougher pastures bordering the marsh attract Goldfinches. House and Tree Sparrows also form flocks. Formerly a few Corn Buntings occurred, but sadly these are a very rare sight on the Dee nowadays. Skylarks feed out on the marsh, as do many Reed Buntings, although these birds are less prone to flocking than finches. Lapland Buntings visit the marsh each winter. They spend much of their time farther out, but high tides occasionally bring them 'inland'. These dumpy, short-tailed buntings are usually seen only in flight, when their distinctive call – "tic tic" followed by a whistled "teu" – betrays their presence.

Rock Pipits move onto the Dee in October and remain until April. They feed along the gutters and forage among debris at the high-water mark. Counts of 100 to 200 are possible. A few Water Pipits may also be seen below the car park at Parkgate, particularly around the south end of Neston reedbed area. By March and early April the Water Pipits have often developed the beautiful pink flush of their summer plumage.

The profusion of birds feeding on the marsh and the mudflats attracts predators, making this one of the best sites in the region to see raptors. Sparrow-hawks steal in low from the landward side hoping to snatch an unwary finch and Kestrels hover in search of small mammals. One or two Hen Harriers may quarter the marsh systematically and are sometimes joined by a Merlin, apparently taking advantage of the harrier's flushing of larks and small waders that the falcon then pursues. Peregrine Falcons hunt the area, and can generally be seen during a morning's watch. Another characteristic predator of the marshes from autumn to spring is the Short-eared Owl. Numbers fluctuate in response to vole populations: in some winters almost none are seen; in a good year 10 or more may be present, with several in the air at once. In recent times day-flying Barn Owls have become a feature of "owl watching" on the marshes, particularly from Denhall Lane. Raven and Common Buzzard are now seen regularly.

One final feature of winter birdwatching on the Dee estuary is the flooding of the marshes by the highest tides, particularly at Parkgate. As normally dry parts of the marsh become inundated, small mammals break cover and swim for higher ground. Shrews, voles, mice and rats all fall victim to the owls and harriers, or to the more numerous gulls and Grey Herons that line the advancing tide. Water Rails, too, are driven out of the cord-grass. If the marsh floods completely they fly up onto the seawall and take cover under parked cars or in fields and gardens. Not all the rails make it to safety: some fall prey to Grey Herons. Finches, larks and buntings are also displaced from the marsh and move to coastal fields, as do Common Snipe and a few short-billed Jack Snipe.

Northern Wheatears appear along the seawall from March, when Meadow Pipits pass over in large numbers. White Wagtail may be numerous in April, but Yellow Wagtail has declined greatly. April and May bring a light passage of marshland waders, some of which have attained smart breeding plumage by the latter month. If a high-pressure system becomes established over the continent at this time, south-east winds may bring a Marsh Harrier in place of the departing Hen Harriers. A Garganey or two may appear at this season.

A few Mallards and Shelducks nest on the marshes, and small numbers of Teal, Shoveler and other duck species may spend the summer at Inner Marsh

Farm RSPB Reserve. Redshank and Oystercatcher nest in small numbers. Several hundred pairs of Black-headed Gulls inhabit the reserve. Common Terns nest just over the border in Clwyd and often fish in the Dee or on pools on the marsh. The reedbed at Neston holds breeding Reed and Sedge Warblers, with further pairs of the latter species and a few Grasshopper Warblers in rushbeds elsewhere along the edges of the marsh. The reedbed has also played host to breeding Bearded Tit and wintering Cetti's Warbler recently; whether these will become regular only time will tell. Reed Bunting and Skylark nest commonly. Quail are heard in many summers uttering their soft "whet-whet-whet" call from the marsh or nearby cornfields. In summer Hobby can be seen in the area.

Marshland waders are rather more conspicuous on spring passage than in winter, but the largest numbers occur in autumn. Maximum counts of Greenshank roosting off Parkgate or at Inner Marsh Farm at this season have varied between 30 and 70. Up to a dozen or so Spotted Redshanks may be seen and in the 1970s counts in excess of 100 off Burton were not exceptional. Black-tailed Godwit may be present in hundreds in almost any month. Curlew Sandpiper and Little Stint are noted annually in small numbers. Ruff occurs more reliably with up to 40 in good years. Scarce or rare species are found from time to time, including Wood and Pectoral Sandpipers, Grey, Red-necked and Wilson's Phalaropes, Black-winged Stilt, Temminck's Stint and Long-billed Dowitcher in recent years. Spoonbills have visited on a number of occasions and Spotted Crake is almost annual at Inner Marsh Farm RSPB Reserve. Great White Egret and Common Crane have occurred. As at Red Rocks and Hilbre, diurnal movements of thrushes and finches may be heavy given easterly winds in late autumn.

Timing

The marshes may appear quiet between tides, but activity increases as the river channel floods and waders are forced onto the marsh to roost. Raptors and owls then become more active. Only the very highest tides of 33 feet (10 to 11 m) or more are now likely to flood the marsh, although a low pressure system

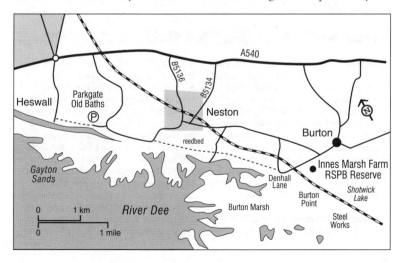

producing a south-west wind on the day of a high tide might still have the same effect. On high tide days the car park at Parkgate fills up with birdwatchers very quickly, so it is advisable to take up a good position an hour or two before high tide. Evening visits give views of harriers entering the roost there when the light fades. Prolonged east or southeast winds in May are a sign that passage harriers may occur, or perhaps even some overshooting southern migrants. September or October may bring scarce and rare waders to the pools.

Access

Access is essentially restricted to a series of lanes and footpaths that run the length of the landward side of the marshes from Burton northwestward to Gayton. The whole area lies to the west of the A540 Chester to Hoylake road. To view Burton Marshes, take Denhall Lane westward from Burton village until the marshes, here grazed by sheep, appear in front (SJ302736). Pools here may hold waders at any time and Eurasian Wigeon and Common Teal in winter. An unmade road runs north from here to Neston, with good bird-watching all the way. The Decca pools beyond Denhall House Farm are particularly productive. The other main vantage point is the site of the old baths at Parkgate, now a car park. From Parkgate village take the road northwest along the front until it swings away from the marsh. Here fork left along a side road with speed ramps. This leads to the car park (SJ273791). Watch from here for raptors, owls and possibly rails on flooding tides. Walk north along the seawall for further views of finches and occasional Water Pipit. A path leads inland from the car park and connects to the Wirral Way.

Walk southwards from Parkgate along the edge of the marsh to reach Neston reedbed. Raptors may be seen here in winter. Water Pipit is regular and particularly easy to see in early spring. Warblers summer here. Shotwick fields are viewed by taking the industrial estate road west off the A550(T) south of Shotwick village (SJ338708).

Inner Marsh Farm RSPB Reserve is open to RSPB members only. Access is currently from Burton Point Farm off Station Road, running from Burton village down to the marsh and Denhall Lane. Check with the RSPB for future access details.

CALENDAR

All year: Shelduck, Oystercatcher, Redshank and Northern Lapwing breed; Black-headed Gull always present and many pairs nest; Black-tailed Godwit usually present, particularly at Inner Marsh Farm RSPB Reserve. Reed Bunting and Skylark nest commonly, with perhaps Stonechat. Grey Herons stalk the shoreline and more recently Little Egrets can be seen along the marsh, particularly at Parkgate and Inner Marsh Farm RSPB Reserve. Raven, Peregrine Falcon and Common Buzzard are often seen.

December–February: Flocks of finches gather along edge of marsh – Chaffinch,

Brambling, Greenfinch, Linnet, Twite and Goldfinch are joined by House and Tree Sparrow, and perhaps Corn Bunting; hundreds of Skylark and Reed Bunting on marsh; Rock and a few Water Pipits in creeks. A small flock of Lapland Buntings winters on the marsh, but they are usually seen only when the marsh is flooded. Snipe, Jack Snipe and Water Rail may be flushed into view by a high tide. Grey geese and more regularly wild swans sometimes join Northern Lapwings and European Golden Plovers at Burton or Shotwick. Pintail, Common Teal and Eurasian Wigeon winter in thousands out on the marsh, and Shelduck on the flats. Spotted Redshank and Greenshank occasional. Peregrine Falcon, Merlin, Hen Harrier and Short-eared Owl hunt the marshes, with Kestrel and Sparrowhawk.

March–May: Wildfowl mostly depart in March. Wader flocks disperse a little later. A sprinkling of stints or shanks pass through in April or May and may include the occasional Temminck's Stint at Inner Marsh Farm RSPB Reserve in May. Raptors are regular to early April, then progressively more scarce. Marsh Harrier occurs annually in May. Summer plumaged Water Pipits present in March and early April. Easterly winds in May can bring Black Terns in good numbers.

June–July: A few Pintail, Common Teal and Shoveler linger along with small numbers of non-breeding waders such as Bar-tailed and Black-tailed Godwits. Common Terns fly out from Shotton (Clwyd) to fish the Dee. Grasshopper, Reed and Sedge Warblers occur in Neston reedbed. Quail visits the marshes in some years.

August–November: Wader passage in August may bring Spotted Redshank and Greenshank in large numbers; in September joined by Little Stint and Curlew Sandpiper. Rarer waders are most likely in September and October, when raptors also start to return. Spotted Crake is almost annual in August or September, particularly at Inner Marsh Farm RSPB Reserve.

77 HILBRE ISLAND AND THE DEE MOUTH

OS Landranger Map 108
SJ18, 28

Habitat

At just under 12 acres (5 ha) and with cliffs rising to 55 feet (17 m) on the exposed western side, Hilbre is the largest of a group of three islands lying about 1 mile (1.6 km) west of the north-west tip of Wirral in the mouth of the Dee estuary. At low tide the islands are accessible with caution across the sands from West Kirby, but at high tide they are cut off from the mainland. All three islands are composed of red sandstone and topped with rough grassland. Apart from some blackthorn, a few bushes and trees on Hilbre and some bracken on Middle Eye, there is little cover for birds and, other than an old, roofless lifeboat house and a seawatching hide (built by Hilbre Bird Observatory), even less shelter for birdwatchers. Hilbre Bird Observatory was established in 1957 and for over 50 years has recorded, ringed and analysed the islands' birds as well as other aspects of natural history. West Hoyle Bank, a large sandbank to the west of the islands, is used regularly by Grey Seals, which haul themselves out of the water there; up to 600 have been recorded in recent years. At high tide the seals often bob around the main island. At low tide sands are exposed stretching from Hoylake and West Kirby to Hilbre and south down the Dee estuary, but there are a number of deep gutters that can trap the unwary. These extensive flats are the feeding grounds for thousands of shorebirds. Sea ducks are seen off Hilbre.

Species

260 species have been recorded at Hilbre, but only a few breed because of the restricted habitat. Shelducks are seen throughout the year. Cormorants rest on sandbanks at low tide, often in large numbers. Vast flocks of waders winter in

the estuary. In late July the first Dunlins, perhaps a thousand or more, return from the arctic tundra. They are joined by flocks of Sanderling, particularly in August, on the way to their winter quarters on African beaches. Up to 20,000 Oystercatchers and sometimes more arrive in August. They remain in similar or even larger numbers through the winter. August sees the peak of Ringed Plover passage. Dunlin, Curlews and Redshanks increase and early Knot, some of them red summer-plumaged birds, black-bellied Grey Plover and godwits of either species may arrive. Turnstones reach 200 to 300 on Hilbre in August and September, flicking over seaweed and pebbles in their search for food. Grey Plover numbers may exceed 1,000 in September. Knot numbers increase, reaching several thousands by October. A speciality of the island is a flock of Purple Sandpipers that builds up from mid October into November, reaching perhaps as many as 70 birds in total (in recent years this number has fallen below 30). Winter Knot flocks have also reduced in size but occasionally still exceed 10,000. There may be 10,000 to 20,000 Dunlin and up to 1,000 Curlews and several thousand Redshanks in the Caldy/West Kirby/Hilbre area. Hundreds of Grey Plovers and a smaller number of Ringed Plovers will also be present. Oystercatchers remain abundant and highly conspicuous.

Not all of these birds will use the outer estuary at any one time. Many commute between the Dee and the Alt or Ribble estuaries. High-tide roosts may gather on the two lesser Hilbre islands, which should be left undisturbed at high tide for this purpose. The high tide wader roost has also improved between West Kirby and Red Rocks thanks to the perseverance of the Dee Estuary Voluntary Wardens. Quite often the roosts are disturbed by a Peregrine, several of which hunt the estuary daily in winter. Rather less often a Merlin appears.

Numbers of waders in the estuary are falling by March. In April and May the Purple Sandpiper flock returns north, perhaps to Greenland (Hilbre Bird Observatory had a ringing recovery there). By June only a few Oystercatchers, Curlews and Turnstones remain with occasional birds of other species.

A modern feature of winter is a large flock of Pale-bellied Brent Geese around Hilbre. This flock increased from only four birds in the winter of 1995/96 to over 100 just 10 years later. Small numbers of Dark-bellied Brent Geese have always occurred and continue to do so, although their paler cousins from the west now outnumber them hugely. A favourite haunt for these birds during low tide is around the Tanskey Rocks south of Little Eye, where Wigeon may be seen resting over the high tide. Large numbers of dabbling ducks winter on the marshes of the inner Dee, but only a few wander this far out. Occasionally parties of Pink-footed Geese fly over on their way to or from

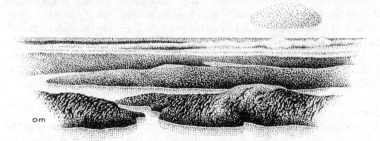

DM

Knot flock

the Lancashire mosslands and Pintail may fly over from Gayton Sands.

Scaup are now seen infrequently off Hilbre. Up to 400 have been counted in the past, but this species is now sadly rare at Hilbre and its former haunt off Caldy. Red-breasted Mergansers are regular. Sometimes Common Goldeneye or even a Long-tailed Duck are present. Common Goldeneye are regular on West Kirby Marine Lake in winter where the other three species of sea ducks mentioned may occur from time to time.

Visitors to Hilbre often go there specifically for seawatching. Two or three days of strong northwesterlies in autumn are almost guaranteed to produce Leach's Storm-petrels. Ideal conditions are infrequent – non-existent in some years – but most autumns produce at least a handful of birds. Outstanding counts in the last 30 years include 959 passing by on 27 September 1978, 337 on 14 September 1980, 265 on 19 October 1983 and 243 on 13 September 1987. Most birds beat westward into the wind close by the north end of the island. Exhausted birds may settle for a while on the sea. European Storm-petrels occur only rarely among the larger Leach's during September to November, but have become more regular during the summer in recent times with as many as 30 seen on 21 July 2005 and 42 seen on 16 August 2007.

Autumnal storms produce other exciting seabirds. Arctic Skuas – which pass occasionally in spring and at any time from July to October – are most numerous at such times, with a few Great Skuas and a chance of the delicate Long-tailed or heavy Pomarine. One or two Long-tailed Skuas are reported during prolonged windy spells in autumn. Grey Phalaropes are not seen every year but may appear under such conditions. And as Kittiwakes stream past look out for the stunning tri-coloured wing pattern of the rare Sabine's Gull. A winter flock of Little Gulls in Liverpool Bay varies greatly in size from year to year, and these birds may be blown inshore. In the last decade or so a strong passage of Little Gulls has been observed at Hilbre from March to April. They have recently taken to roosting on the West Hoyle Bank, albeit rather distantly observed from Hilbre. The largest count is an incredible 628 on 20 March 2006.

Seawatching from Hilbre is productive at any time of year. Divers occur from September to May, although daily totals seldom rise above 20. Red-throated Diver is by far the most numerous: up to 100 can be recorded in a day. Great Northern Diver is seen on a handful of days each year. Black-throated is even less regular although spring (March through to May) is a good time. The smaller grebes also occur, albeit rarely with only three or four records a year; Slavonian and Red-necked Grebes are more likely than Black-necked, which is the scarcest of the trio at Hilbre.

Fulmars fly within sight of land between March and October when the wind blows from the west or northwest. Manx Shearwaters appear under similar conditions between June and September and several hundred may be counted on good days, with the occasional Sooty Shearwater thrown in. Gannets are seen from March to November. Few ducks frequent the open sea off the Dee mouth, but Common Scoters may be seen in any month (perhaps least often in late winter and early summer). Occasionally rafts of up to 100 bob offshore, but more usually small parties fly past in lines well out near the wind farm. Recent counts of up to two or three thousand have been recorded. Velvet Scoter is rare but does occur.

Terns can be seen offshore from Hilbre from April to October. Common Tern is generally the most numerous, and occurs throughout the summer.

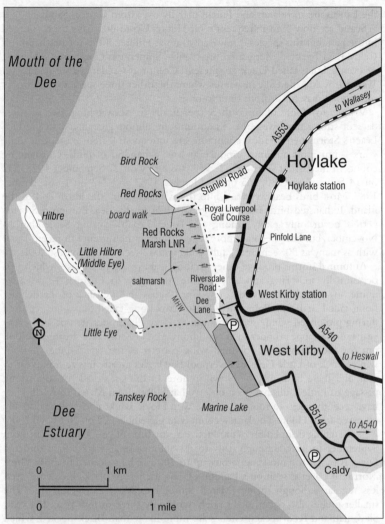

Dozens may be counted on spring days, with much larger numbers from July to September. Arctic Terns pass through in small numbers, particularly in spring and autumn.

Little Terns visit from late April to early September and are probably birds from the nearby colony at Point of Ayr. Noisy Sandwich Terns are the first to arrive, in March, but peak numbers occur in July and August when several hundred roost on the sandbanks along with other terns. A few late birds hang around into October. Roseate Tern is a very scarce migrant with an occasional spring or summer record. Black Terns are a little more frequent, particularly during early autumn seawatches.

A small flock of Common Guillemots and Razorbills moult in Liverpool Bay during summer. Only single figures of either are likely on any day from December to August, but larger numbers may come within range given onshore winds in the autumn. Other auks – Puffin in spring, Little Auk in late autumn/winter and Black Guillemot at any time of year – are less than annual.

Movements of passerine migrants have been studied intensively at Hilbre. Spring passage begins in early March or even February with Stonechats usually heralding the start. The first Chiffchaffs, Northern Wheatears and perhaps a Ring Ouzel arrive in March. A spectacular movement of Meadow Pipits reaches a peak in late March or early April, when a couple of thousand birds may pass in a day. Migration is at its height in late April or early May when, given suitable conditions (usually southeast winds), the bushes may be full of migrants shortly after dawn. Willow Warbler is the principal species involved.

Spring passage at Hilbre is more varied than in autumn. Sedge and Grasshopper Warblers, Common and Lesser Whitethroats, Common Redstart and Whinchat are typical spring migrant species. Tree Pipit and Yellow Wagtail are also frequent. Many other summer visitors occur in smaller numbers. Recent rarities include a Red-rumped Swallow in May 1988, a Melodious Warbler caught in May 1994 and two male Subalpine Warblers in April (1988 and 2006). The shortage of vegetation cover on Hilbre means that migrants are unlikely to stay for more than a few hours or a day at most. Considerable numbers of finches pass through in April and May, with Goldfinch, Lesser Redpoll, Linnet and Siskin the principal species. Tree Sparrow occurs in very small numbers. Late spring is largely quiet, but Spotted Flycatcher occurs in mid May to early June and there are occasional rarities at that time, such as a European Bee-eater in June 1990.

Emigration of summer visitors picks up in August, when the largest autumn totals of Willow Warblers occur. Over 100 of these dainty birds may descend on Hilbre; there was an exceptional arrival of as many as 400 on 5 August 2004. There is less variety on the island during autumn passage, but Garden Warblers occur more often at this season than in spring and Pied Flycatcher is sometimes seen. A few Black Redstarts are noted each year, either in spring or late autumn. Yellow-browed Warblers have made appearances several times in late September and October, and Icterine and Melodious Warblers have visited. A Yellow-breasted Bunting in September 1994 and a Pallas's Warbler in October 1997 were exceptional west-coast records. Relatively few diurnal migrants pass over Hilbre compared with the mainland coastline. However, immigrant winter thrushes and Starlings fly over the island in large numbers from October onwards, when finch movements may also be heavy. Renewed movement of plovers, larks and thrushes may follow winter frosts. Snow Buntings are seen regularly in some winters and occasionally in others.

Timing

For seawatching, strong winds from the northwest are ideal. A persistent blow for two or more days in September or October will bring in storm-petrels, Little Gull, skuas and shearwaters. Consult tide tables and time your visit around high tide, but pay particular attention to the state of the tide when visiting this tidal island (see Access). In April and May the largest arrivals of warblers and other passerines take place with southeast winds. Birds arrive shortly after dawn, rest and feed briefly then move on. Few remain by mid morning. In autumn east or northeast winds bring in the birds. Severe winter weather may bring large westward movements of birds seeking milder conditions. A thaw following prolonged cold induces return movements.

Access

Permits are no longer necessary to visit the island, except for groups of more than six persons in which case apply to the Wirral Borough Council Ranger Service, Visitor Centre, Wirral Country Park, Station Road, Thurstaston, Wirral, L61 0HN. The centre is open daily from 10 am until 5 pm (tel: 0151 648 4371/3884). The walk across the sands to Hilbre can be tricky and should not be attempted in foggy conditions. From junction 2 of the M53 follow signs for West Kirby, then the brown signs for the Marine Lake which lead to Dee Lane.

It is usual to set out from the end of Dee Lane at least three hours before high tide and head for the left-hand side of the southernmost (left-hand) island, Little Eye, thereby avoiding treacherous gutters. Follow the western side of Little Eye and then eastern side of Middle Eye to Hilbre. Visitors must then remain on the island until at least two hours after high tide when a return to the mainland is again possible. The marine lake at West Kirby is obvious from the end of Dee Lane and should be checked for waterfowl and gulls.

CALENDAR

All year: Few nesting species. Cormorant and Kestrel present for much of the year.

December–February: Vast flocks of estuarine waders such as Dunlin, Oystercatcher, Curlew and Knot as well as rock-dwellers Turnstone and Purple Sandpiper around Hilbre. Large wintering flock of Pale-bellied Brent Geese and smaller numbers of Dark-bellied. Common Scoter, Red-breasted Merganser and other sea ducks. Peregrine Falcon and Merlin hunt the waders. Red-throated Diver and Great Crested Grebe are likely on the sea, and a chance of scarcer divers and grebes. Severe weather brings westward movements of Northern Lapwings, European Golden Plovers, Skylarks and thrushes. Wandering Pink-footed Geese. Snow Bunting is a possibility.

March–May: Winter ducks; Brent Geese and wader flocks disperse. Spring passage brings Sanderling, Whimbrel, Common Sandpiper and other wader species. Purple Sandpipers depart by early May. Seawatching improves, with possibility of Fulmar, Gannet and Kittiwake from March onwards, and less likely a skua. Terns appear during April. Passerine migration starts in March; heavy movements of Meadow Pipit in late March and early April. Passage peaks late April to early May with

falls of Willow Warbler, other warblers and chats. White and Yellow Wagtails are regular. Steady passage of hirundines. Northern Wheatear passes through in good numbers.

June–July: Common, Sandwich and Little Terns offshore. Fulmar, Gannet, Manx Shearwater and European Storm-petrel in appropriate windy conditions. Small numbers of non-breeding waders summer in the estuary; by late July Sanderling and other species start to return.

August–November: Wader flocks increase. Early birds may be in breeding plumage. Purple Sandpiper return in October and November. Northwesterly gales in September and October (even early November) bring Leach's Storm-Petrel; Arctic, Great, perhaps Pomarine and possibly Long-tailed Skuas; Kittiwake and Little Gull with the occasional Sabine's Gull. Manx Shearwater until end of September, Fulmar and auks into October, and Gannet until November; Common Scoter throughout. Large gathering of terns in early autumn. Falls of warblers in August or September mostly Willow Warbler or Chiffchaff, with the occasional rarity. Diurnal passage in October and November involves winter thrushes, Starling, Chaffinch, Linnet and Greenfinch, and buntings (which may include Snow Bunting).

78 RED ROCKS, HOYLAKE

OS Landranger Map 108
SJ20-88

Habitat

Red Rocks, at Hoylake, is the northwest tip of mainland Wirral and consists, like Hilbre Island (site 77), of a sandstone outcrop. The farthest point, Bird Rock, is cut off by the tide and is then popular with roosting waders, provided anglers do not occupy it. Private gardens at the point contain a number of bushes and trees attractive to migrants. Around the corner into the estuary a line of mature sand dunes runs south to West Kirby, separating the Royal Liverpool golf course from the shore. Just south of the gardens on Stanley Road between the dunes and the beach lies Red Rocks Marsh, a Cheshire Wildlife Trust reserve with a reedbed and alder thickets. On the beach itself the expanding West Kirby saltmarsh runs north to south along the beach from West Kirby to Red Rocks.

Species

Red Rocks, like Hilbre, is one of the richest areas for birdwatching in Cheshire and Wirral. Sedge, Reed and Grasshopper Warblers are the main breeding birds of note. Many of the Dee's estuarine waders can be seen feeding off the marsh and, as the tide rises, in flight out of the estuary past the point. These birds used to roost on the beach here and due to the efforts of the Dee Estuary Voluntary Wardens, they have been returning in the last decade or so. Peregrines are frequently seen hunting waders over the estuary. As at Hilbre, movements of passerine migrants have been studied, albeit not so intensively, and although there is a great deal of similarity between movements at the two sites there are also some stark differences.

March brings the first spring visitors, with Goldcrests visiting the gardens. Meadow Pipit passage is heavy in early spring (as on Hilbre). Westward passage of Collared Doves is a feature at Red Rocks in April, with up to 100 or more on some days. Conditions suitable for a fall are infrequent, but prolonged southerly winds and poor visibility may ground Willow Warblers and small numbers of other migrants at the point soon after dawn. Such days are rare, however, and the vast majority of migrants pass straight through. White Wagtails are seen more regularly on the west coast of Wirral than anywhere else in Cheshire. It seems probable that these pale, slender wagtails are moving up the west coast of Britain towards Icelandic rather than continental breeding grounds. Up to 45 or so may frequent the beach at Red Rocks between mid April and mid May, with a couple of hundred counted on several occasions. The best area for these is now the North Wirral beach between Red Rocks and the Old Baths at Hoylake. Spring rarities have included Bluethroat, Dartford Warbler, Tawny Pipit, Savi's Warbler, Serin and three Red-backed Shrikes. Hoopoe has occurred on several occasions. Red Rocks can be difficult to cover as the gardens and golf course – both very productive for migrants and rarities – are private with severely restricted access.

Seawatching at Red Rocks can be good given onshore winds. Fulmars and Gannets are visible offshore between March and June and again in autumn. Manx Shearwaters pass in small numbers between June and September.

Occasional larger scale movements characteristic of this species are increasingly accompanied by sightings of Mediterranean Shearwater. Autumn gales may bring Leach's Storm-petrel, skuas and other exciting species. Be warned, though, that there is little shelter here for seawatchers and there is little or no elevation.

Diurnal autumn migrants following the coastline southwards start with swifts in July. Sizeable movements of hirundines may follow as autumn progresses and have included a Red-rumped Swallow. Tree Pipit may be picked up overhead by their rough "teez" call and are much more regular here in autumn than Hilbre (where they are almost absent at this time of year). Easterly winds in autumn, as in spring, may also bring in rarities. These have included Yellow-browed Warblers, several Richard's Pipits and Red-throated Pipit. Extreme rarities recorded at Red Rocks include the amazing record of a Black-billed Cuckoo from America.

From mid September to mid October parties of Blue Tit fly westward along the north coast of Wirral and either drop into the reeds at Red Rocks or turn south and follow the Wirral coast or head high west. They are accompanied by smaller numbers of other tits and sometimes a Treecreeper or woodpecker. Ringing has shown these to be local birds dispersing after the breeding season. Large numbers of immigrant winter visitors fly over the Dee mouth from late September into November. Movement is most concentrated at the point in the second half of October. Hundreds, even thousands of Starlings, Redwings, Fieldfares and Chaffinches may be counted in a day, with smaller numbers of Linnet, Greenfinch and other species. Snow Buntings may also join in these movements and a Lapland Bunting may sometimes be heard passing overhead or flushed from the saltmarsh. Winter frosts may initiate cold-weather movements. With the onset of severe weather European Golden Plovers, Northern Lapwings, Skylarks, thrushes and other birds fly west into Wales, perhaps on their way to Ireland.

Timing

Waders can be seen roosting again on West Kirby shore in recent years, but birds can also be watched feeding from various points as the tide rises and falls. Spring arrivals of migrant passerines are assisted by winds from a southerly quarter. Dawn visits are advisable at Red Rocks, although a search of the bushes here and along the coast may reveal migrants lingering later in the day. In autumn east or northeast winds bring in the birds.

Dispersal movements may be witnessed at Red Rocks on any fine morning in the autumn, but for diurnal movements of long distance migrants weather conditions are more critical. Low cloud with a fresh or strong breeze from a southerly quarter will result in heavy visible passage, particularly for the first two hours after dawn, but movement may continue throughout the day. There is little passage with strong wind, mist or fog, and with clear skies and light wind the birds will fly too high to be seen. Birders are advised to get to Red Rocks early as it is definitely a morning site.

Access

From the Hoylake roundabout on the A553 turn north onto a minor road then first left into Stanley Road (SJ214889). Park at the far end and either walk right to the point (SJ203886) for seawatching and to scan the flats or turn left for the marsh, which is soon obvious between the beach and the golf course.

Migrants may frequent the reedbed or bushes in the dunes. The best cover is a small poplar plantation at the north end of the marsh. Please do not enter the private areas or Red Rocks marsh itself.

CALENDAR

All year: Waders may be present all year with non-breeding birds summering in the estuary.

December–February: Wader flocks and Shelduck offshore, with hunting Peregrine Falcon. Severe weather brings westward movement of Northern Lapwing, European Golden Plover, Skylark and thrushes, with wandering Pink-footed Goose. Stonechat along the dunes and Snow Bunting a possibility.

March–May: Passerine migration starts in March, peaking late April–early May. Similar species involved as at Hilbre, but White Wagtail along Red Rocks shore and large movements of Collared Dove. Fulmar and Gannet in onshore winds, with terns from April.

June–July: Common Tern offshore and Manx Shearwater on passage days. Small numbers of non-breeding waders. Grasshopper Warbler along the coast. Mediterranean Gull is seen with some regularity, particularly from King's Gap, Hoylake.

August–November: Falls of common warblers in early autumn, with perhaps the odd rarity. Tits and other species on dispersal are seen in good numbers. Diurnal passage of winter thrushes in October and November. Starling, Chaffinch, Linnet, Greenfinch and buntings, which may include Snow Bunting. Seawatching can be excellent at this season, with skuas and storm-petrels after strong westerlies.

79 NORTH WIRRAL SHORE OS Landranger Map 108
SJ29

The north shore of Wirral, running east from Hoylake to New Brighton, is largely given over to market gardens defended from the sea by a fixed dune system and a man-made sea defence that runs from Dove Point all the way through to New Brighton. The whole area may prove attractive to migrants given the right weather conditions. Rarities have included Great Grey Shrikes, Red-breasted Flycatcher, Richard's and Red-throated Pipits, Pallas's Warbler, Yellow-browed Warblers, Savi's Warbler and Britain's fourth Desert Warbler from 28 October to 22 November 1978. During northwest gales the entire coastline offers good seawatching, especially at high tide in autumn. Vehicular access to the top is limited, but is possible at a number of sites including Dove Point, The Gunsite and New Brighton.

79A DOVE POINT, MEOLS   OS ref: SJ234907

Dove Point is reached by driving to the easternmost point of Hoylake promenade. Storm-petrels, skuas and shearwaters may be seen here after north-west gales in September and October. Leach's Storm-petrels often come close to shore, beating their way between the moored boats and yachts. Dove Point, like New Brighton, allows the luxury of seawatching from a car (an important factor in a gale). The state of the tide is critical: passing birds will be too distant

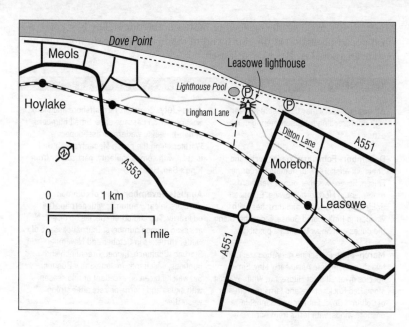

for adequate views unless the East Hoyle sandbank is flooded completely. On less windy days the sandbank is worth checking, particularly in August when numerous gulls and terns roost on its easternmost end. In recent years, Mediterranean Gulls have been seen regularly between here and Hoylake.

79B MEOLS THROUGH LEASOWE LIGHTHOUSE   OS ref: SJ262918

This area lies between Dove Point and the Leasowe lighthouse (SJ262918). Lingham Lane runs south from the lighthouse. The hedges on either side of this lane are probably the easiest section to cover. Separated slightly from other sites on the north shore, Ditton Lane runs east-west between the A551 coast road and the Birkett (SJ258913). The patch of willow and alder cover can be full of migrants, but covering it often proves frustrating for a single observer and perhaps this is why it has produced little of interest over the years.

In migration periods, the coastal fields immediately behind the seawall are particularly good for Northern Wheatear, Whinchat, Ring Ouzel and pipits. Stonechat is a regular breeding species. Skylark and Northern Lapwing also breed. The hedges and ditches are attractive to warblers, with Grasshopper Warbler a regular breeder. Access to the market gardens is limited, but they can be viewed from the public footpath and private road (which is a public right of way).

This is a large geographical area within which there are many fields, hedges and copses that are all worth a look. The row of sycamores and silver poplars that runs northwest to southeast down the side of Stone Cottage just prior to the lighthouse is excellent. As well as providing cover for the usual summer migrants, such as Grasshopper Warbler and Pied Flycatcher, the trees have attracted singing Serin in spring and Yellow-browed Warbler in autumn.

The car park is a favourite area for Stonechats and other common migrants during a spring fall. The horse paddock at the very beginning of Lingham Lane (usually full of daisies in April) is excellent for wagtails, pipits, buntings and finches. Ring Ouzel is always a prize find.

Farther down the lane there is a bridge that crosses the Birket. Here Spotted Flycatcher, Grey Wagtail and Kingfisher can be found with a little effort. Through Lingham Farm is the now almost completely in-filled old brick pit. This site has in the past produced Ring-billed Gull and Black-throated Diver. Now it is a mass of bricks and rubble and looks ideal habitat for Black Redstart, so might still be worth a look.

The whole length of the lane is exciting and has produced such rarities as Firecrest and Yellow-browed, Pallas's, Barred and Subalpine Warblers.

Back at the entrance of the lane there is a public footpath that runs between the inland fields on the left and coastal fields on the right. This path runs east to west and continues all the way through to Meols. Once again these fields are a magnet for Yellow Wagtails and Wheatears in the spring, especially when flooded. Short-eared Owls may be seen in the winter and many waders use these fields in which to roost over high tide. Unusual species in the fields have included Stone Curlew, Short-toed lark, Red-throated, Tawny and Richard's Pipits (the last two relatively frequently) and Lapland and Little Buntings.

79C GUN SITE CAR PARK (LEASOWE)

Access
Take the A554 from Junction 1 of the M53 towards New Brighton. After the second slip road there is a sign saying North Wirral Coastal Park. Turn left here into Green Lane. Follow the lane all the way, passing two car parks on the left until eventually arriving at the car park by the sea defence, where access is easy because you can drive on to and park at the very edge of the sea defence. Being able to seawatch from a car is most definitely a plus, especially if it is raining. The slightly elevated position allows better viewing and from here you can see birds both exiting the Mersey mouth and flying straight along the coast. The only drawback is that telescopes can vibrate somewhat when resting on the open car window or attached to a window clamp.

Take care on particularly high tides with very strong winds as the waves come over the top and flood the car park. When that happens it is probably time to go home and batten down the hatches.

A good blow in July and August should produce storm-petrels, Arctic Skua and possibly Sooty Shearwater. The same conditions in September and October are good for Leach's Storm-petrel and Pomarine and Great Skuas. Sabine's Gull and Grey Phalarope are possible.

80 NEW BRIGHTON AND THE OUTER MERSEY ESTUARY

OS Landranger Map 108

Habitat

The former holiday resort of New Brighton stands on the corner of the Mersey estuary at the east end of the north Wirral shore. Unusually for the area, the beach here is rocky. A sewage outfall is an attraction for touring gulls. New Brighton itself has little to offer and birdwatchers stand with their backs to the town looking out. A mixture of gulls and terns follow the Mersey ferries at Seacombe jetty to the south.

Between Rock Ferry oil terminal and New Ferry, 5 to 6 miles (8 to 10 km) up river from the mouth, is another stretch of muddy beach, with some rocky areas and with a developing saltmarsh at its southern end. During autumn and winter there is a small roost of waders by the saltmarsh. In midwinter up to several hundred Common Teal and Pintail are present regularly and over 1,000 each of Knot and Dunlin appear on occasion. There is a rubbish tip to north of Bromborough Pool that attracts large numbers of gulls, many of which rest on the river.

Species

New Brighton is best known for the shelters on its promenade that provide cover for seawatching during autumn storms. The Irish Sea is largely land-locked, so contains fewer seabird species than more exposed Atlantic or North Sea coasts. Northwest gales can produce birds in any month, but the chief attraction is in autumn when hundreds of Leach's Storm-petrels may appear offshore. The Mersey mouth lies in the angle between the Lancashire and North Wales/Wirral coasts, so persistent gales lasting over two or more days funnel birds into the river. Under such conditions storm-petrels may be seen upriver as far as Seacombe Ferry. Odd birds appear even over inland meres and flashes. Many beat out of the river mouth past Fort Perch Rock, some of them being

Leach's Petrel

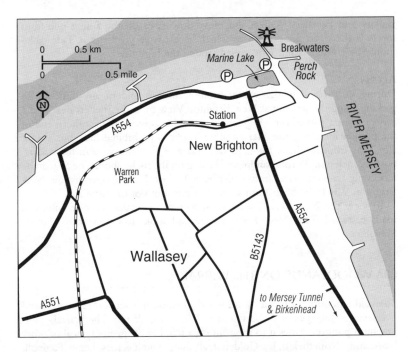

blown back to make further passes. The range of other seabirds involved is similar to those at Hilbre or Seaforth. Pomarine and Long-tailed Skuas and Sabine's Gulls are regular given suitable conditions, which may be less than annual.

From late summer to spring Turnstones frequent the rocky beach, and may be joined in winter by a few Purple Sandpipers. Common Eiders are occasionally seen off Fort Perch Rock. Gulls around the sewage outfall may include uncommon species. Birds following the Mersey ferries at Seacombe have included Little and Mediterranean Gulls as well as Kittiwakes. Little Gulls are very often present in the river, although more usually on the Liverpool side. The river mouth is at its narrowest here, so watches at passage times allow reasonable views of terns, including Black Tern, following easterly winds. Rarer gulls and terns have been recorded.

The New Ferry wader roosts consist chiefly of Redshank, Curlew, Oystercatcher, Knot and Dunlin, but many other estuary species appear from time to time. Common Teal and Pintail are present along the shore in winter, the latter offering close views at times. Glaucous and other gulls join the throng scavenging at the tip or loafing offshore.

Timing

For seawatching, strong winds from a northwesterly quarter are ideal, and a persistent blow for two or more days in September or October will bring in storm-petrels, Little Gulls and skuas. At low tide the sea retreats a considerable distance from the shore, although watching is still practicable from New Brighton, During the strongest blows storm-petrels may be seen flying over the beach at Leasowe. The shore at New Ferry is narrower and birds are more likely to be driven into view by a rising tide. Roosts are largest here during

January and February. Waders also move downriver on the falling tide from roosts farther into the estuary to which access is very restricted. Tide tables should be consulted and visits timed around the high tide.

Access

During storms and in the winter months there is seldom any difficulty in parking along the seafront at New Brighton. View from the shelters near to the fort or from a parked car. The sewage outfall lies towards the southern end of the promenade along the Mersey shore. Traffic is prohibited here, but a walk along the front to check the gulls will also give a chance to scan for waders, possibly including Purple Sandpiper, feeding on the rocky shore. The Seacombe ferries ply across the river from a pier head 2 miles (3.2 km) upriver from New Brighton. Watch the boats from vantage points south of the terminal.

To view the New Ferry wader roost and winter wildfowl, take suburban roads eastward from New Ferry village and look down the clay cliffs at SJ343855.

80A WOODLANDS ON THE WIRRAL

To avoid repetition of species from wood to wood this section gives a general overview of the species to be found in Wirral woodlands. The Wirral's geographical position causes it to miss out on a number of species typical of other woodlands. Nonetheless, Jay, Goldcrest, all three woodpeckers, Lesser Redpoll, Siskin, Goldfinch, Chaffinch and all the English tits occur. Fieldfare, Redwing, Woodcock, Chiffchaff, Willow Warbler, Blackcap and Garden Warbler can all be found in most Wirral Woodlands. The following is a list of the better woodlands on the Wirral. Any specialty of that particular woodland is highlighted.

ARROWE PARK

Access

From junction 3 of the M53 take the first exit and continue on this road past Asda on your right up the hill. The park can be accessed via the gate opposite the Arrowe Park public house.

Species

Firecrest and Tawny Owl.

STAPLEDON WOODS

Access

Take the A540 from West Kirby heading south. Proceed past the boys grammar school on the left and about 300 yards (275 m) on the right is Kings Drive North. Park and enter the woods here.

Species

Wood Warbler and Lesser Spotted Woodpecker particularly near the bottom and middle tracks. Migrants occur during spring and autumn and rarities have included a White-throated Sparrow in May 2003.

ROYDEN PARK/THURSTASTON

Access
Continue along the A540 as above you reach a roundabout. Turn left here up Montgomery Hill and then right opposite the Farmers Arms public house to bring you to the entrance for Royden Park. Alternatively continue straight over the roundabout through the sandstone cutting and access Thurstaston on the left where there is ample parking. This is quite a large area to cover.

Species
Pied Flycatcher, Green Woodpecker, Woodcock and Lesser Redpoll.

STORETON WOODS

Access
Take Junction 4 Birkenhead exit off the M53 and continue along this road until you reach Red Hill road on your left. Park in this road and enter the woods.

Species
Lesser Spotted Woodpecker, Siskin, Lesser Redpoll; Grey Partridge and Pheasant in surrounding farmland.

EASTHAM WOODS

Access
Take Junction 5 off the M53 and follow the A41 in the direction of Birkenhead until you reach Eastham village road on the right. Follow the road all the way, continuing along Ferry Road until you reach the country park car park at the end.

Species
Owls, Pied Flycatcher and Firecrest.

BURTON WOODS

Access
Take Mudhouse lane off the A540 at Burton, which continues into Burton village and park. Enter the wood via a small lane called Mill Lane.

Species
Common Crossbill, Wood Warbler (occasional).

BIDSTON HILL

Access
Take junction 1 off the M53. Follow the Bidston link road towards Birkenhead then the A553 Hoylake Road towards Birkenhead. Turn right by the church up Worcester Road then right into Vyner Road North where the wood can be accessed at a number of points.

Species

Green Woodpecker and Firecrest. Golden Oriole and Pallas's Warbler have occurred in the past.

BROTHERTON WOODS/DIBBINSDALE

Access

Take Junction 4 off the M53. Follow the B5137 towards Bromborough along Spital Road turning right at the mini roundabout. The entrance is on the right. A great woodland with easy access.

Species

Lesser Spotted Woodpecker, Firecrest and Garden Warbler.

RIVACRE VALLEY

Access

Take Junction 7 off the M53. Go down the B5132 Netherpool Road and back on your self onto Rivacre Road (still the B5132). Park in the ample car park at the Country Park for relatively easy access.

Species

Kingfisher, Lesser Spotted Woodpecker and Firecrest.

81 WIRRAL WAY

Habitat

The Wirral Way is a public footpath that runs from West Kirby in north Wirral down the whole of west Wirral to Parkgate, where it turns inland towards Willaston and eventually ends in Hooton. This route has some mixed evergreens, pines and deciduous trees between tracks of farmland, but the bulk is made up of hedges of which hawthorn is a particular feature.

Species

There is no particular best spot along this route. Thurstaston is excellent for Lesser Whitethroat and Green Woodpecker, and there has been a Hoopoe nearby in the past. Both Willow and Marsh Tits have been recorded just at the back off the Wirral Way at Thurstaston Country Park visitor centre. Willow Tit can also be found in the Heswall area near Pipers Lane. The arable land is always worth checking for Grey and Red-legged Partridges, although the latter is scarce. During the summer months listen for the quiet "quip" of Quail as they arrive back from Africa.

Access

Access the Wirral Way at one of many points along its length from the start at West Kirby (on the A540 opposite the end of Orrysdale Road) to Hooton.

Isle of Man

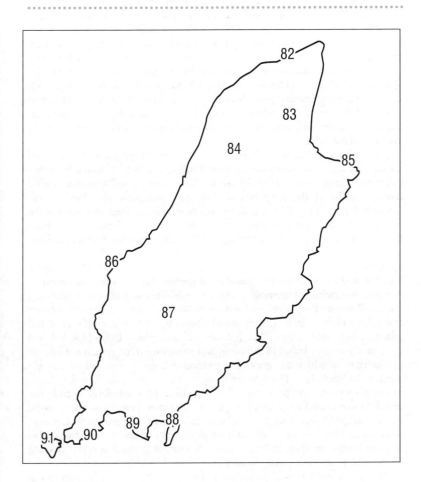

82 The Ayres
83 Glascoe Dub
84 Ballaugh Curragh
85 Maughold Brooghs
86 Peel

87 Eairy and Kionslieu Dams
88 Langness and Derby Haven
89 Strandhall and Poyll Vaaish
90 Chasms and Sugar Loaf
91 Calf of Man

From a birdwatcher's point of view, the main focus of attention has to be the coast, from the sheer cliffs and rocky shores of the south to the long sandy and pebbly beaches of the north. But, there are many inland attractions, too. The hills are mostly rounded in outline and are reminiscent more of the adjacent parts of Ireland than the Cumbrian Mountains. They are traversed by excellent roads and are easily explored by car, but the Snaefell Mountain Railway is the only form of public transport providing access. The unclassified road linking the B10 with Ballaugh is particularly recommended. Of the many wooded glens, Silverdale is the richest in birdlife, but Ballaglass, Tholt y Will, Glen Helen and Glenmaye offer the finest scenery. The larger reservoirs are disappointing and Kerrowdhoo alone attracts a modest variety of wildfowl.

The Manx passion for motor sports should be borne in mind by visitors looking for peace and quiet. The TT Races and Manx Grand Prix each occupy two-week periods, starting in late May and late August respectively. These take place on the Mountain Course (clearly marked on the OS map) and the roads are closed during practice periods and races. Similarly the Southern Hundred course, to the west of Castletown, is closed on occasions during the summer. Elsewhere, rallies will from time to time necessitate closure of sections of highway island-wide.

The island can be reached by sea from both Heysham and Liverpool throughout the year and seasonally from Dublin and Belfast. Ronaldsway has direct connections with many airports in Britain and Ireland. Car Hire can be arranged easily at the Airport and there is a comprehensive bus service. Additionally, the Isle of Man Railway operates a steam train summer service between Douglas and Port Erin, and the Manx Electric Railway runs from Douglas via Laxey to Ramsey throughout the year (www.iombusandrail.info).

Species

The Isle of Man is home to a number of species that are scarce or absent in north-west England. Foremost is the Chough. This is a common breeding species all around the rocky coast and forms flocks of up to 100 during autumn and winter. There is an increasing population of Ravens, both on the coast and inland, where tree nesting has become commonplace. Both Hooded and Carrion Crows occur and hybridise to an increasing extent, producing a range of plumages in which the grey of the Hooded Crow is replaced by variable amounts of black. Hen Harriers are spared persecution on the island and nest in good numbers on the moors; they also hunt over farmland outside the breeding season and roost communally at three sites. Peregrines are plentiful and can often be seen over Douglas and other towns. Manx Shearwaters have returned to breed on the Calf in recent years and pass the west coast of Man in considerable numbers in late summer. Seawatching can also reveal Basking Sharks and a variety of cetacean species.

One of the most typical passerines is the Stonechat, which is abundant at coastal sites at all seasons with smaller numbers inland during the summer months. The Whinchat favours the bracken-rich upper valleys of the Laxey (SC4186), Cornaa (SC4389) and Glen Auldyn (SC4291) rivers. Several pairs breed at each site.

Whooper Swans are annual visitors to the northern plain, with herds of up to 60 settling in the Ballacain area (SC3596) and on farmland to the west. Smaller numbers appear from time to time at the Bishop's Dub, to the south-west of Ballaugh (SC333929), and on Kionslieu. Flocks of over 50 Goldeneye are present through the winter off Ramsey Vollan (SC454962).

During the last decade the Eider has become a familiar species, especially along the west coast, where large groups of young are frequently seen. Purple Sandpipers have several favoured wintering sites, notably the rocks by Peel Castle, Niarbyl (SC211777), Port St Mary Point and Port Jack on Douglas Bay.

There are four Kittiwake colonies, Black Guillemot is a Manx speciality, but Puffins are rather scarce.

Grey Wagtail is the most characteristic inhabitant of the rocky streams that often visits the coast as well as towns and gardens during winter. Common Sandpipers occur only on passage. Dippers are curiously absent. Goosanders are now becoming regular winter visitors to the lower stretches of the Glass and Sulby Rivers.

The Manx avifauna perhaps has more in common with Ireland than with Cumbria and Galloway: woodpeckers and Tawny Owl are effectively absent and, as in Ireland, Long-eared is the common owl. Pied Flycatcher, Marsh and Willow Tit and Nuthatch are all missing. Although well represented in most of the other areas bordering the Irish Sea, Jay and Bullfinch are absent.

82 THE AYRES: POINT OF AYRE TO THE LHEN

OS Landranger Map 95
NX30, NX40

Habitat
The area of maritime heath that stretches for six miles from the Point of Ayre to the mouth of the Lhen Trench, is known as the Ayres. At its eastern, broader end there is extensive lichen heath that gives way as it narrows to the west to a carpet of grass and in many places burnet rose. Along its inland margin there are marshy slacks with a growth of willow, which are separated from the adjacent farmland by fixed dunes covered with gorse, bramble and bracken. There is a small conifer plantation. Marram-covered dunes lie between the heathland and the shore.

The most obvious feature of the Point of Ayre is the imposing but very bare storm beach, a broad, layered area of large pebbles beyond which there is an impressive tide race. Moving westward, the pebbles become smaller and the proportion of sand increases. After Ballaghennie, the foreshore contains a mix of stones and sand with a scatter of sessile vegetation. Lower down extensive sands are revealed at low tide. In the extreme west the sluggish Lhen Trench cuts through the dunes before it tumbles over the shingle to join the sea.

To the south and west of the Point of Ayre there are extensive gravel pits. The fully worked pits east of the road were used for landfill and have now been covered with sand. The western pits are still worked in places, but there remain areas of shallow water and emergent vegetation. The creation of islands, together with appropriate planting will, it is hoped, make this an outstanding nature reserve.

Species
Waders particularly favour the shoreline three-quarters of a mile (1.2 km) to either side of Rue Point. Numbers are modest by mainland standards, but Oystercatcher, Ringed Plover, Golden Plover, Sanderling, Dunlin and Curlew can reach three figures. Turnstone is also regular, and small numbers of Grey Plover, Knot, Whimbrel and sometimes Curlew Sandpiper also occur.

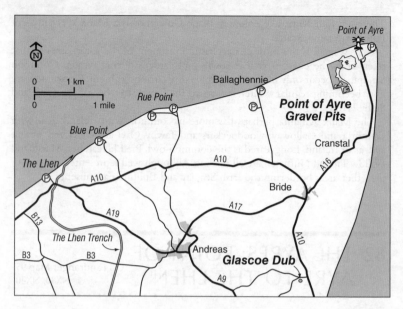

Gannets can be seen fishing here throughout the summer. Considerable numbers of northbound Manx Shearwaters pass here and at the Point of Ayre. Parties of Eiders, rafts of Common Scoter and all three divers feed offshore, particularly in autumn. Of the skuas, the Arctic is the most common, but Great and Pomarine are seen with reasonable frequency. Mediterranean and Little Gulls also turn up occasionally. In excess of 100 Sandwich Terns are often present from April to October and are joined on the beach by comparable numbers of Kittiwakes in late summer. Little Terns breed annually, but have a high failure rate. Small numbers of Arctic and Common Terns can often be found.

Hen Harrier, Kestrel, Merlin, Peregrine and Short-eared Owl sometimes hunt over the heath and Long-eared Owls nest in the Plantation. Skylarks and Meadow Pipits are plentiful, Wheatears occur particularly in the warren to the east of Blue Point, while Stonechats and, in summer, Whitethroats are prominent in the shrubby areas. Yellowhammers, once common, are now very scarce along the farmland margins.

The Point of Ayre is an excellent place for seawatching. Arctic Terns nest on the higher parts of the beach and a careful study of this zone can often reveal surprising numbers of Ringed and Golden Plovers. This is one of the best sites on the island for Snow Bunting, and Twite winter in the area in increasing numbers.

The gravel pits to the west of the road attract an increasing number and variety of species. Greylag Geese are now reaching pest proportions and Pink-feet are regular winter visitors. Flocks of Wigeon, Mallard, Pochard, Tufted Duck and Coot frequently exceed 100. Smaller numbers of Teal and Golden-eye also occur. Occasional visitors include Gadwall, Pintail, Shoveler, Scaup and Long-tailed Duck. Shelduck and Eider both breed.

Apart from Lapwing, and on spring passage Common Sandpiper and Whimbrel, waders although varied, are not plentiful; Ruff, Black-tailed Godwit and Greenshank are the most likely of the scarcer species. The most abundant breeding gulls are Herring and Lesser Black-backed, with just a few pairs of Great Black-backed and Common, and the possibility of the re-establishment of a Black-headed Gull colony.

Recent rarities in the area have included Red-crested Pochard, Ring-necked Duck, King Eider, Surf Scoter, Ruddy Duck, Wilson's Phalarope, Long-tailed Skua and Southern Grey Shrike of the Steppe subspecies.

Timing

Spring and more especially autumn are the best times for the Ayres shore, both for waders and for sea-watching. Three hours on either side of low tide is preferable, as the birds are remarkably difficult to pick out once they move on to the stony part of the beach. Winter presents a good chance of Twite and Snow Bunting around the Point of Ayre. Golden Plovers often use the fields alongside the lighthouse road. Summer is best for Little Terns, but they are sensitive to disturbance and visitors should take this into account.

Access

The principal access road for the area is the A10, which leads north from Ramsey to Bride and then west and south, eventually joining the A3 at Ballaugh. The Point of Ayre is signposted to the right at Bride Church and after 3.5 miles (5.6 km), just before the lighthouse, a metalled track leads to a parking area overlooking the eastern shore. Other tracks lead off to the north and west, where there is also easy parking.

From Bride the A10 can be followed westward with a right turn, signposted Ballaghennie and shore only at NX440019. This road passes a wooded parking place on the edge of the Ayres and continues for a further quarter of a mile (400 m) to another parking place by the visitor centre. At NX412019 there is an access road to Rue Point (no signpost) and the heath to the west, with easy parking in many places. The Blue Point access road is at NX398015. The Lhen can be reached from NX380014 by parking by the dunes and then walking about quarter of a mile (1.2 km), either through the Cronk y Bing Reserve or along the shore, to the river mouth. There is at present no public access to the gravel pits, although plans are in place for the erection of a number of hides and creation of footpaths once commercial operations cease. Buses from Ramsey serve Bride and the A10 as far as the Rue Point turning to Smeale (not Sundays). There is a twice-daily service to the Point of Ayre.

83 GLASCOE DUB

OS Landranger Map 95
SC447988

Habitat

"Dub" is the Manx name for a pond of any size, and Glascoe is one of many such ponds scattered over the northern plain. Their origin is uncertain, some are kettle holes while others are the result of extraction of marl or clay. From the birdwatchers point of view, Glascoe is far and away the best, both in terms of access and ornithological reward. It is effectively no more than a farm pond, with grazing land to the east and a damp meadow overgrown with sedge to the west. There are no reeds, but the northern end has some cover from low bankside bushes. At the southern end are muddy shallows.

The neighbouring fields are liable to flooding, in particular the field bordering the A10 to the east of the dub, and to a lesser degree the field to the south-west overlooked by Grenaby Farm.

Species

Glascoe Dub and floods have long had peaks of several hundred Wigeon and Teal, but it is only since 1995 that Pink-footed Geese have become regular winter visitors, with a peak of 73 birds at the end of 2004. This is the best place to see Shoveler, which are generally rather scarce on the island. A pair of Shelducks is often present in spring. Gadwall, Pintail and Pochard are all seen occasionally. Snipe are usually present in winter and both Oystercatcher and Redshank use the shallows at the southern end of the dub. Sand Martins, which nest in the sand cliffs to the south of the Dog Mills, feed over the dub.

Timing

Glascoe is most rewarding in winter, when wildfowl numbers are at their peak and flooding may expand the habitat considerably. Sun position dictates that the dub itself is best studied in the afternoon; the light is best for the floods in the morning.

Access

Leaving Ramsey by the A10, take the second left turn after the Dog Mills at SC449989. The dub appears behind the low stone wall at the junction by the old chapel. Watch from the road. To view the main floods, stop on the A10 about 100 yards (100 m) before the Glascoe turn and scramble up the hedge to look west across the field. The smaller Grenaby flood can be seen on the right hand side of the road about a quarter of a mile (400 m) south-west of the dub.

---

84 BALLAUGH CURRAGH   OS Ref: SC3694, SC3695

Habitat

"Curragh" is a Manx term for willow carr. Apart from the dominant grey willow, birch is also well represented and extensive areas of marshy grassland are peppered with the aromatic bog myrtle. Recently designated a Ramsar Site, Ballaugh Curragh covers 478 acres (190 ha) and includes Manx National Heritage's 202 acre (82 ha) reserve and the Manx Wildlife Trust's Close Sartfield Reserve (31 acres/12.6 ha). The latter reserve includes some curragh, but is made up largely of the drier periphery and is characterised by carefully managed hay meadows, where in spring there is a spectacular display of orchids. The curragh is traversed by the sluggish Killane river, which receives a number of small tributaries. There is much standing water, shaded by willows in the eastern part of the Manx National Heritage Reserve, as well as a picturesque shallow dub at SC363951.

Red-necked Wallaby is a surprise resident of the curragh, having escaped from the nearby Curraghs Wildlife Park many years ago. There is a small self-sustaining population.

Timing

The great harrier roost is occupied from late September into April, with October probably attracting the greatest numbers. Watching from the Close Sartfield Hide should commence at least one hour before sunset and continue as long as the light permits. Still, crisp evenings with fine visibility tend to be associated with lower counts than in stormy conditions. Several hundred Greylag Geese will be seen flighting at dusk, Water Rails squeal from a number of places and there is always a chance of seeing Merlin and Long-eared Owl. Spring provides an excellent opportunity of seeing roding Woodcock, again around sunset. Early summer is best for passerines, including the resident Siskin and Redpoll. The call of the Curlew is one of the special curragh sounds and Cuckoo can be heard occasionally; Corncrake might also, with luck, be heard on summer evenings.

Access

The two most interesting parts of the curragh – the Manx National Heritage Reserve centred on Pennyholdings Lane and the Manx Wildlife Trust's Close Sartfield Reserve – are accessed from different points.

Approaching from the south on the A3, turn left immediately after Ballaugh

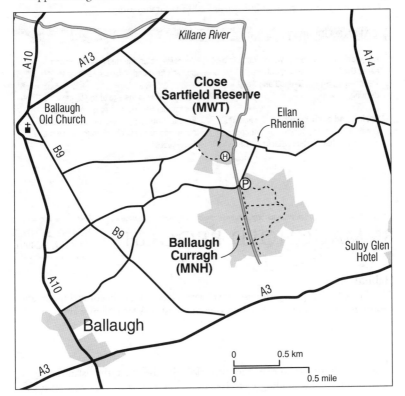

Bridge onto the A10 and take the second right turn after about 1 mile (1.5 km) at SC343945. Cross the B9 after half a mile (800 m) and continue, ignoring turns first to the right and then the left (at Palm Cottage). There are metalled tracks with a central grassy area and deep ditches on either side. After about three-quarters of a mile (1.2 km) the lane crosses a bridge, beyond which there is an obvious space for several cars to park and a large slate indicating Ballaugh Curragh. This is the start of Pennyholdings Lane, which leads to marked paths that traverse the marshes, with extensive boardwalks where necessary. One can also walk back along the lane about 100 yards (100 m) to view a shallow dub just to the south.

Travelling from Douglas via the A18 and A14, cross the A3 at the Sulby Glen Hotel (a source of good food) and after about 1 mile (1.5 km), turn left at SC378958 onto a lane that meanders through a succession of meadows to Ellan Rhennie (SC365955). Here a left turn takes one quickly to the start of Penny-holdings Lane (SC363952). From Ramsey, leave the A3 at the Sulby Glen Hotel.

From Ballaugh, start as above for Close Sartfield, but turn left on reaching the B9. At the next right turn a sign indicates Windmill Road, leading to Close Sartfield. Close Sartfield Reserve is indicated by a very discrete sign at ground level just under 1 mile (1.5 km) from the B9. Turn right into the car park (SC361956). An excellent boardwalk leads past hay meadows and through waterlogged woodland to the public hide. If approaching from the east by the A14, keep straight ahead at Ellan Rhennie and after 300 yards (300 m) turn left. The reserve car park is 200 yards (200 m) farther on.

CALENDAR

All year: Greylag Goose, Water Rail, Long-eared Owl, Long-tailed Tit, Goldcrest, Treecreeper, Siskin, Redpoll and Reed Bunting.

Spring and early summer: Corncrake, Woodcock, Curlew, Cuckoo, Grasshopper Warbler, Sedge Warbler, Blackcap, Chiffchaff,

Willow Warbler, Spotted Flycatcher and possibly Teal and Shoveler.

Winter: This is the site of the largest communal Hen Harrier roost in Western Europe. Counts in excess of 100 have been made and peak counts of up to 60 are made most years.

---

85 MAUGHOLD BROOGHS   SC4792, SC4892, SC4992, SC4991

Habitat
The brooghs are grassy slopes above slate cliffs, which become higher and sheerer from west to east. They host one of the island's four main seabird breeding sites.

Species
Nesting seabirds are the prime attraction. In the west the island's largest Cormorant colony, holding over 100 nests, covers a large area of low rocks.

Fulmars, Shags, Razorbills and Black Guillemots nest here and there along most of the site and a few Puffins can usually be seen on the sea. The most abundant species are Kittiwakes and Guillemots, which particularly occupy the ledges between St Maughold's Well and Gob ny Skeg. Ravens have nested here since time immemorial, several pairs of Chough occupy this stretch of coast and a pair of Peregrines favours the high cliffs around Traie Curn in the east. Stonechats are particularly plentiful all along the brooghs and on the adjacent gorse scrub. This is also a good place to see Loghtan Sheep. Post-breeding assemblies of Grey Seals, hauled onto the lower rocks, can approach 100.

Timing

The Ravens justify a visit from February onward, but this is essentially a late spring and early summer site for seabirds.

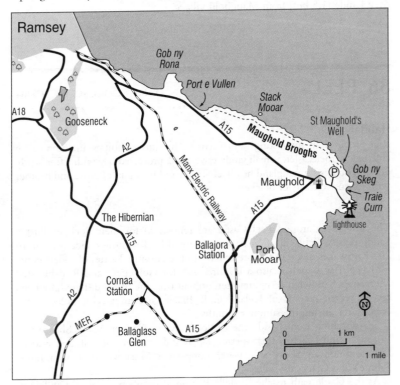

Access

Leave Douglas on the A2. Seven and a half miles (12 km) north of Laxey, turn right onto the A15, signposted Ballaglass Glen, Cornaa, Ballajora. Ignore the right turn for Ballaglass and Cornaa after nearly a mile. Fine views of the Cumbrian Mountains soon appear. Farther on, take a sharp right turn, ignoring the road of the Scarffe's Ridge, Bayr, Dreeyn Skerry and drop down past Ballajora station and then up to Maughold village green. Turn right then sharp left at the church gates and follow the lane around the north side of the churchyard before taking a sharp left turn up to a large grassy car park.

Looking towards the sea there are two gates: on the left leading to the long-distance coastal path Bayr ny Skeddan and on the right to St Maughold's Well and a rather dangerous but rewarding path towards the lighthouse. It is possible to drive on toward the lighthouse, but this is not recommended. From the first, deeply rutted parking place there are fine views to cliffs overlooking a small cove, Traie Curn. The second parking place, above the lighthouse, is little more than a turning bay.

From Ramsey, leave the town by the A2 and after 1.25 miles (2 km) take a left turn signposted Port e Vullen and Maughold (A15). After a further mile climbing up from Port e Vullen there is a footpath to the left. This follows the brooghs to the Maughold car park. Continuing along the A15 takes one directly to Maughold village. There is a good bus service between Ramsey and Maughold (not Sundays). Ballajora station on the Manx Electric Railway is just over 1 mile (1.5 km) from Maughold village.

86 PEEL

OS Ref: SC2383, SC2384, SC2484

Habitat

Peel provides an interesting assortment of maritime habitats, including slate cliffs, a low rocky islet, a small sandy cove and a protected bay with a fine sandy beach. There is some upland heath, characterised by a mix of gorse and heather with extensive tracts of bracken.

Species

The low rocks around Peel Castle are renowned for their flock of Purple Sandpipers, which will often be accompanied by Turnstones. Flocks of up to 200 Kittiwakes frequent the breakwater in the autumn. Parties of Eiders come into Peel Bay, which is also a favoured site for Goldeneye and Red-breasted Merganser. Sandwich Terns are often present over the bay and there have been several recent records of Iceland Gull. Black Guillemots visit holes in the breakwater during the summer months.

Sea-watching from beside the castle can yield Gannet, Manx Shearwater, European and Leach's Storm-petrels, skuas and a variety of gulls and waders. Less common are Sooty Shearwater, Long-tailed Skua, Mediterranean, Little, Sabine's and Glaucous Gull.

As the Castle path reaches Fenella Bay, good numbers of Black Guillemots can be seen on the sea and visiting the low-lying rocks towards Traie Dullish. Farther south, a few Puffins may be seen on the sea, but the main attraction is the rocky outcrop of Cashtal Mooar, where ranks of Guillemots, as well as Kittiwakes, can be seen during the summer. All along this coast one is likely to encounter Peregrine, Raven and Chough. The hill is an ideal Stonechat site.

Timing

Seawatching, especially for Manx Shearwaters, is most productive in south-westerly or westerly winds between early May and the end of September, with

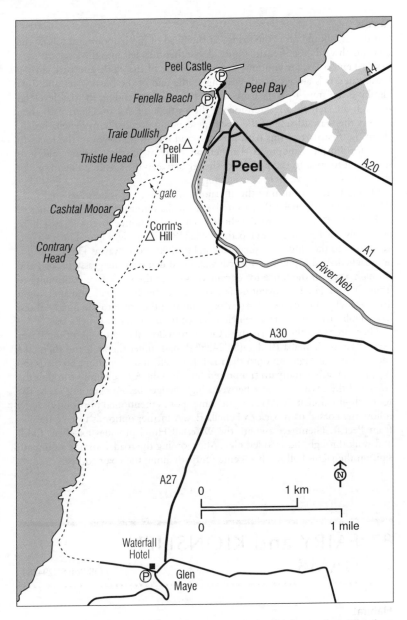

the greatest numbers between mid-August and mid-September. The best period for Leach's Storm-petrels is from the second week in September through to mid-October. Purple Sandpipers are usually absent in June and have only token numbers in July and August, but there are good numbers during all the other months. Numbers in general seem to have declined recently. The state of the tide is unimportant: just study the rocks carefully all the way from the breakwater to Fenella Bay.

Access

Car drivers should cross the bridge at the head of the harbour and follow the quay northward. Just after the footbridge, either turn left into the large car park beside Fenella Bay or continue around the side of the castle and park on the breakwater. It is always worth walking to the end of the breakwater and then climbing the steps to walk back along the wall. Descending to road level, go through an arch in an extension of the castle wall. An excellent path then follows the seaward side of the castle, descending eventually to Fenella beach. From the first part of this path it is easy and safe to go down to the rocks to look for Purple Sandpipers. Farther on there is a safety railing and it is important to stick to the path. Take shelter between the Castle wall and one of the buttresses for excellent seawatching.

Owing to the position of the afternoon sun, the coast is best explored from the south. From Fenella Bay, a number of paths traverse Peel Hill. A concrete path climbs to cross a broad vehicle track and continue over the two hills, eventually reaching the coastal path at SC231826. Turn right here. The path gets very close to the cliffs at Cashtal Mooar, but then veers away as Thistle Head is approached. At this point it is worth walking down over the grassy broogh and through a gap in the fence for decent views over the sea before continuing to Traie Dullish. The less adventurous should go through the gate and after about 100 yards (100 m) follow a narrow path through the gorse to the quarry above Traie Dullish, from where a vehicle track continues towards Fenella Bay.

There are two other alternatives. One is to follow the east bank of the River Neb as far as Glenfaba Bridge (SC242831), pass under the arch and then take the steps on the right up onto the road. Turn left, and after about 50 yards (50 m) join the public footpath signposted on the right. A lane climbs through the trees and then winds its way between high hedges before climbing up to the footpath junction at SC231826 (the same spot as mentioned previously). Now follow the coastal path back to Fenella Bay. A further option is to take the bus from Peel to Glenmaye (where the Waterfall Hotel provides excellent food) and walk through the wooded glen. After joining the road, look for a footpath sign on the right. Follow this scenic footpath along the coast to Peel.

87 EAIRY and KIONSLIEU DAMS
OS Ref: SC294780

Habitat

The Eairy Dam is a 5.5 acre (2.2 ha) freshwater lake with marginal vegetation. The sloping west bank is covered mostly with gorse. Mature trees line the east bank. At the northern end the reedy shallows extend into a 600-yard (600 m) stretch of willow carr, which ends at the raised eastern bank of Kionslieu Dam (9½ acres/3.8 ha). Kionslieu has a considerable intrusion of marginal vegetation, including a rich growth of horsetails along its north side, behind which there is a mature conifer plantation. Gorse and willow line the raised

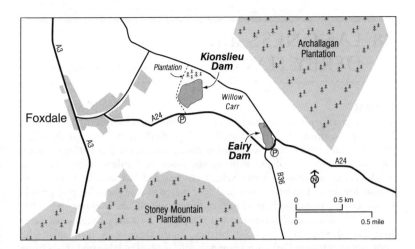

east and west banks and the outflow incorporates a further small area of willow carr. There is also a small island.

Timing
Both dams are worth visiting throughout the year. The sun makes morning observation at Kionslieu difficult. Look for Common Sandpiper on the Eairy in spring and young Tufted Duck on Kionslieu in late June.

Access
Follow the A24 from Douglas. It passes the southern end of Eairy Dam, from which observation is straightforward. Walk back along the minor road that skirts the east bank and use the cover of the trees to study the northern shallows. To reach Kionslieu turn right at once, continue for half a mile (800 m) and park by the rough ground on the left. Cross the road to the footpath, which follows the west bank of the dam. The A24 can also be accessed in Foxdale from the A3 Castletown–Kirkmichael–Ramsey road. The bus service from Douglas to Peel via Foxdale passes both dams, while that from Port Erin and Castletown to Peel necessitates a walk from Foxdale. (Neither service runs on Sundays).

CALENDAR

All year: Breeding Tufted Duck, Coot, Goldcrest, Long-tailed Tit, and Treecreeper. Ruddy Duck.

Pintail (occasional), Pochard (quite scarce), Scaup (occasional), Goldeneye, Little Grebe, Water Rail and Snipe.

Winter: Whooper Swan, Cormorant, Wigeon, Gadwall (occasional), Teal (regular flock on Eairy Dam), Green-winged Teal (one record),

Spring and summer: Common Sandpiper (passage), hirundines, Sedge Warbler and Willow Warbler.

88 LANGNESS and DERBY HAVEN

OS Ref: SC2866,2867,2966,2967

Habitat

The Langness peninsula is attached to the south-east corner of the Isle of Man by a narrow isthmus. It stretches southward, gradually narrowing, for about 1.5 miles (2.4 km), ending in a westward-pointing succession of low barren rocks. On the western side of the isthmus, the sands of Castletown Bay cease at Sandwick, giving way to rocks, which are revealed at low tide. These rocks extend for about 1 mile (1.5 km) and are covered in seaweed. A strip of gravely beach, often covered with great rolls of rotting wrack, finally ceases about 200 yards (200 m) south of Sandwick and is replaced by a very rough grassy area interspersed with rocky pools. Farther south there is a tidal inlet, the eponymous Stinking Dub, also known simply as The Pool. Beyond this a stone wall stretches somewhat uncertainly seaward, separating the pool from an area of saltmarsh, overlooked by the ruined Langness farmhouse (Haunted House). After a grassy area, low cliffs develop and extend to the Point. The eastern side is made up entirely of low cliffs. The central body of the peninsula incorporates a large cultivated field, an elevated rocky area with much gorse and, in its northern part, a golf course. Scattered stretches of dense shrubbery, made up of gorse and bramble, flank the lighthouse road.

Derby Haven is a shingle-bordered bay with quite extensive intertidal mud, well protected by Fort Island and a detached breakwater. Fort Island, a Manx National Heritage site, is a low rocky islet beyond a narrow causeway. It has two notable ruins: the circular 17th century fort and a chapel dating from the early part of the 11th century. At its northern end Derby Haven curves eastward to form a small peninsula beyond which is another tidal pool – the Wigeon Pool – beside the flying club. The whole area is bordered by the grassy margins of Ronaldsway Airport.

Species

Wildfowl and waders contribute equally to the appeal of this excellent site. Wigeon, Teal and Mallard all reach peaks of several hundred. Eider, Goldeneye and Red-breasted Merganser are regular visitors in small numbers and Pintail, Shoveler and, in Derby Haven, Long-tailed Duck occur from time to time. A recent development is the regular wintering of up to 40 Brent Geese, which particularly favour Derby Haven. Shelduck are present for most of the year and several pairs breed. Derby Haven is also the best site for Great Crested, Red-necked and Slavonian Grebes. The bay often holds Great Northern Diver and several Black Guillemots.

Oystercatcher, Golden Plover, and Curlew are the most abundant waders, but Ringed Plover, Dunlin, Redshank and Turnstone also form good flocks. Small numbers of Grey Plover particularly favour the area below the Golf Links Hotel. Lapwings have become rather scarce. Little Egret, Greenshank and Ruff, as well as parties of Knot and Bar-tailed and Black-tailed Godwits occur regularly. Scarcer visitors include Little Stint, Curlew Sandpiper and Spotted Redshank. Snipe winter on the salt marsh. Oystercatcher, Ringed Plover and sometimes Redshank breed.

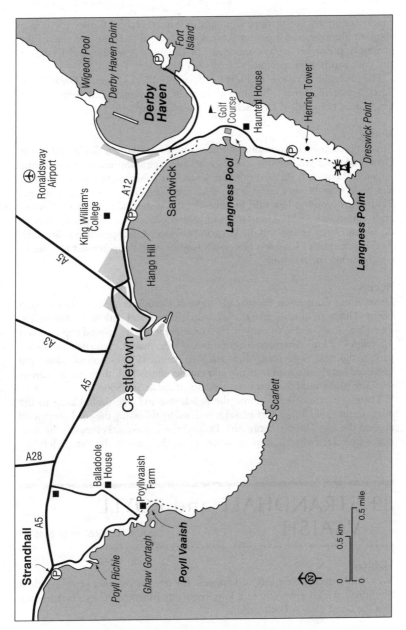

Passerines are well represented here, with good numbers of Skylarks, Meadow and Rock Pipits, Stonechats, Linnets and Reed Buntings throughout the year. This is a good place for migrants. Sedge Warblers and Whitethroats stay on to breed, while numerous Wheatears as well as Redstart, Whinchat and Grasshopper Warbler are regular on passage. White Wagtails occur in good numbers along Sandwick shore in both spring and autumn. The banks of wrack can attract 60 or more Choughs in winter. Hybrid Crows occur in a range of plumages and a pair of Ravens nests annually on the east side of the peninsula. Inevitably raptors are drawn to Langness: Peregrine and Kestrel at any time and Merlin and Short-eared Owl in winter.

The catalogue of rarities includes Green-winged Teal, Garganey, Great White Egret, Spoonbill, Avocet, Temminck's Stint, White-rumped and Buff-breasted Sandpipers, Long-billed Dowitcher and Calandra Lark.

Timing
Any time of year is interesting. Winter is best for Chough flocks and Brent Geese and other wildfowl, as well as grebes and raptors. Spring brings passerine migrants. Autumn is the best time for waders. At Langness, the flocks of ducks and waders can be very difficult to see on the weed-covered rocks at low tide. Sandwick is good at low tide, but elsewhere a higher tide is preferred, when birds congregate in Stinking Dub and waders come onto the grassy areas to the north. Derby Haven and the Wigeon Pool can be disappointing at low tide. As the best areas of Langness face south west or west, the peninsula is easier to watch during the morning.

Access
Drive along Castletown Promenade towards Derbyhaven. Soon after passing Hango Hill with its ruin, take the second right turn and park above the beach. From here it is possible to explore the entire peninsula in a round trip of about 4.5 miles (7.2 km). Alternatively, continue to Derbyhaven, turn right and either park at the next right turn (short track to Sandwick) or continue along the unfenced lighthouse road over the golf course, after which there are numerous stopping places until the main car park is reached at SC283660.

There is a private area around the lighthouse and one should keep to the edges of the golf course. Fort Island is reached by following the road southward around the bay. There is a car park beyond the causeway. Following the road north from Derbyhaven, stop anywhere up to the gates of the flying club.

---

89 STRANDHALL and POYLL VAAISH
OS Ref: SC238687 to SC244675

Habitat
Very similar to the west side of Langness, the site consists of a sandy beach at Strandhall, which gives way to a low, frequently indented, rocky coast, ending in a sheltered cove at Poyll Vaaish.

Species
Wildfowl are the principal attraction, with Wigeon peaking recently at almost 500. Teal and Mallard are also plentiful and parties of Eider are seen, especially in spring. This is also an excellent area for Shelduck: several pairs breed and most of the island's non-breeders summer around Strandhall and Poyll Richie. Oystercatcher and Ringed Plover also breed. Curlews are present in good

numbers during winter. A flock of Golden Plover alternates between fields around Poyll Vaaish and the margins of Poyll Richie, and one or two Grey Plover can often be found on the sands at Strandhall. Stonechat and Chough are ever-present and Wheatears are common on passage.

Timing

The area is at its best between October and March. At low tide there are extensive wrack-covered rocks where ducks and waders collect. They can be difficult to see, so two hours either side of high water is preferable.

Access

Strandhall is roughly half way between Port Erin and Castletown on the A5. From Strandhall a narrow but well-maintained lane follows the coast in a south-easterly direction to Poyll Vaaish Farm. There are several places to park, such as on the verge before the farm, then walk through to view Poyll Vaaish. A sharp left turn just before the farm returns to the A5 at Balladoole Farm (SC249686).

90 CHASMS and SUGAR LOAF

SC1866, SC1966
SC2066, SC2067

Habitat

The site embraces Bay Stacka and continues northward as far as Callooway. There is a fine series of slate cliffs, the most dramatic feature being the aptly named Sugar Loaf stack. Tiers of narrow ledges are a feature both of the Sugar Loaf and the adjacent cliffs. The Chasms are a series of very deep clefts in the rocks that overlook the Sugar Loaf. Sheep-grazed fields border the coast to the east of the Chasms, while inland there is a stretch of heath. To the west of the Chasms a mosaic of irregularly shaped sod hedges enclose rough pastures.

Species

Writing in the mid 17th century, John Ray wrote evocatively that the "Manks"men likened the Guillemots on these cliff ledges to the pots on the shelves of an apothecary's shop. Guillemots and Kittiwakes crowd the ledges on both the Sugar Loaf and the cliffs nearby, and are the major attraction here. Just east at the Anvil there is a smaller colony of Kittiwakes. Fulmars and Razorbills are widely scattered, Puffins are now extremely scarce, but there are fair numbers of Black Guillemots between Kione y Ghoggan and Callooway. Kestrels and Peregrines frequent the cliffs and there is every chance of seeing a Hen Harrier hunting over the heath or hedge-hopping along the rough pastures. Breeding passerines include Skylark, Meadow Pipit, Stonechat, Wheatear (around Kione y Ghoggan) and Whitethroat, as well as Chough and Raven in the immediate vicinity of the Chasms.

Timing

The site should be visited between March and July. June is the optimum month.

Access

The simplest approach is along the Howe Road (A31) from Port St Mary. After climbing for about 1 mile (1.6 km), pass a large quarry car park on the right and turn left through Cregneash village. A narrow metalled lane continues due south to the Radio Beacon Station, where there is a further car park. A footpath with steps descends to a gate, beyond which are the Chasms.

Several paths lead to the cliff edge. Proceed with caution: this is a dangerous area as some of the deep clefts are partly concealed by vegetation. The views from the cliff top to the Sugar Loaf are magnificent. From here a path traverses the fields towards Callooway, but it is just as easy to walk with care along the cliff top, examining in particular the Anvil (also known as the Pulpit). From the Chasms it is also possible to follow a footpath west. This continues spectacularly via Black Head and Spanish Head to the Sound. Other footpaths north of Black Head meander back through the fields to Cregneash. The bus service can be used here to good advantage using stops at Port St Mary, Cregneash and the Sound. The coastal footpath from Port St Mary to the Sound is an ideal way of covering the site.

91 THE CALF OF MAN   OS Ref: SC16

Habitat

The Calf is administered by Manx National Heritage as a bird sanctuary and nature reserve. It lies about 600 yards (600 m) off the south-west tip of the Isle of Man. The intervening stretch of water, the Sound, is interrupted by a rocky islet, the Kitterland. Little Sound separates the Kitterland from the main island, and is no more than 100 yards (100 m) wide. The coastline of the Calf is made up of slate cliffs of varying height that reach 300 feet (100 m) in places. The total length of the indented coastline approaches 5 miles (8 km). Much of the Calf is covered in heather, but there are also some extensive patches of bracken and perhaps 100 acres (40 ha) of abandoned cultivation enclosed by dry stone walls. More than half of the island is over 200 feet (70 m) above sea level; the highest point at 421 feet (128 m) is close to the steep western cliffs.

The Calf is partly divided by a shallow valley, the Glen, which runs from north to south and embraces most of the old pastures. At the head of the Glen is the former farmhouse, now the Bird Observatory, and here an assortment of trees and shrubs have been planted. In the centre of the Glen a marshy area develops into a small freshwater pool and a stream drains through the willow withy into a deep gully, the Mill Giau. In addition to the Observatory there are two early 18th century lighthouses, now abandoned. Between them is a modern lighthouse. A fourth lighthouse, also abandoned, occupies the Chicken Rock, which is about 1000 yards (1 km) offshore to the south west.

The Bird Observatory was officially established in 1962. It is manned by two wardens between March and November; they census the breeding birds annually as well as keeping a daily log of migration through the island. Birds are caught by mist netting and in two Heligoland traps. By the end of 2004, more than

206,000 birds had been ringed, with 2,570 recoveries. Seawatching is another important activity.

Species and Timing

Over the years between 30 and 35 species have bred annually, although the overall total of species that have at some time bred is well over 60. Seabirds include Fulmar, Manx Shearwater, Shag, Lesser Black-backed, Herring and Great Black-backed Gull, Kittiwake, Guillemot and Razorbill. Mallard, Eider and Moorhen are regular breeders. Water Rails bred for several years in the mid 1990s, but no longer do so. Breeding raptors include Hen Harrier, Kestrel, Peregrine and Short-eared Owl. Up to 14 pairs of Chough may breed and there are usually two pairs of Raven. Among the smaller passerines, pride of place numerically goes to Meadow Pipit, followed by Wren, Wheatear, Stonechat and Linnet.

Early migrants are likely to include a few Snipe and Woodcock, followed by Goldcrests and Chiffchaffs in late March and early April, then Willow Warblers, Wheatears and Ring Ouzels. May sees hirundine passage at its spring peak, starting with Sand Martins and followed by Swallows and then House Martins. Grasshopper Warbler, Sedge Warbler and Whitethroat pass through in good numbers in early May, but have a negligible showing on return passage. Redstart, Whinchat and Spotted Flycatcher come later in May and reappear at the end of August. Of the scarce migrants Hoopoe, Bluethroat, Nightingale, Subalpine Warbler and Golden Oriole are almost exclusively spring visitors, while Hobby, Red-breasted Flycatcher and Red-backed Shrike occur fairly evenly in both seasons. Until 1992 Common Rosefinch records had occurred exclusively during the first three weeks of June, but this is now an almost regular autumn visitor. Another rare visitor, seen most often in June is the Greenish Warbler.

Return movement of Willow Warblers is a feature of August and this is the most likely month for Melodious Warbler. Icterine Warblers tend to arrive a little later. Garden and Barred Warblers, as well as Wryneck, are typical of September. October is the month for wagtails, thrushes, finches and Goldcrest, with a fair chance of Firecrest, Yellow-browed Warbler and Lapland Bunting. Scarcer autumn visitors include Richard's and Tawny Pipits.

Sea-watching is most rewarding in late August and early September when, among the thousands of Manx Shearwater, one should search for Cory's and Sooty Shearwaters. Skua movement continues until early October, with every chance of Pomarine and the possibility of Long-tailed. Sabine's Gull can be expected from mid September to the end of October.

It is reasonable to suppose that anything might turn up on the Calf, but the following records were exceptional: Bridled Tern, Mourning Dove, Scops Owl, Pechora Pipit, White-throated Robin, Black-eared Wheatear, Sardinian Warbler, Dusky Warbler, Yellow-rumped Warbler, Song Sparrow, Black-headed Bunting and Baltimore Oriole.

Mammals provide an additional attraction. There is a large flock of native Loghtan Sheep. Grey Seals relax on the rocks bordering the Sound. Less welcome are those long-tailed fellers – the superstitious Manxman does not use the accepted name for the larger of the two most common rodents – which allegedly escaped during the 19th century from a wrecked Russian merchantman. They are held responsible for the decimation of the great shearwater colony and remain a threat to ground-nesting species.

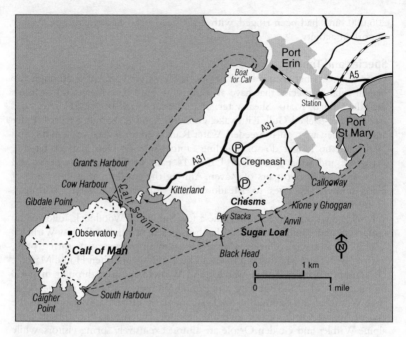

Access

The Calf can be reached by boat from Port Erin and Port St Mary. Between April and September there are usually three trips daily from Port Erin. Times are shown on a board by the jetty. Contact Ray Buchan on 01624 832339. The trip takes about 30 minutes and allows three to four hours on the island.

Landing takes place on the Calf either at Cow or Grant's Harbour on the Sound, or at South Harbour. It should be remembered that there are no toilet facilities for day trippers. Alternatively, contact Juan Clague on 01624 834307 to arrange transit from Port St Mary. He also does a weekly supply trip on Tuesdays.

It is also possible to stay at the Observatory, where there are two rooms with two bunks each and a third room with four bunks. Blankets are provided, but it is wise to take a sleeping bag. There are cooking facilities, but visitors need to take their own provisions. Intending visitors should apply to Manx National Heritage, Manx Museum, Douglas, Isle of Man (Telephone: 01624 648000).

It is important to bear in mind that weather conditions may prevent a planned return to the main island. There is no emergency alternative to sea travel and one could possibly be marooned for several days.

SELECTED BIBLIOGRAPHY

The authors wish to thank the authors and organisations for a source of information from the following publications.

Books

Bell, T. H. (1962) *The Birds of Cheshire*. John Sherratt and Son

Bell, T. H. (1967) *A Supplement to 'The Birds of Cheshire'*.

CAWOS, *Cheshire & Wirral Bird Reports (1963-2005)*. Cheshire & Wirral Ornithological Society (formerly COA)

Conlin, A. (2003) *Birding the Wirral Penninsula*. Where and When.

Conlin, A. & Williams, S. (2004) *Rare Birds in Cheshire & Wirral*. CAW Birding

Cooper, J.H. & Wood, J.C. (1986) *A Checklist of the Birds of Bolton*. Bolton RSPB Group.

Coward, T. A. (1910) *The Vertebrate Fauna of Cheshire and Liverpool Bay*, Volume 1, Witherby & Co

Craggs, J.D. (1982) *Hilbre: The Cheshire Island*. Liverpool University Press.

Cullen, J.P. & Jennings, P.P. (1986) *Birds of the Isle of Man*. Bridgeen.

Firth, A. (2005) *Site Guide: Sandbach Flashes*, Birding North West (Volume 1:12)

Green, G. & Cade, M. (2001) *Where to watch birds in Dorset, Hampshire and the Isle of Wight*, Christopher Helm.

Garrad, L.S. (1972) *The Naturalist in the Isle of Man*. David & Charles.

Guest, J., Elphick, D., Hunter, J.S.A., & Norman, D. (1992) *The Breeding Bird Atlas of Cheshire and Wirral*. Cheshire and Wirral Ornithological Society.

Hardy, E. (1979) *Birdwatching in Lancashire*. Dalesman.

Harrison, R. & Rogers, D.A. (1977) *The Birds of Rostherne Mere*. NCC.

Holland, P., Spence, I., & Sutton, T. (1984) *Breeding birds in Greater Manchester*, Manchester Ornithological Society.

Hutcheson, M. (1985) *Cumbrian Birds*. Frank Peters, Kendal.

Madders, M. (1985) *Birdwatching in the Lake District*. Bartholomew Guides.

Madders, M. & Welstead, J. (2002) *Where to watch birds in Scotland*. Christopher Helm.

Mitchell, W.R. & Robson, R.W. (1973) *Pennine Birds*. Dalesman

– (1974) *Lakeland Birds*. Dalesman.

Prater, A.J. (1981) *Estuary Birds of Britain and Ireland*. T.&A.D. Poyser.

Sharpe, C.M. *et al.* (2007) *Manx Bird Atlas*. Liverpool University Press.

Sharrock, J.T.R. *et al.* (1976) *Rare Birds in Britain and Ireland*, T.&A.D. Poyser.

Spencer, K.G. (1973) *The Status and Distribution of Birds in Lancashire*, Turner & Earnshaw, Burnley.

Wilson, J. (1974) *The Birds of Morecambe Bay*. Dalesman.

Wilson, J.D. (1985) *Birds and Birdwatching at Pennington Flash*, Pennington Flash Joint Committee.

Wright, M. (1973) *'Island'* in *Birdwatchers'Year*, T.&A.D. Poyser.

Wright, M. (1976) *'The Calf of Man'* in *Bird Observatories in Britain and Ireland*. T.&A.D. Poyser.

Annual Reports

Ayres National Nature Reserve Annual Report. Isle of Man Government Department of Agriculture, Fisheries and Forestry.
Bird News. Cheshire and Wirral Ornithological Society.
Birds in Cumbria. Cumbria Naturalist Union.
Birds in Greater Manchester. Greater Manchester Bird Recording Group.
Calf of Man Bird Observatory Annual Report. Manx National Heritage.
CAWOS (various), Bird News, Cheshire and Wirral Ornithological Society
Cheshire and Wirral Bird Reports. Cheshire and Wirral Ornithological Society.
Fylde Bird Club Reports.
Hilbre Bird Observatory Annual Reports.
Lancashire Bird Reports. Lancashire and Cheshire Fauna Society.
Lancaster and District Birdwatching Society Annual Reports.
Peregrine: The Manx Bird Report. Manx Ornithological Society.
Seaforth Bird Reports. Lancashire Wildlife Trust.
Walney Bird Observatory Annual Reports.

Websites

www.manchesterbirding.com
www.deeestuary.co.uk
www.hilbrebirdobs.co.uk

CODE OF CONDUCT FOR BIRDWATCHERS

Today's birdwatchers are a powerful force for nature conservation. The number of those of us interested in birds rises continually and it is vital that we take seriously our responsibility to avoid any harm to birds.

We must also present a responsible image to non-birdwatchers who may be affected by our activities and particularly those on whose sympathy and support the future of birds may rest.

There are 10 points to bear in mind:
1. The welfare of birds must come first.
2. Habitat must be protected.
3. Keep disturbance to birds and their habitat to a minimum.
4. When you find a rare bird think carefully about whom you should tell.
5. Do not harass rare migrants.
6. Abide by the bird protection laws at all times.
7. Respect the rights of landowners.
8. Respect the rights of other people in the countryside.
9. Make your records available to the local bird recorder.
10. Behave abroad as you would when birdwatching at home.

Welfare of birds must come first
Whether your particular interest is photography, ringing, sound recording, scientific study or just birdwatching, remember that the welfare of the bird must always come first.

Habitat protection
Its habitat is vital to a bird and therefore we must ensure that our activities do not cause damage.

Keep disturbance to a minimum
Birds' tolerance of disturbance varies between species and seasons. Therefore, it is safer to keep all disturbance to a minimum. No birds should be disturbed from the nest in case opportunities for predators to take eggs or young are increased. In very cold weather disturbance to birds may cause them to use vital energy at a time when food is difficult to find. Wildfowlers already impose bans during cold weather: birdwatchers should exercise similar discretion.

Rare breeding birds
If you discover a rare bird breeding and feel that protection is necessary, inform the appropriate RSPB Regional Office, or the Species Protection Department at the Lodge. Otherwise it is best in almost all circumstances to keep the record strictly secret in order to avoid disturbance by other birdwatchers and attacks by egg-collectors. Never visit known sites of rare breeding birds unless they are adequately protected. Even your presence may give away the site to others and cause so many other visitors that the birds may fail to breed successfully.

Disturbance at or near the nest of species listed on the First Schedule of the Wildlife and Countryside Act 1981 is a criminal offence.

Copies of Wild Birds and the Law are obtainable from the RSPB, The Lodge, Sandy, Beds. SG19 2DL (send two 2nd class stamps).

Rare migrants

Rare migrants or vagrants must not be harassed. If you discover one, consider the circumstances carefully before telling anyone. Will an influx of birdwatchers disturb the bird or others in the area? Will the habitat be damaged? Will problems be caused with the landowner?

The Law

The bird protection laws (now embodied in the Wildlife and Countryside Act 1981) are the result of hard campaigning by previous generations of birdwatchers. As birdwatchers we must abide by them at all times and not allow them to fall into disrepute. The Isle of Man has its own legislation (Wildlife Act 1990) which affords protection to nesting birds, their eggs and dependent young.

Respect the rights of landowners

The wishes of landowners and occupiers of land must be respected. Do not enter land without permission. Comply with permit schemes. If you are leading a group, do give advance notice of the visit, even if a formal permit scheme is not in operation. Always obey the Country Code.

Respect the rights of other people

Have proper consideration for other birdwatchers. Try not to disrupt their activities or scare the birds they are watching. There are many other people who also use the countryside. Do not interfere with their activities and, if it seems that what they are doing is causing unnecessary disturbance to birds, do try to take a balanced view. Flushing gulls when walking a dog on a beach may do little harm, while the same dog might be a serious disturbance at a tern colony. When pointing this out to a non-birdwatcher be courteous, but firm. The non-birdwatchers' goodwill towards birds must not be destroyed by the attitudes of birdwatchers.

Keeping records

Much of today's knowledge about birds is the result of meticulous record keeping by our predecessors. Make sure you help to add to tomorrow's knowledge by sending records to your county bird recorder.

Birdwatching abroad

Behave abroad as you would at home. This code should be firmly adhered to when abroad (whatever the local laws). Well behaved birdwatchers can be important ambassadors for bird protection.

This code has been drafted after consultation between The British Ornithologists' Union, British Trust for Ornithology, the Royal Society for the Protection of Birds, the Scottish Ornithologists' Club, the Wildfowl Trust and the Editors of *British Birds*.

USEFUL ADDRESSES

County Bird Recorder

Cumbria:

Cumbria (County), Colin Raven, 18 Seathwaite Rd, Barrow-in-Furness, Cumbria, LA14 4LX Email: colin@walneyobs.fsnet.co.uk

Cumbria (South), Ronnie Irving, 24 Birchwood Close, Kendal, Cumbria, LA9 5BJ, Tel: 01539 727523 Email: ronnie@fenella.fslife.co.uk

Cumbria (North East), Michael Carrier, Lismore Cottage, 1 Front Street, Armathwaite, Cumbria, CA4 9PB Tel: 01697 472218

Cumbria (North West), Jake Manson, Fell Beck, East Rd, Egremont, Cumbria, CA22 2ED Tel: 01946 822947 Email: jake.manson@btinternet.com

Lancashire, inc. North Merseyside:

Steve White, 102 Minster Court, Crwon Street, Liverpool, L7 3QD Tel: 0151 7072744 Email: stephen.white2@tesco.net

Greater Manchester:

Mrs A. Judith Smith, 12 Edge Green Street, Ashton-in-Makerfield, Wigan, WN4 8SL Tel: 01942 712615 Mob: 07970 778024 Email: judith@gmbirds.freeserve. co.uk

Cheshire and Wirral:

Hugh Pulsford, 6 Buttermere Drive, Great Warford, Cheshire, SK9 7WA Tel: 01565 880171 Email: Hugh.Pulsford@astrazeneca.com

Isle of Man:

Dr Pat Cullen, Troutbeck, Cronkbourne, Braddan, Isle of Man, IM4 4QA Tel: 01624 676774 Email: bridgeen@mcb.net

Assistant Recorder (Rarities)

Ian McKerchar, 42 Green Ave, Astley, M29 7EH

Tel: 01942 701758 Mob: 07958687481 Email: ian@mckerchar1.freeserve. co.uk

Assistant Recorder (Database)

Steve Atkins, 33 King's Grove, Wardle, Rochdale OL12 9HR Tel: 01706 645097 Email: steveatkins@tiscali.co.uk

BTO Regional Representatives

Cumbria:

North RR, Clive Hartley, Marsh Cottage, Burgh-by-Sands, Carlisle, CA5 6AX Tel: 01228 576349 Email: clivehartley@marshcott.freeserve.co.uk

Lancashire:

East RR. Tony Cooper, 28 Peel Park Avenue, Clitheroe, Lancs, BB7 1ET Tel: 01200 424577 Email: tonycooper@beeb.net

North and West RR, Keith Woods, 2 Oak Drive, Halton, Lancaster, LA2 6QL Tel: 01524 811 478 Email: woods.keith@btopenworld.com

South RR, Philip Shearwood, Netherside, Green Lane, Whitestake, Preston, PR4 4AH Tel: 01772 745488 Email: phil.shearwood@virgin.net

Manchester:

Stephen Suttill, 94 Manchester Rd, Mossley, OL5 9AY Tel: 01457 836360
   Email: steve@marctheprinters.org (work) suttill.parkinson @virgin.net
   (home).
Regional Organiser for the Breeding Bird Survey, Manchester Region: Mrs
   A.J. Smith, address above.

Cheshire and Wirral:

Charles Hull, Edleston Cottage, Edleston Hall Lane, Nantwich, Cheshire
   CW5 8PL Tel: 01270 628194 Email: edleston@yahoo.co.uk
   The 10km squares SJ78, SJ88 and SJ98 are in this region although large
   parts of them are in Greater Manchester.
Paul Miller Tel: 01928 787535
   Email: huntershill@worldonline.co.uk

BTO Regional Development Officer

Jim Jeffery, 20 Church Lane, Romiley, Stockport SK6 4AA
Tel: 0161 494 5367 Email: jim_jeffery1943@yahoo.co.uk
Chris Sharpe, 33 Mines Rd, Laxey, Isle of Man, IM4 7NH Tel: 01624 861130
   Email: chris@manxbirdatlas.org.uk

WWT Wetland Bird Survey Organiser

Adrian Dancy, Flat 5, Kensington Court, Bury New Rd, Salford M7 4WU
Tel: 0161 278 5381 Email: a.dancy@ntl.com
Dee Estuary – Colin E Wells, Inner Marsh Farm RSPB Reserve, Burton
   Point Farm, Burton, Cheshire, CH64 5SB Tel: 0151 3367681
   Email: Colin.Wells@rspb.org.uk
Duddon Estuary – Bob Treen, 5 Rydal Close, Dalton-in-Furness, Cumbria,
   CA13 0YR Tel: 01229 464789
Mersey Estuary – Graham Thomason Email via: webs@bto.org
North Lancashire (inland) Peter Marsh, Leck View Cottage, Ashle's Farm,
   High Tatham, Lancaster, LA2 8PH Tel: 01524 264944 Email:
   pbmarsh@btopenworld.com
Ribble Estuary – Mike Gee, Ribble Estuary, National Nature Reserve,
   Reserve Office, Old Hollow, Marsh Rd, Banks, PR9 8DU Tel: 01704
   225624 Email: english-nature@ribble-nnr.freeserve.co.uk

CLUBS

Cheshire and Wirral Ornithological Society
Contact: David Cogger, Membership Secretary, 113 Nantwich Road,
   Middlewich, Cheshire, CW10 9HD. Tel: 01606 832517

Greater Manchester Bird Recording Group
Contact: County Recorder.

Hale Ornithologists
Contact: Diana Grellier, 8 Apsley Grove, Bowdon, Altrincham WA14 3AH

Leigh Ornithological Society
Contact: Raymond Meredith, 24 Samuel St., Hindsford, Atherton M46 9AY
Tel: 01942 793555 Email: raymond.meredith@ntlworld.com

Liverpool Ornithologists Club
Contact: Tony Duckels, 24 Dunes Drive, Formby, Lancashire, L37 1PF. Tel: 01704 876676

Manchester Ornithological Society (was Greater Manchester Bird Club)
Contact: Bob Sandling, 17 Range Rd, Stalybridge, SK15 2HH Tel: 0161 338 6971

Stockport Birdwatching Society
Contact: Dave Evans, 36 Tatton Rd South, Stockport, SK4 4LU Tel: 0161 432 9513 Email: windhover@ntl.com

Wirral Bird Club
www.wirralbirdclub.com <http://www.wirralbirdclub.com>

RSPB MEMBERS' GROUPS – Group Leaders or contacts:
Blackpool: Alan Stamford Tel: 01253 859662 E-mail: alanstamford140@msn.com
Bolton: Mrs C. Johnson, 65 Lever Park Ave, Horwich, Bolton BL6 7LQ Tel: 01204 468850
Carlisle: Bob Jones Tel: 01228 561684 E-mail: bob@onethirty.force9.co.uk
Chester: Roger Nutter Tel: 01829 782237 E-mail: lexeme@onetel.com
Cuerden: David Beattie Tel: 01772 313231 E-mail: www.explorers.freeuk.com
Daisy Nook: Jane Downall Tel: 01706 622587
High Peak: Peter Griffiths, 17 Clifton Drive, Marple SK6 6PP Tel: 0161 427 5325
Lancaster: Jill Blackburn Tel: 01539563280 E-mail: jill.blackburn@dsl.pipex.com
Leighton Moss: Keith Nelson Tel: 01254 814174 E-mail: keith.nelson@btinternet.com
Macclesfield: Tina Hanak Tel: 01625 503572
E-mail: wex@macclesfieldRSPB.org.uk
Ray Evans Tel: 01625 432635 Daytime E-mail: ray@macclesfieldRSPB.org.uk
Manchester: Peter Wolstenholme, 31 South Park Rd, Gatley SK8 4AL Tel: 0161 428 2175
North Cheshire: Paul Grimmett Tel: 01925 268770 E-mail: paulw@ecosse.net
North Fylde: Don Rusling Tel: 01253 866 010 E-mail: donald472@btinternet.com
South Lakeland: Martin Baines Tel: 01539 732214
Stockport: Brian Hallworth, 69 Talbot St, Hazel Grove, SK7 4BJ Tel: 0161 456 5368
West Cumbria: Neil Hutchin Tel: 01900 825231 E-mail: marjorie.hutchin@btinternet.com
Wigan: Graham Tonge, 29 St Andrew's Drive, Wigan WN6 7RQ Tel: 01942 248238

NATIONAL
British Birds Rarities Committee
Colin Bradshaw, 9 Tynemouth Place, Tynemouth, Tyne and Wear NE30 4BJ

Telephone: 0191 257 2389.
Email: secretary@bbrc.org.uk
Website: www.bbrc.org.uk

British Trust for Ornithology
The Nunnery, Thetford,
Norfolk IP24 2PU.
Telephone: 01842 750050.
Email: info@bto.org
Website: www.bto.org

Environment Agency
Millbank Tower, 25th floor,
21/24 Millbank,
London SW1P 4XL.
Telephone: 08708 506506.
Website: www.environment-agency.gov.uk

Forestry Commission
Silvan House, 231 Corstorphine Road, Edinburgh EH12 7AT.
Tel: 0131 3340303.
Email: enquiries@forestry.gsi.gov.uk
Website: www.forestry.gov.uk

Friends of the Earth
26-28 Underwood Street,
London N1 7JQ. Tel: 020 7490 1555.
Website: www.foe.co.uk

Greenpeace
Canonbury Villas,
London N1 2PN.
Telephone: 020 7865 8100.
Email: info@uk.greenpeace.org
Website: www.greenpeace.org.uk

National Trust
PO Box 39,
Warrington WA5 7WD.
Telephone: 0870 4584000.
Email: enquiries@thenationaltrust.org.uk
Website: www.nationaltrust.org.uk

Natural England (formerly English Nature)
Northminster House,
Peterborough PE1 1UA.
Telephone: 01733 455000.
Email: enquiries@natural-england.org.uk
Website: www.natural-england.org.uk

Ordnance Survey
Romsey Road,
Southampton SO16 4GU.
Telephone: 08456 050505.
Email: customerservices@ordnancesurvey.co.uk
Website: www.ordnancesurvey.co.uk

Royal Society for the Protection of Birds
The Lodge, Sandy,
Bedfordshire SG19 2DL.
Telephone: 01767 680551.
Website: www.rspb.org.uk

Woodland Trust
Autumn Park, Dysart Road, Grantham, Lincolnshire NG31 6LL.
Telephone: 01476 581111.
Email: conservation@woodland-trust.org.uk
Website: www.woodland-trust.org.uk

INDEX OF PLACE NAMES

Locators are site numbers

INDEX OF SPECIES

Locators are site numbers